IMAGES
of America

Around Egg Harbor City and Pleasantville

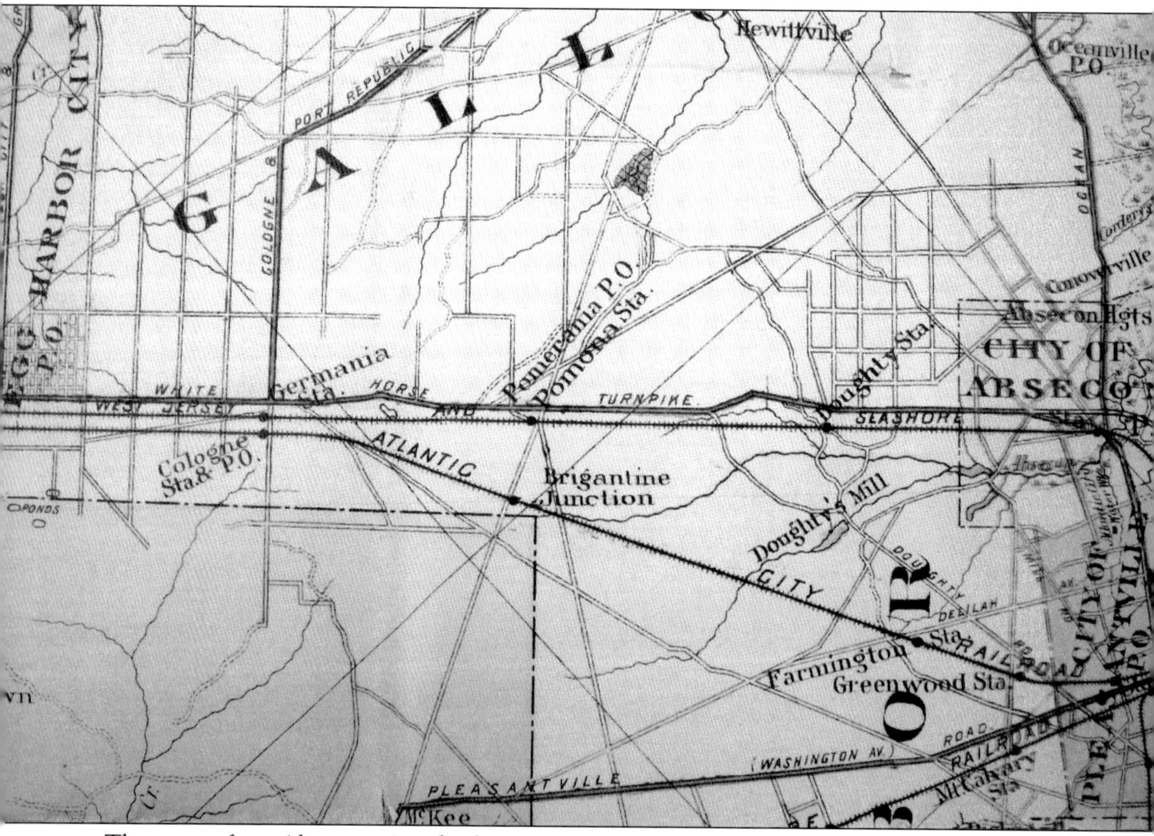

This map is from *Absegami: Annals of Eyern Haven and Atlantic City 1609–1904*, which was written and published by Alfred M. Heston in 1904. Railroads were an integral part of life in South Jersey. A closer look at the map reveals how easy it once was to travel from Egg Harbor City to Pleasantville on the Atlantic City Railroad. (Courtesy of Felix Amador and James Davidson.)

On the Cover: From left to right, Emilie Kirscht, Clara Kirscht, and Mabel Heinzer pose next to Herman Kirscht's photography studio on Cincinnati Avenue in Egg Harbor City about 1909. For 17 years, Herman operated his business from this location, producing cabinet cards, postcards, and other imagery for an entire generation. For more than three decades, Herman and his son Max captured much of an ever-changing Atlantic County on film. (Courtesy of Felix Amador and James Davidson.)

IMAGES
of America

Around Egg Harbor City and Pleasantville

Dennis M. Niceler
Foreword by James Davidson

ARCADIA
PUBLISHING

ISBN 978-1-4671-2073-9

Published by Arcadia Publishing
Charleston, South Carolina

Printed in the United States of America

Library of Congress Control Number: 2013942429

For all general information, please contact Arcadia Publishing:
Telephone 843-853-2070
Fax 843-853-0044
E-mail sales@arcadiapublishing.com
For customer service and orders:
Toll-Free 1-888-313-2665

Visit us on the Internet at www.arcadiapublishing.com

To Margaret A. Niceler, my mother

Contents

Foreword

I have a love of history and genealogy, and Kirscht photographs have always had a special draw on me. The two are often intertwined, for an understanding of our ancestors requires an understanding of the world in which they lived.

My interest in Herman and Max Kirscht began with a single postcard. The image was about 100 years old—just a moment in time. I began to see the changing world of many small towns. The postcards they produced featured several small towns in Atlantic County, some of which I grew up in and visited. These images also reflect the everyday life and the tremendous changes they witnessed in their lifetimes. The Kirscht images capture the evolution of small-town South Jersey. Once a quiet, small place sees growth and the movement of great numbers of people, things change—and not always for the better. No longer content or able to farm or fish, new opportunities arose around 1900. The train and trolley moved people quickly from place to place. The electric light and telephone made lives easier and more connected. In a few years, the automobile would be seen alongside the horse and buggy. The rate of change must have seemed very rapid for the older generations.

Herman Kirscht and his son Max were there to capture the changes. Many saw and lived through the period, but their work captured the transition. Over decades, the Kirschts saw and captured on film quiet rural towns as they became bustling, energized small cities.

As you wander through the images of such places as Egg Harbor City, Pleasantville, Port Republic, and Absecon, you will find yourself drawn into a world long gone. Make your own discoveries, have your favorites, but do look.

—James Davidson

ACKNOWLEDGMENTS

I have been able to view firsthand how Felix Amador and James Davidson have doggedly put together their Kirscht collection. What is amazing is not their ability to gain the items they deem important or even the fantastic photographs they possess, but their belief that these images should be shared with others. This is not an ideal that they alone enjoy, for I have met others who have the same belief.

It was this ideal that brought about the book you now hold in your hand.

No work such as this is accomplished without all kinds of help. People have shared their postcards, their research, and their advice. A few have shown infinite patience.

I want to particularly thank Felix Amador, Roger Arlan, Bob Barnett, Doris Bugdon, James Davidson, Carl Farrell, Dottie Kinsey, Mark Maxwell, Katie McAlpin, Paul Schopp, the Atlantic County Historical Society, the Egg Harbor City Historical Society, the Hamilton Township Historical Society, the staff at the Atlantic City Cemetery, and the members of the West Jersey Historical Roundtable.

Unless otherwise noted, all images appear courtesy of Felix Amador and James Davidson.

INTRODUCTION

By the 1850s, large numbers of Germans had immigrated in the United States. Some had left their homeland to escape political and religious persecution, and some had left simply to find a better life.

The size of the German population eventually caught the attention of a resurgent anti-immigrant movement known as the American or Nativist Party and commonly referred to as Know-Nothings.

These immigrants were literate, resourceful, and not without the means to improve their lives. They also had a strong sense of community, maintaining social and business organizations in most of the major cities in the country.

Eventually, an ideal coalesced that sought a new German home in America. This would be a place for all like-minded countrymen who wanted to combine and enjoy American freedom with *gemutlichkeit*: German sociability, cordiality, and kindliness. Here, they could develop German folk life and build German businesses and commerce. They were eager to be a part of this rapidly growing country and to reap the benefits of the American dream.

When representatives were invited to view a sprawling 30,000-acre piece of land lying in three municipalities in Atlantic County, New Jersey, known as the Gloucester Tract, it was almost certain that a German community was to be.

After numerous meetings in Philadelphia and elsewhere, the Gloucester Farm and Town Association was incorporated in Camden, New Jersey, on December 18, 1854. A great business and social experiment was about to begin.

The founders had always planned to create an urban core surrounded by a farming district. This urban core would eventually be called Egg Harbor City.

As tradition states, the residents of Egg Harbor City observe September 1855 as the beginning of their history. A number of historians believe that the first settlers arrived at that time.

Economic downturns, the Civil War, squabbling, and mosquitoes did much to impede progress in those early years. A few of the pioneers just left. The association often put forth grandiose and unsustainable plans and can be blamed to a small degree for some of the early failures.

It is amazing that the community survived. But prosperity had come to other towns in Atlantic County, such as Absecon, Hammonton, and a small ocean resort called Atlantic City. Those who remained in the "German district" pressed on, clearing land for farms and continuing to shape their ideal. By 1888, Atlantic City was being serviced by three railroads, and Egg Harbor City was flourishing.

Many of the men who had influenced the settlement in those early years were gone. The industrial and agricultural giant once envisioned was forgotten, and a charming German town had taken its place.

At the same time, the residents of the small communities of Adamstown, Lakestown, Martstown, Pleasantville, Risley Town, and Smiths Landing had been coming to terms with their own identity. Most of the residents were dependent on fishing, clamming, and farming for their survival.

The Pleasantville and Atlantic Turnpike, first proposed in 1853, finally provided a road to the resort. It connected the mainland with the ever popular, ever growing Atlantic City. The Philadelphia & Atlantic City Railway had also come through the area on its way to the "City by the Sea." Within a few years, two other railroads, one from Newfield to Atlantic City and the other from Pleasantville to Ocean City, had also been constructed.

Transportation had done much to bring success to these small villages in Egg Harbor Township. A single identity was the next step. On December 15, 1888, the residents of the proposed borough of Pleasantville voted overwhelmingly to incorporate. A special election was held on January 8, 1889.

By 1909, Pleasantville was no longer a small town but not quite a city. One local newspaper claimed that, at this juncture, it was "most difficult to solve municipal problems." Still, real estate developments, the trolley, and the city's proximity to Atlantic City did much to help the municipality grow. It eventually took on a city form of government and attracted residents from other parts of Atlantic County, including members of the Kirscht family.

The continued success of Atlantic City brought real estate speculators to the adjacent communities. Both cities, especially Pleasantville, owe much to the growth and popularity of that city.

These towns became two of the larger and more industrialized cities in Atlantic County. In addition, the Philadelphia & Atlantic City Railway, later called the Atlantic City Railroad, linked these two municipalities for more than half a century.

Herman and Max Kirscht were photographers in these two cities. Subsequently, the father and son produced many postcards showing scenes in Egg Harbor City, Pleasantville, Absecon, Port Republic, and several other communities.

These postcards and photographs form an eclectic collection. A few of their cards have a variety of different scenes and text. Some have no credit. Unfortunately, a complete catalog of either man's postcards has not been completed, and this book does not represent every postcard produced by them.

Today, these cards are highly prized and command steep prices. They also represent a window through which we can be witnesses to a vanished age.

One

The Kirscht Family

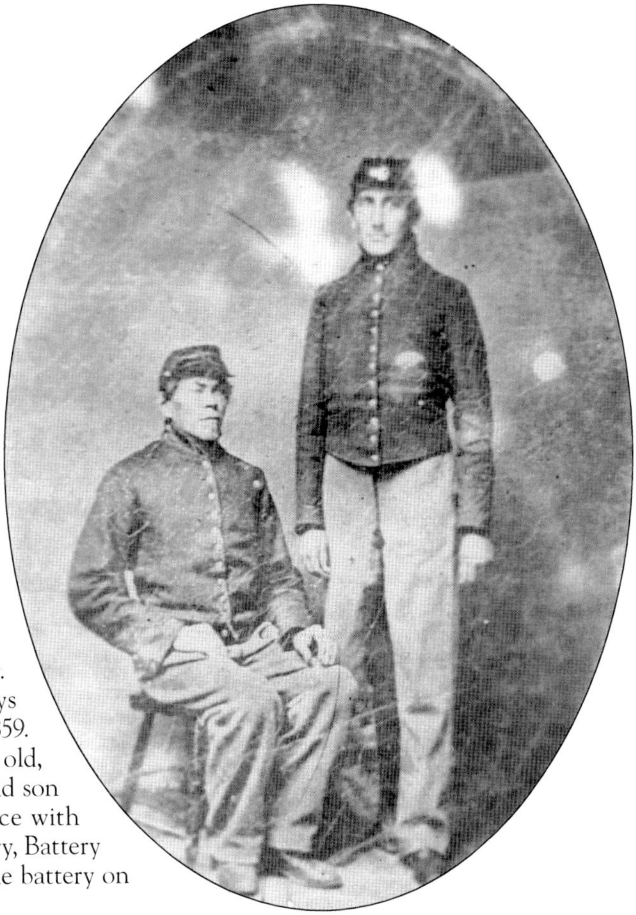

August G. Kirscht (March 31, 1823–August 17, 1891) was a pioneer settler in Egg Harbor City. He became a US citizen in Mays Landing, New Jersey, on April 12, 1859. On October 25, 1864, at 41 years old, August (sitting) and his 18-year-old son Charles (standing), entered service with the 1st Pennsylvania Light Artillery, Battery I. Both men mustered out with the battery on July 1, 1865.

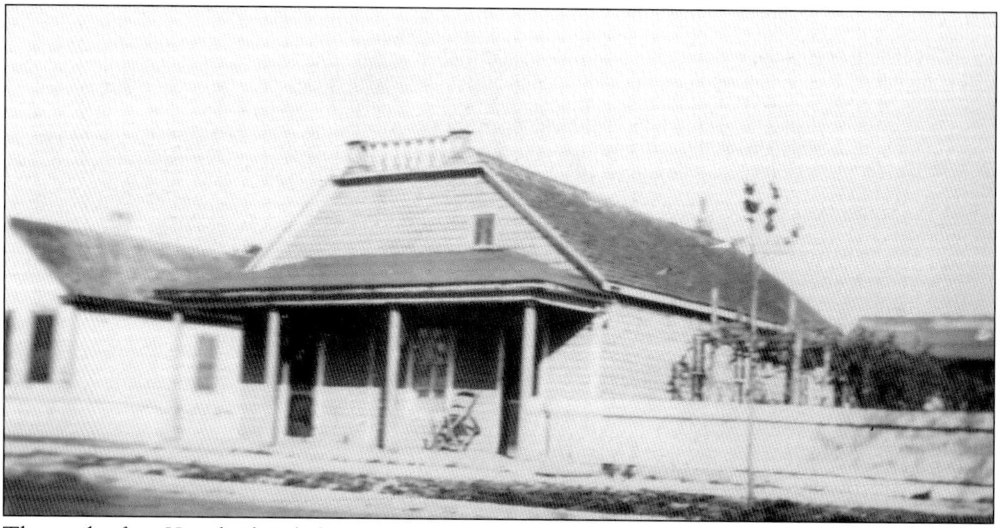

This is the first Kirscht family home, located at 208 St. Louis Avenue in Egg Harbor City. After the Civil War, August sold the property to Henry Gugler, who spent two years in this home engraving a life-size likeness of Abraham Lincoln on a plate of steel. It was the finest portrait of the late president then in existence and possibly the first life-size steel engraving.

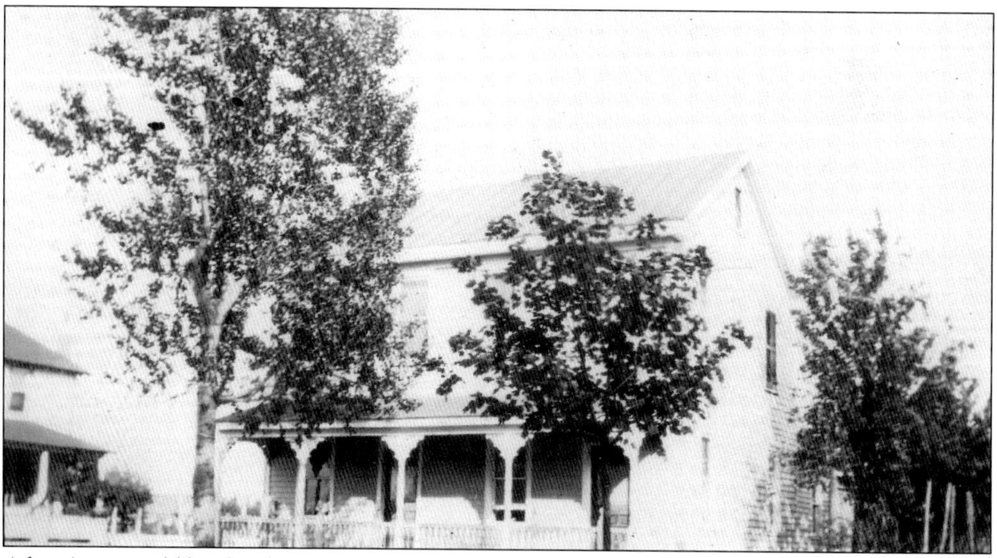

After August sold his first home to Gugler, the family moved to this home at the northeast corner of St. Louis Avenue and Arago Street. A boot maker by trade, August brought all three of his sons into the business. The family lived here for a short time before moving to Atlantic City. The house is still a private residence and has been in the same family for several generations.

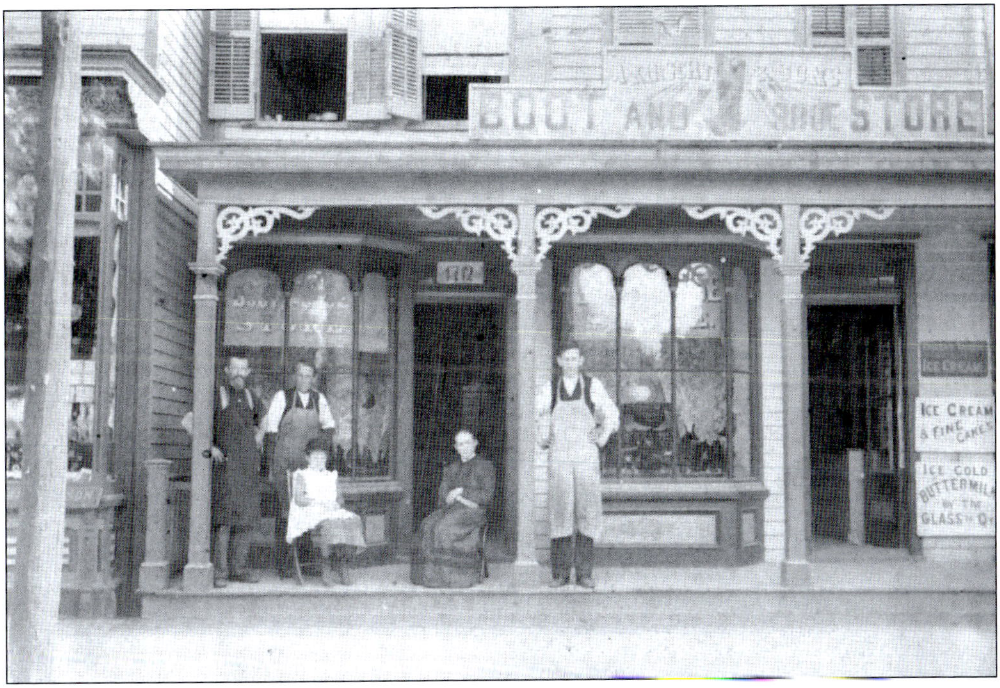

A. Kirscht & Sons Boot and Shoe Store was on the 1700 block of Atlantic Avenue in Atlantic City, between Illinois and Indiana Avenues. Seen here standing are, from left to right, Robert, Charles, and Herman Kirscht. The child and woman are unidentified. Some of the early residents of Egg Harbor City found their fame and fortune in the "City by the Sea."

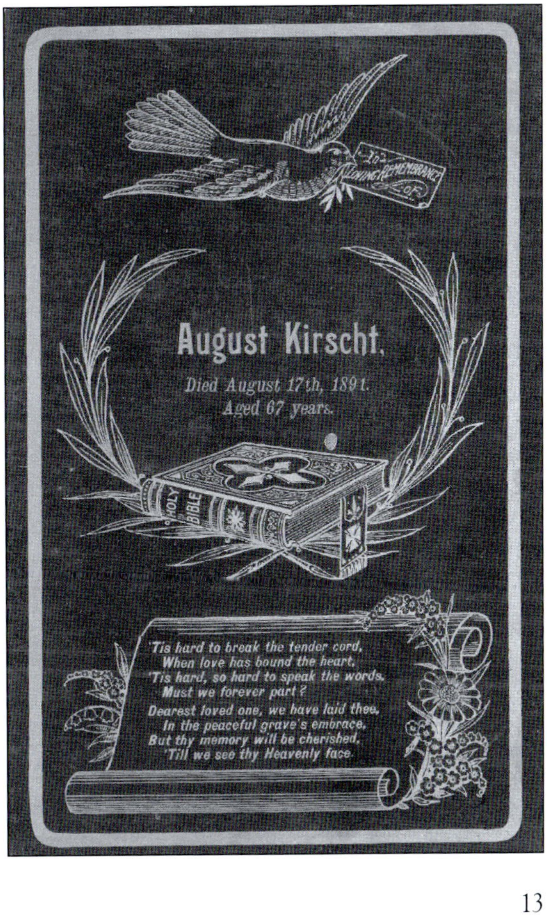

August Kirscht's memorial card is seen here. He and his wife, Amalia (November 19, 1823–May 2, 1884), are buried in Egg Harbor City Cemetery.

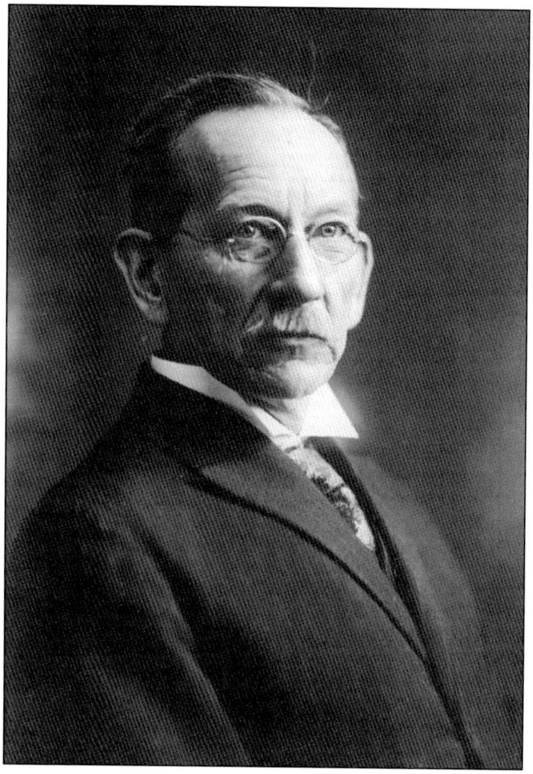

Herman George Kirscht (August 2, 1859–October 14, 1949) was one of three sons of August and Amalia Kirscht, two of whom were born in Egg Harbor City. Herman was a pioneer photographer in Atlantic County. In the 1900 US census, he described himself as a "Capitalist." This is how he looked later in life, when he put together a scrapbook of his experiences and travels, some of which is included in this book.

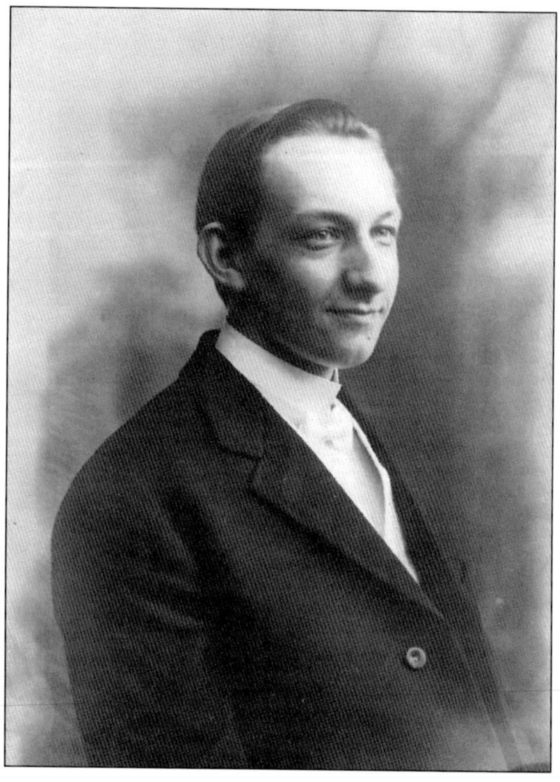

Max Herman Kirscht (January 14, 1885–August 14, 1921) was born in Atlantic City. This picture was taken in 1912, when he was 27 years old. Like his father Herman, Max became a photographer. The *Pleasantville Press* would praise Max as "an artist of exceptional ability . . . his work is far superior to most of that procured in the large cities . . . Pleasantville is fortunate in having such an artist in her midst."

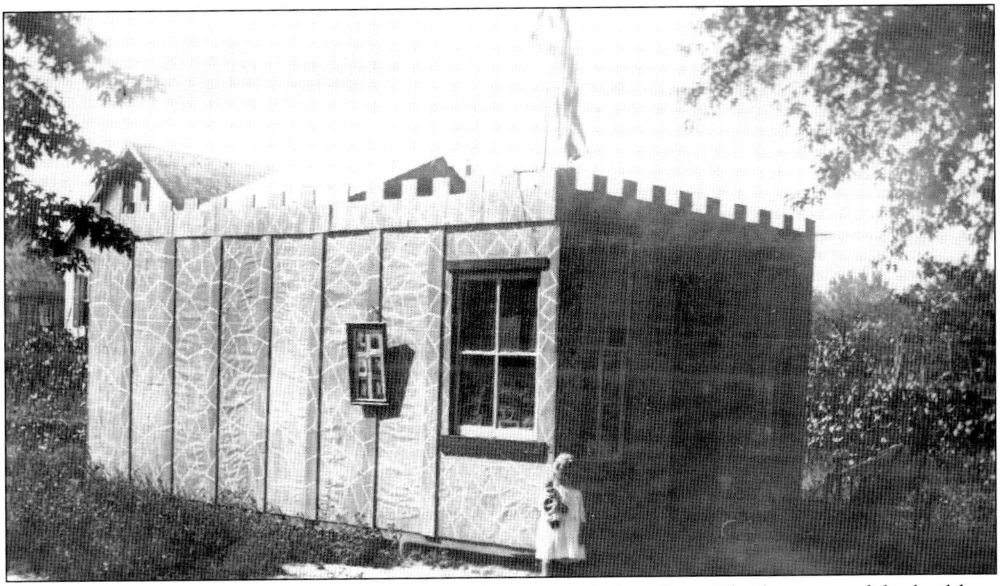

This is Herman Kirscht's first photography studio in Egg Harbor City. The location of the building is unknown, but it may have been behind the family residence on Chicago Avenue. The little girl is Clara Kirscht, Herman's daughter, who appears to be three or four years old, dating the image to either 1898 or 1899. The building is obviously a temporary studio.

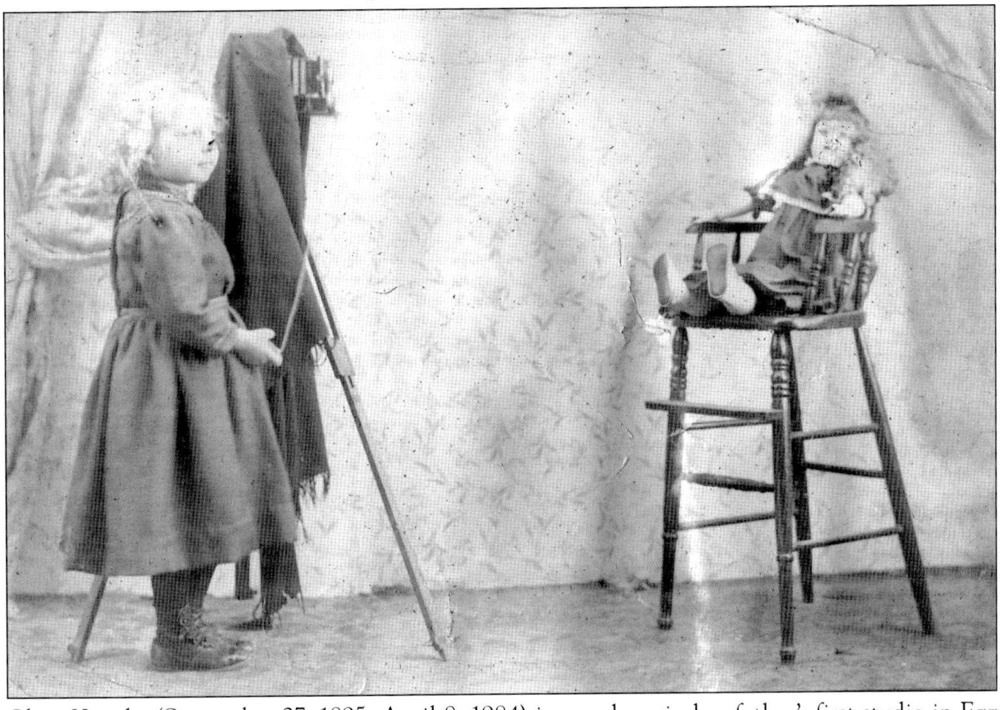

Clara Kirscht (September 27, 1895–April 8, 1984) is seen here in her father's first studio in Egg Harbor City in 1900. This photograph was found in one of her scrapbooks. Written above the picture was "Sweetie and Her Dolly." A number of Herman Kirscht's early images show a certain ease and simplicity both behind and in front of the camera, especially in those that involved members of his family.

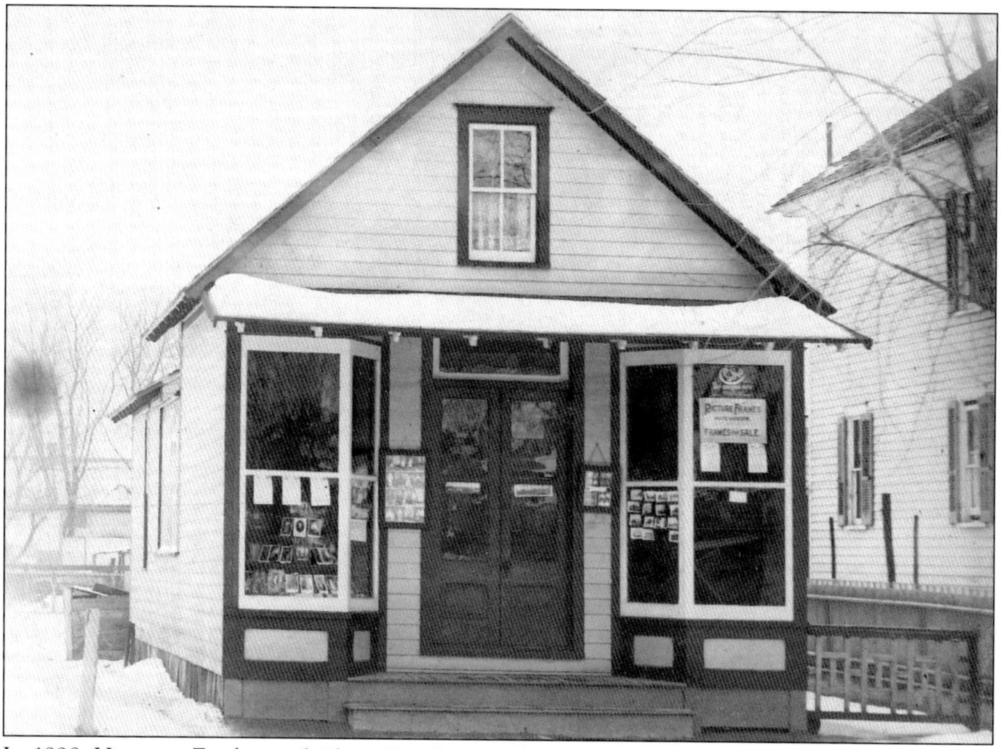

In 1898, Herman, Emilie, and Clara Kirscht were living in Egg Harbor City on what appears to have been a part-time basis. Clara wrote in one of her scrapbooks that the family had a summer home in Egg Harbor City. In 1904, Herman purchased a lot and portions of two adjacent lots on Cincinnati Avenue, between the White Horse Pike and Arago Street, and built a second photography studio.

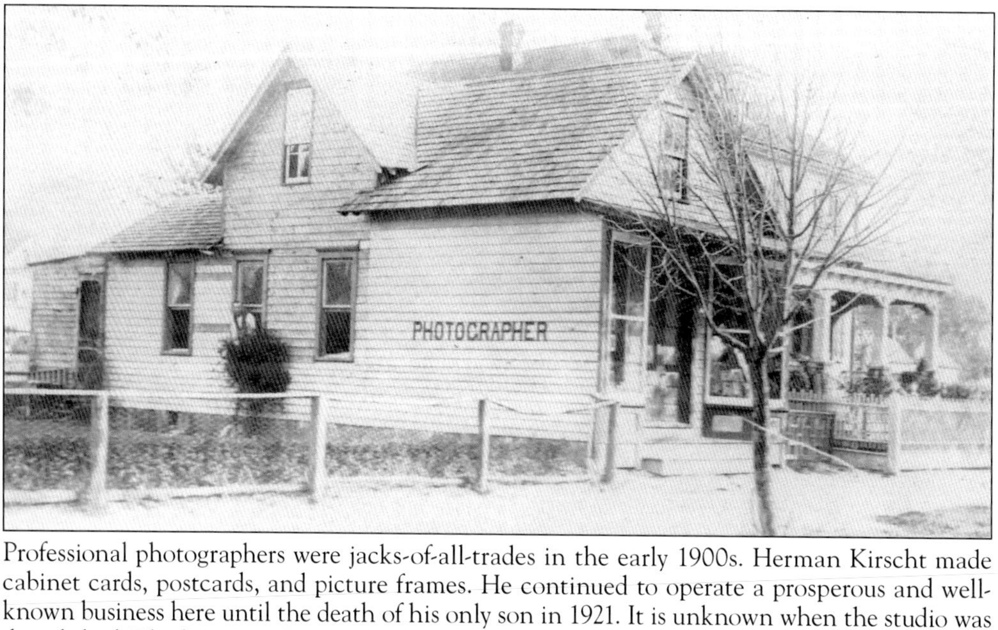

Professional photographers were jacks-of-all-trades in the early 1900s. Herman Kirscht made cabinet cards, postcards, and picture frames. He continued to operate a prosperous and well-known business here until the death of his only son in 1921. It is unknown when the studio was demolished. The house to the right is 238–240 Cincinnati Avenue.

This photograph of Clara Kirscht and her father was taken about 1900 in his first studio. Clara went on to spend much of her working life as a saleslady. She was also very involved in the Presbyterian church in Pleasantville.

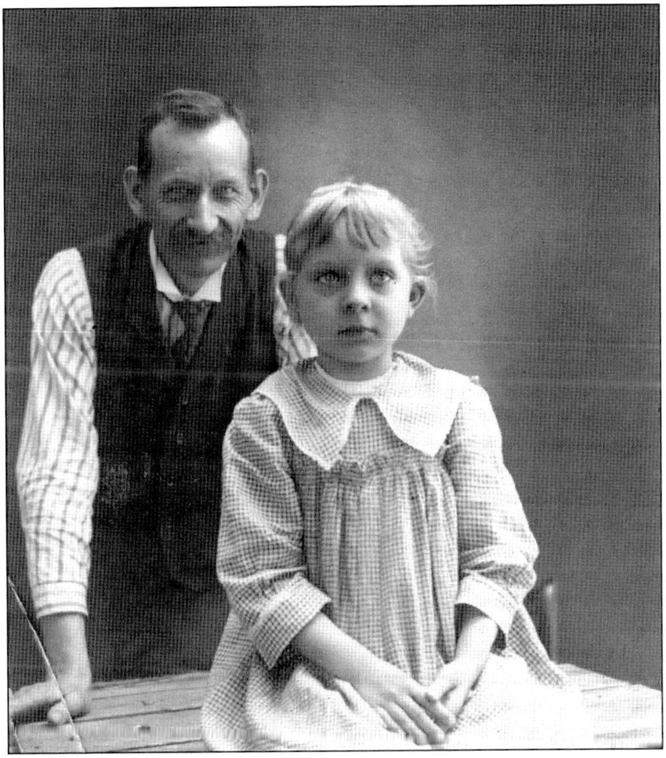

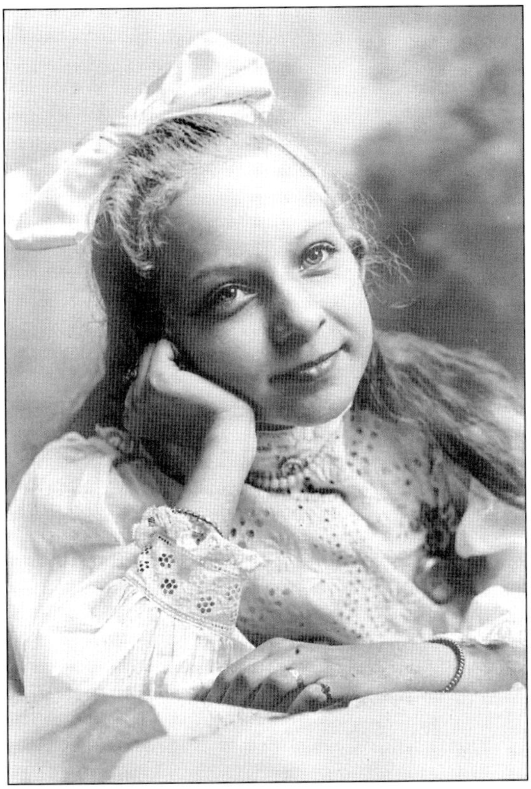

Clara was the only daughter of Herman and Emilie Kirscht. Clara was 13 years old when her father took this photograph. By this time, Herman was a well-known and respected photographer in Egg Harbor City.

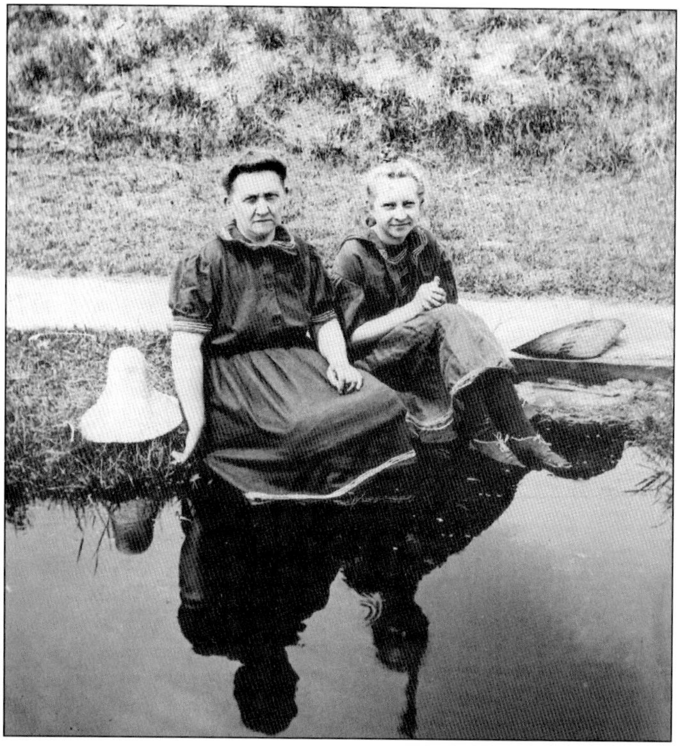

Emilie and Clara Kirscht pose next to the serpentine creek at the Neutral Water Health Resort. Both ladies are dressed in the full outfit required by Dr. Charles Smith. The resort was a popular attraction in Egg Harbor City. Considering the number of photographs and postcards they took there, the Kirschts spent a good deal of time at Dr. Smith's sanitarium.

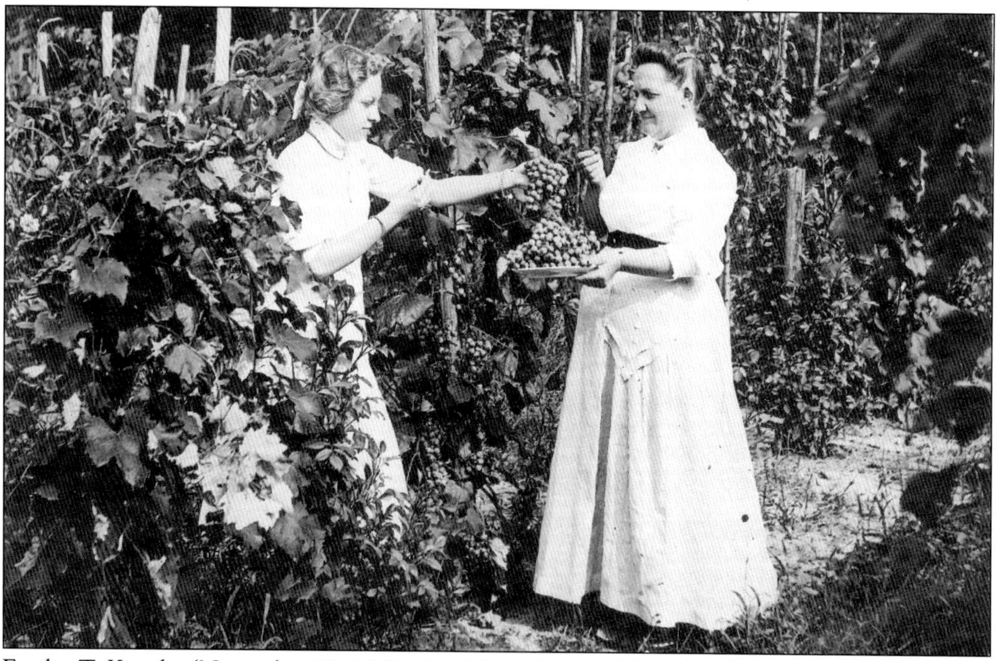

Emilia T. Kirscht (November 11, 1860–April 26, 1944) and her daughter Clara pick grapes in Egg Harbor City in 1911. "Emilie," as she was called, was born in Germany and immigrated in 1883. There was a time when small vineyards could be found throughout Egg Harbor City. Some of the grapes were used for personal consumption; however, most were sold to local wineries for commercial purposes.

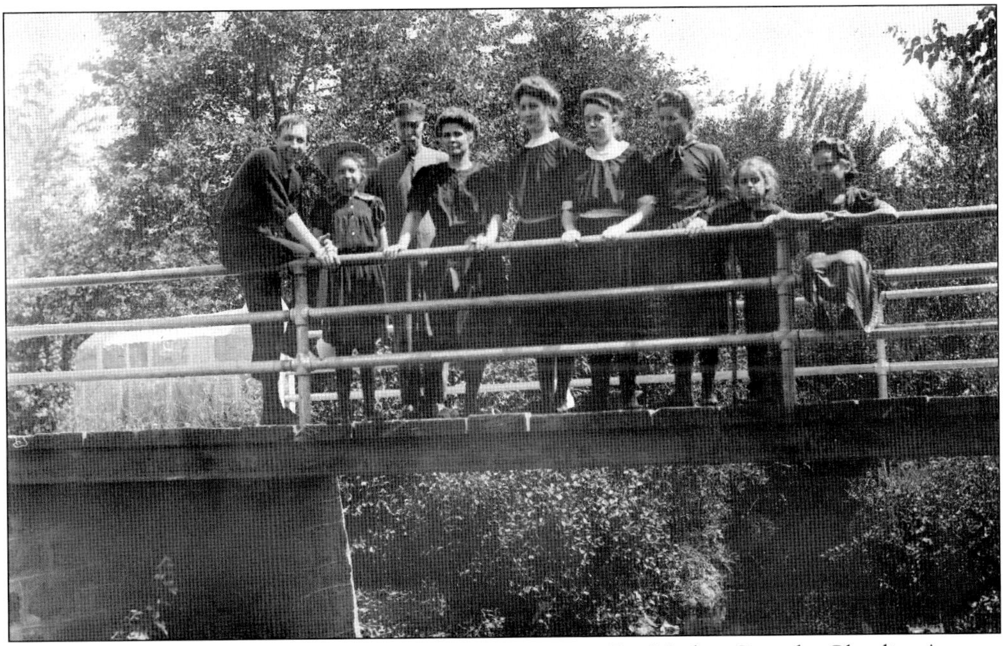

During the early years of Dr. Charles Smith's sanitarium in Egg Harbor City, the Claudius Avenue Bridge was a popular place to pose for photographs. In this image, also found in Clara Kirscht's scrapbook and taken in 1907 or 1908, a small party waits while Herman Kirscht takes their picture. Max and Clara Kirscht are on the far left.

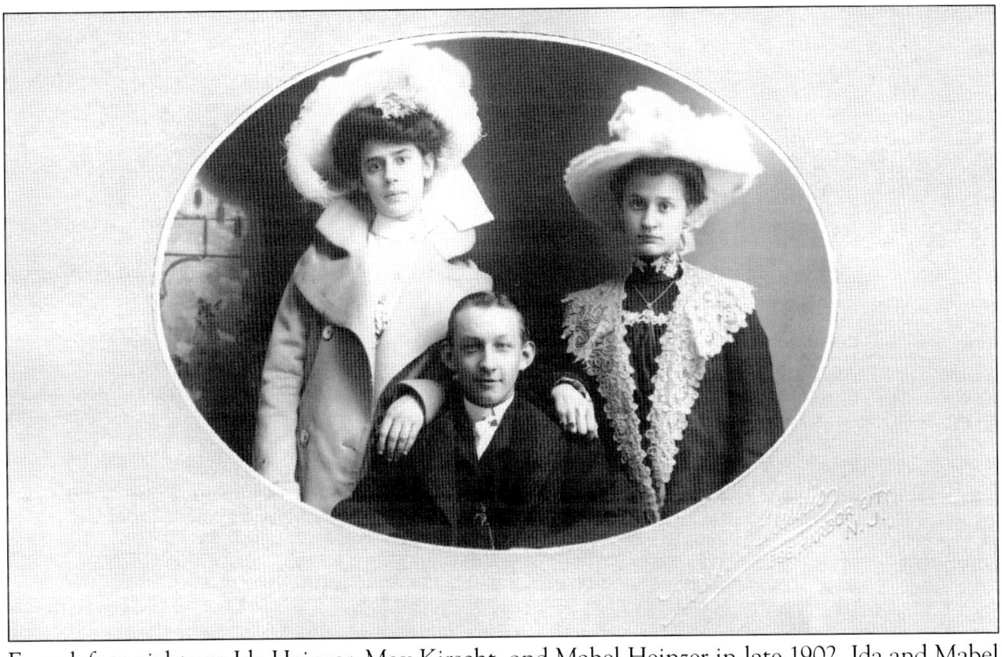

From left to right are Ida Heinzer, Max Kirscht, and Mabel Heinzer in late 1902. Ida and Mabel were sisters, and the Heinzer and Kirscht families were close. Members of the Heinzer family operated bakeries in both Egg Harbor City and Pleasantville, including the Vienna Bakery, which was located at the corner of Washington Avenue and Main Street. The two families remained friends for many years.

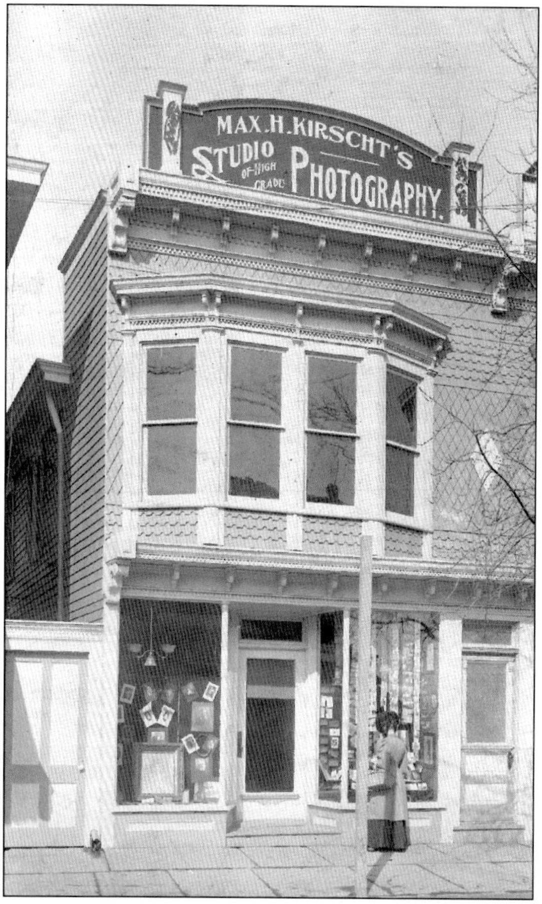

Max Kirscht's photography studio was located at 3 North Main Street in Pleasantville. Around 1905, Nickelodeons—usually makeshift movie theaters operated in storefronts—became popular. Max was the first person to open such a theater in Pleasantville. He charged 5¢ for a show and "did a fair business." The building was razed years ago, and the lot is still empty today.

The interior of Max Kirscht's photography studio is seen here. Nearly all professional photographers around 1900 used view cameras, most of which were handmade wooden devices. Negatives were usually glass plates and rather large, generally in either five-inch-by-seven-inch or eight-inch-by-ten-inch formats. Prints were made by contact printing rather than by enlargement. By 1917, Max was able to produce enlargements and copies of older photographs.

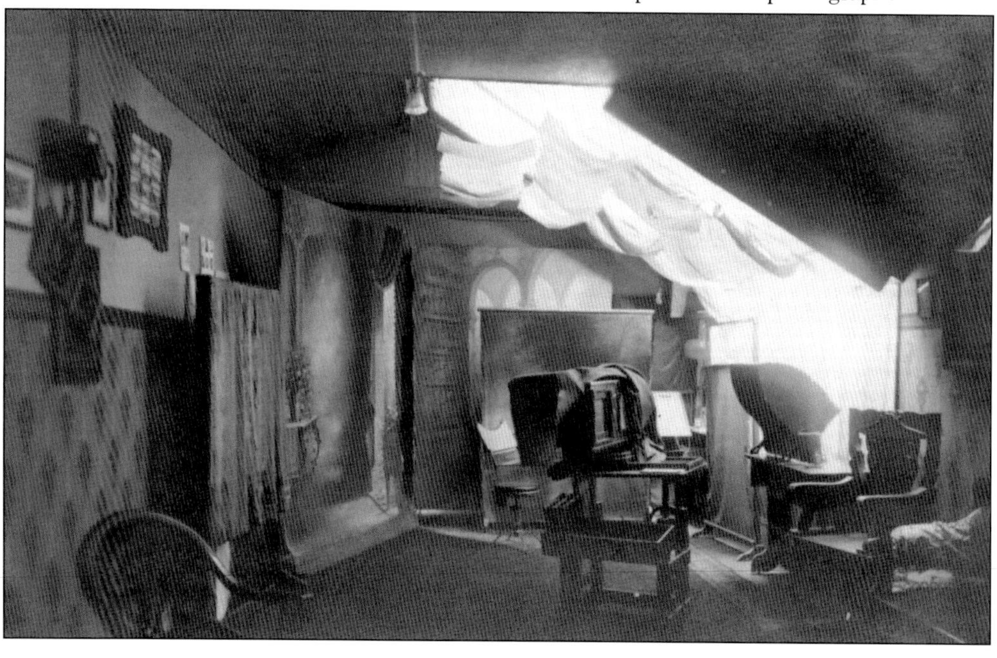

Max Kirscht built this home in 1910 on Brighton Place, which is known today as Abbey Lane. That is him sitting on the front step. Pleasantville was growing rapidly at the time and described as the "Elegant Highland Suburb of Atlantic City." The house still stands.

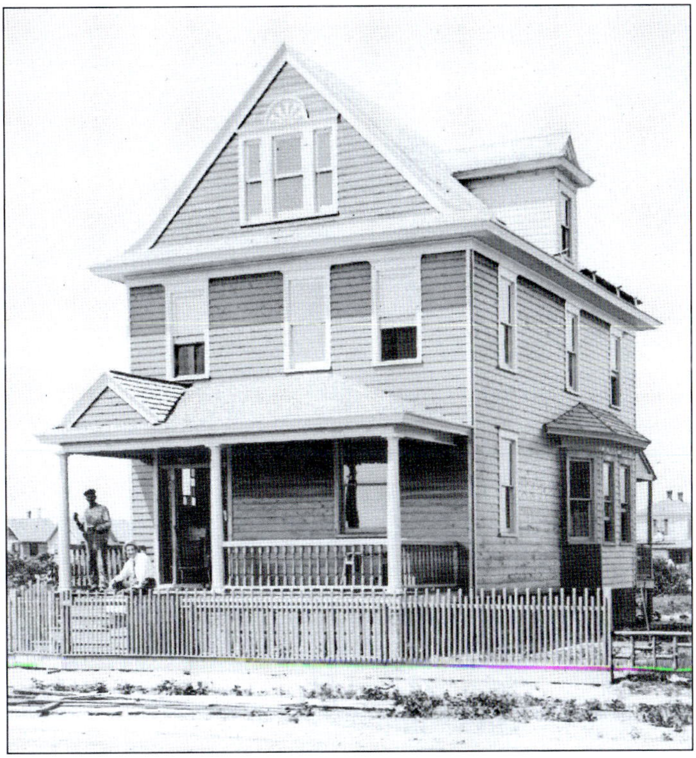

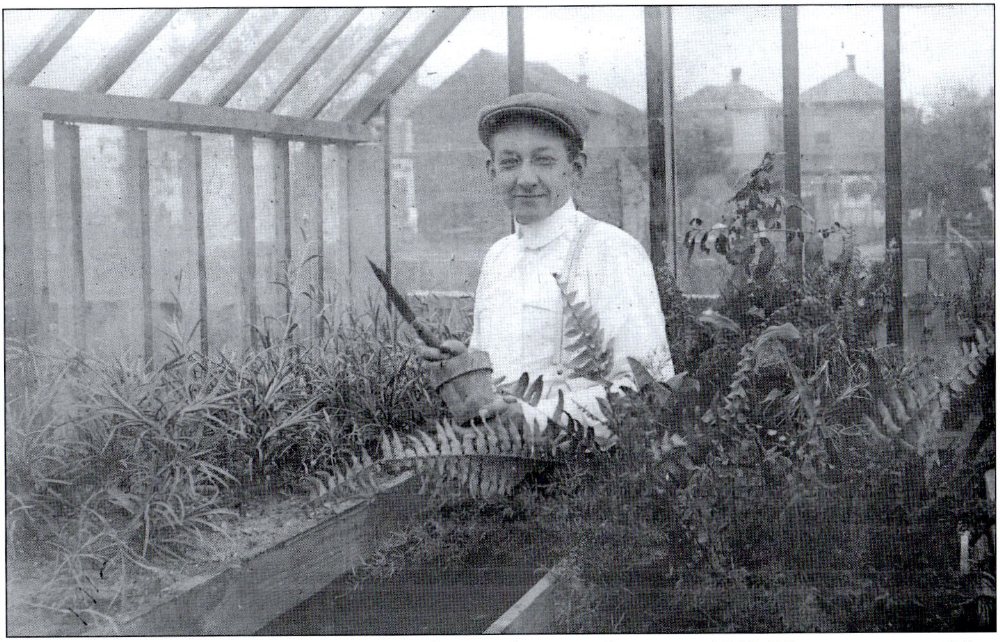

This photograph of Max Kirscht was taken in his greenhouse in 1912. That same year, Max married Lola Frances Gaskill, a local woman. Max contracted typhoid fever about 1918, and his health worsened in June 1921. He died at Sunairy Sanitarium in West Chester, Pennsylvania, on August 14, 1921. The *Pleasantville Press* published his obituary on the front page, noting that the flag at city hall was lowered for several days in his honor.

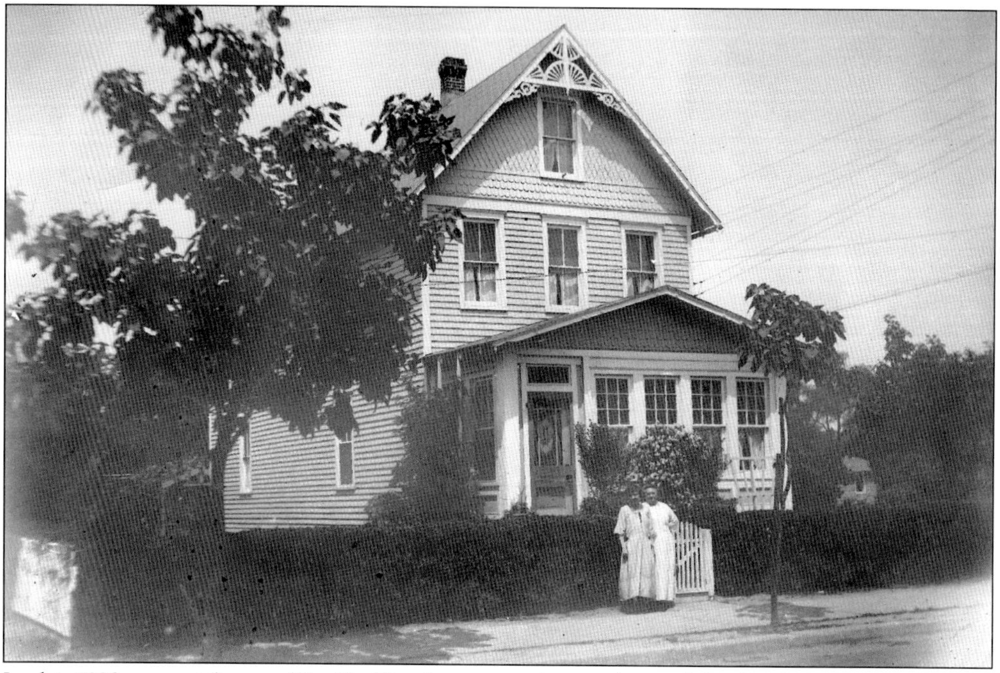

In this 1923 scene, Clara and Emilie Kirscht are standing in front of the family home, at 200 West Washington Avenue. The family lived here for 50 years, summering in Egg Harbor City until 1920. Many years later, a small store called the Novelty Shop operated out of this house, selling handmade wooden novelties, greeting cards, crocheted articles, baby items, earrings, and brooches.

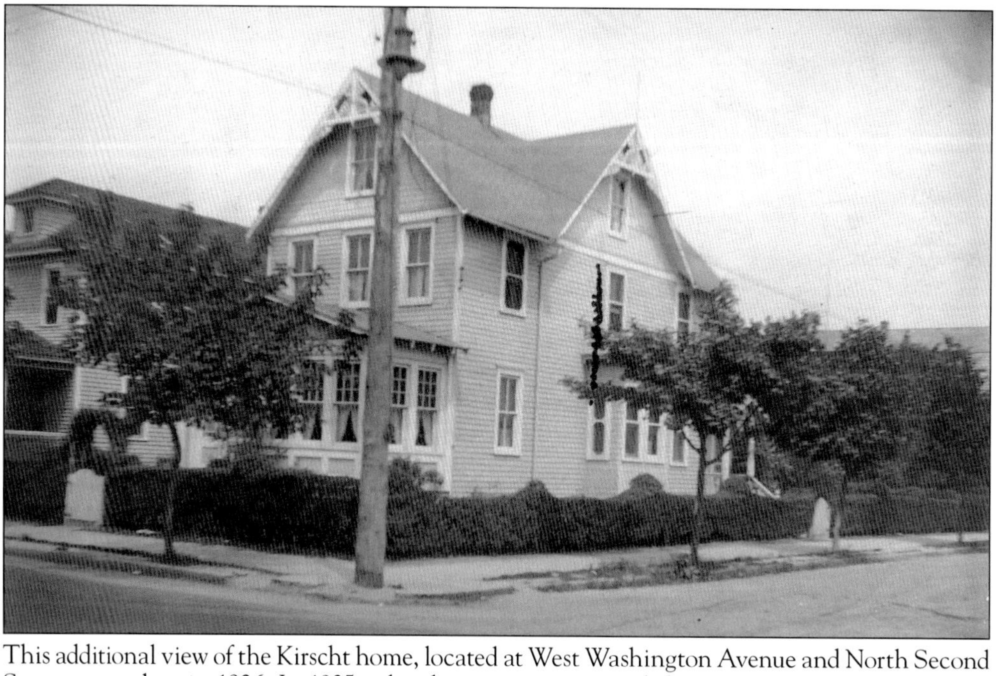

This additional view of the Kirscht home, located at West Washington Avenue and North Second Street, was taken in 1926. In 1935, a local newspaper reported that pranksters had placed a for sale sign on the front lawn on Mischief Night. Considering some of the other tricks that took place that evening, the family must have felt somewhat relieved.

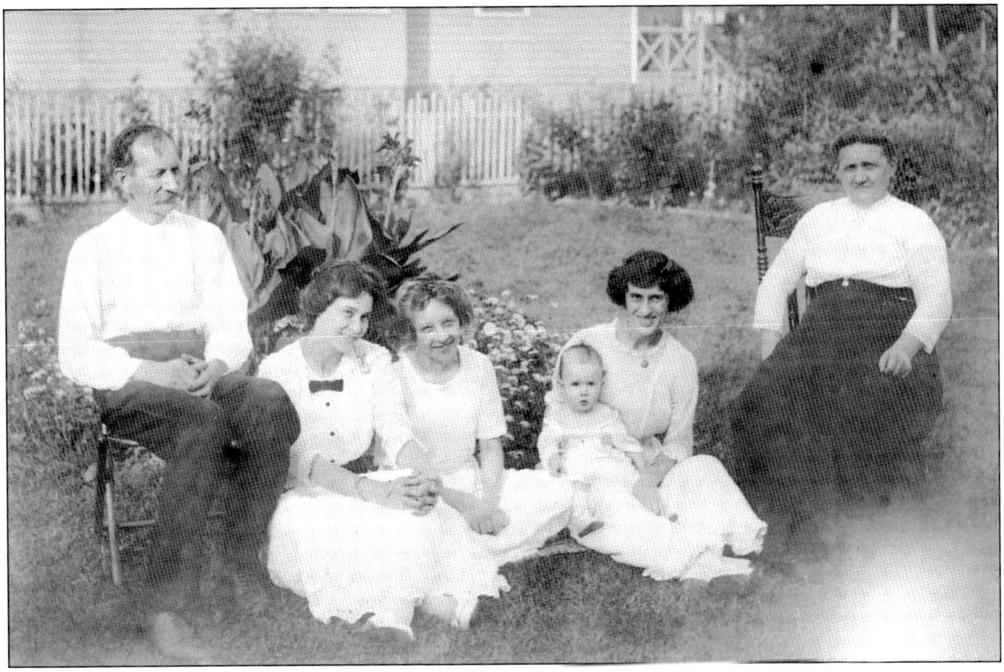

The Heinzer sisters are seen here visiting the Kirscht family at their home in Pleasantville around 1917. From left to right are Herman Kirscht, Mabel Heinzer Brum, Clara Kirscht, Ida Heinzer Steckle, Margaret Steckle, and Emilie Kirscht.

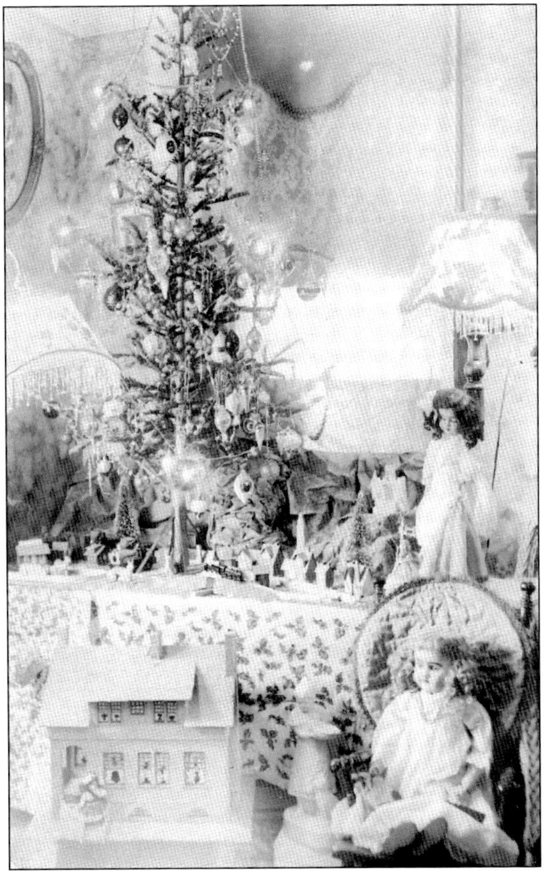

The Kirscht family was known for their elaborate Christmas displays and even lauded in the local newspapers for their holiday decorations. Herman photographed these exhibits, which were sometimes used on postcards.

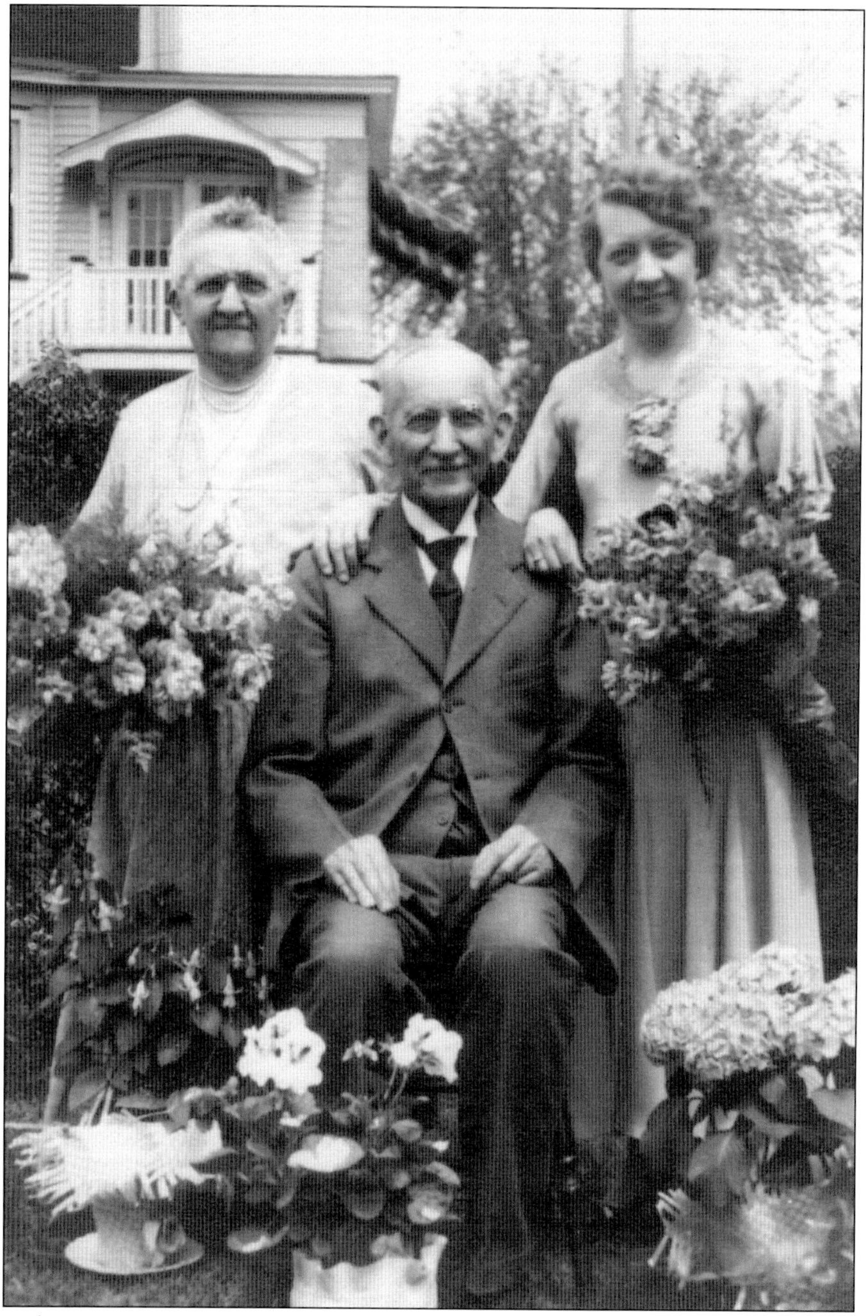

The Kirscht family is seen here in Pleasantville around 1925. In many ways, the Kirscht family migration through Atlantic County was typical of Germans from Egg Harbor City in the second half of the 1800s. When Emilie died of cancer in 1944, the couple was only 12 days shy of their 60th wedding anniversary. She was 83 years old. Herman would live on without her for another five years. He passed away in his home on October 14, 1949. He was 90 years old. Clara married Joseph Bakes but had no children. She would outlive her husband and pass away in Somers Point, New Jersey, on Sunday, April 8, 1984. She was 89 years old and is buried next to her brother. All five are buried in the family plot in Atlantic City Cemetery in Pleasantville.

Two

Egg Harbor City

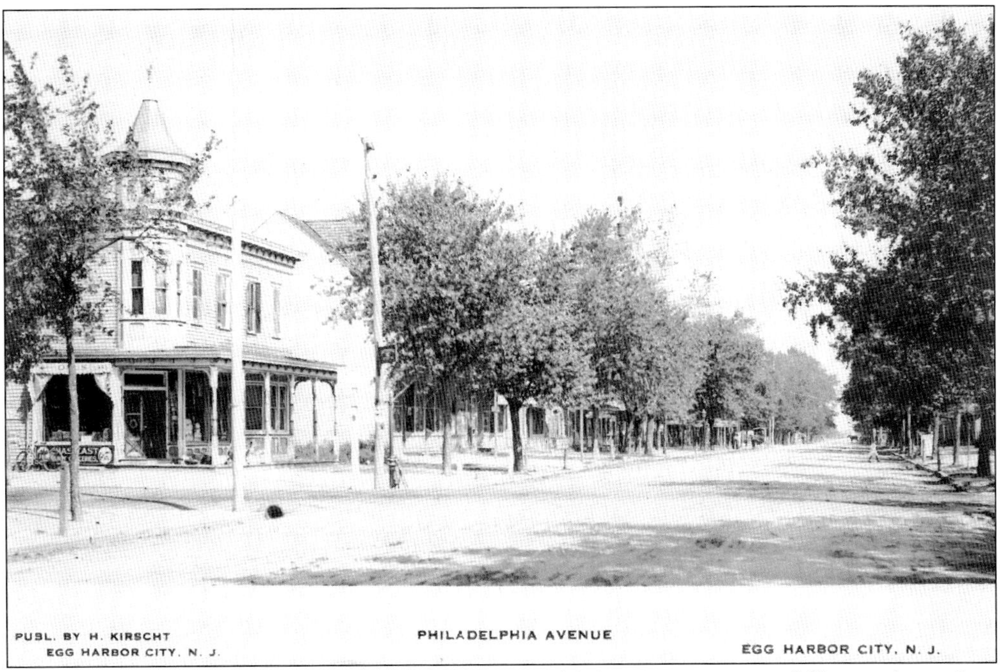

The intersection of the White Horse Pike and Philadelphia Avenue was a different place when this photograph was taken in the early 1900s. Charles Cast's grocery store, on the northwest corner, was modified numerous times over the years. It later became the home of George Otto's Photography Studio and Stationary Store and, later, Atlantic Drug. Recent repairs to this building did not go well, and it was subsequently demolished in April 2010.

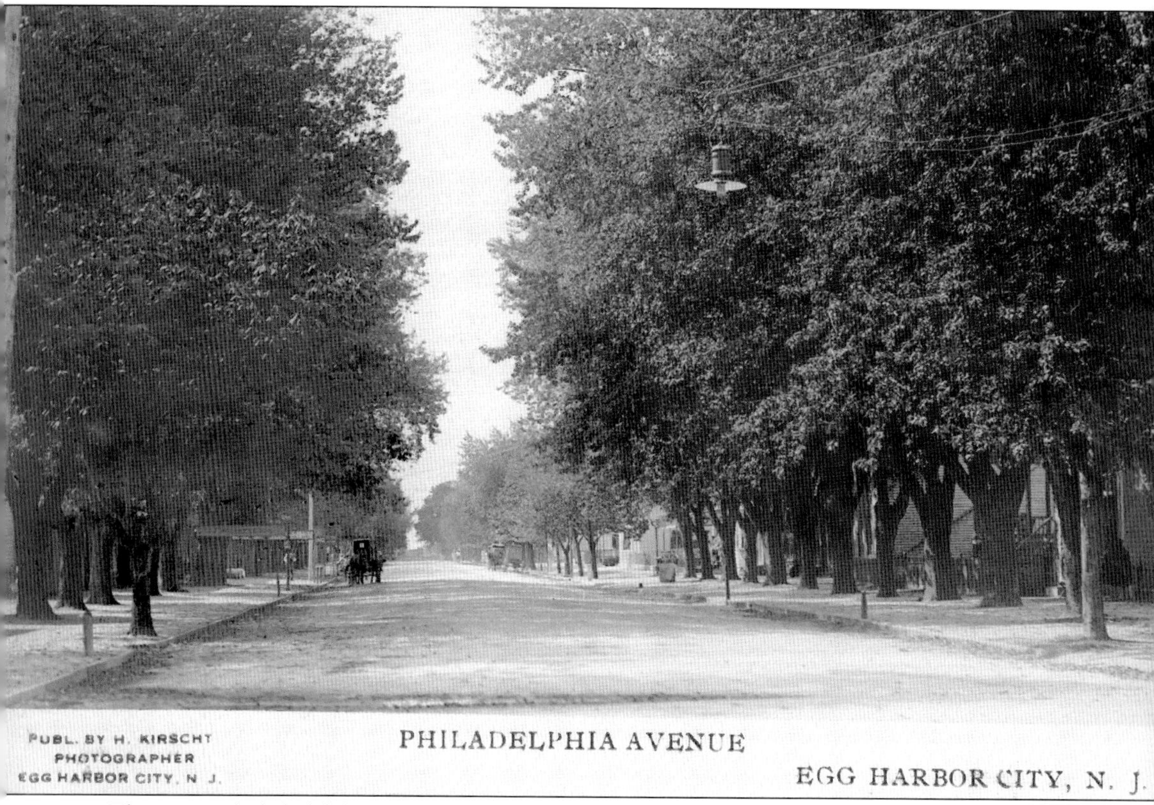

This view of Philadelphia Avenue faces north from Atlantic Avenue. This was considered the city's main thoroughfare since it led from the railroad stations, through the central business district, and to the Mullica River. The avenue is 100 feet wide because a passenger railway was planned to run throughout the city via this roadway.

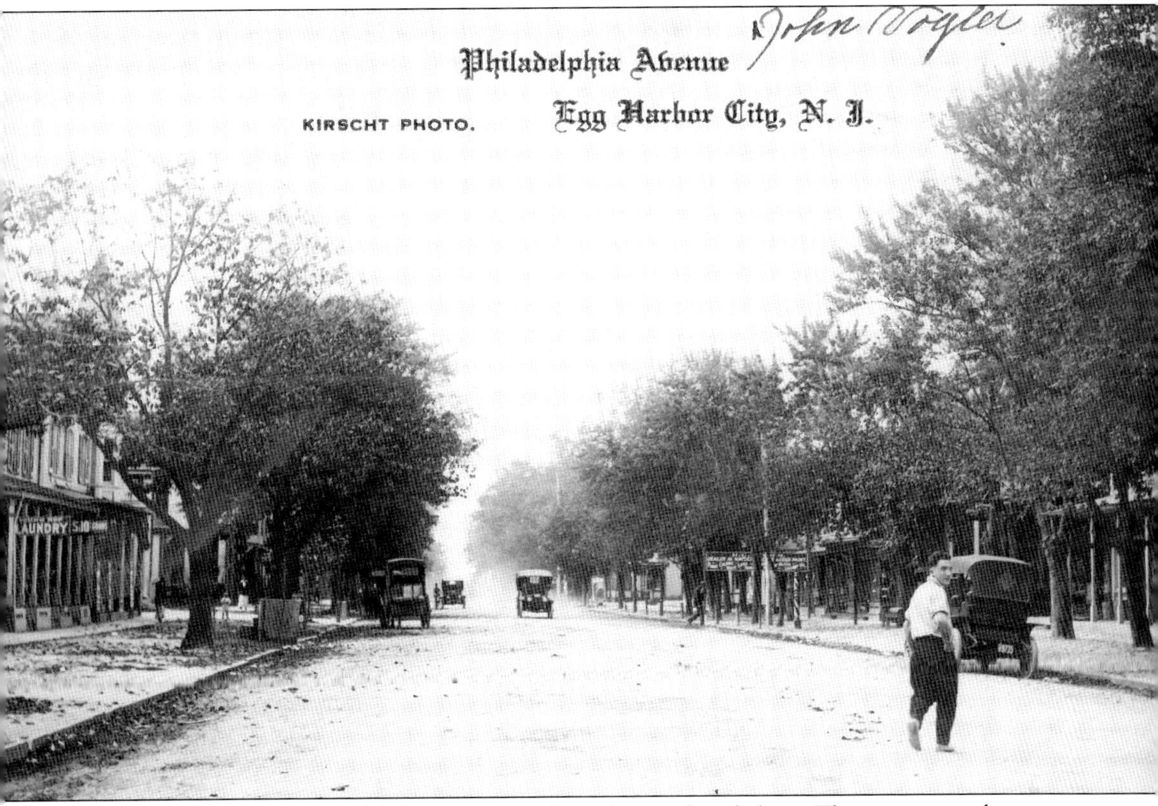

This is another view of Philadelphia Avenue, taken about a decade later. The avenue was known for its wide, tree-lined sidewalks, where folks from all over Atlantic County came to shop and stroll. By 1917, the roadway was dominated by automobiles. In the 1920s and 1930s, many of these trees were removed, which was a point of consternation years later.

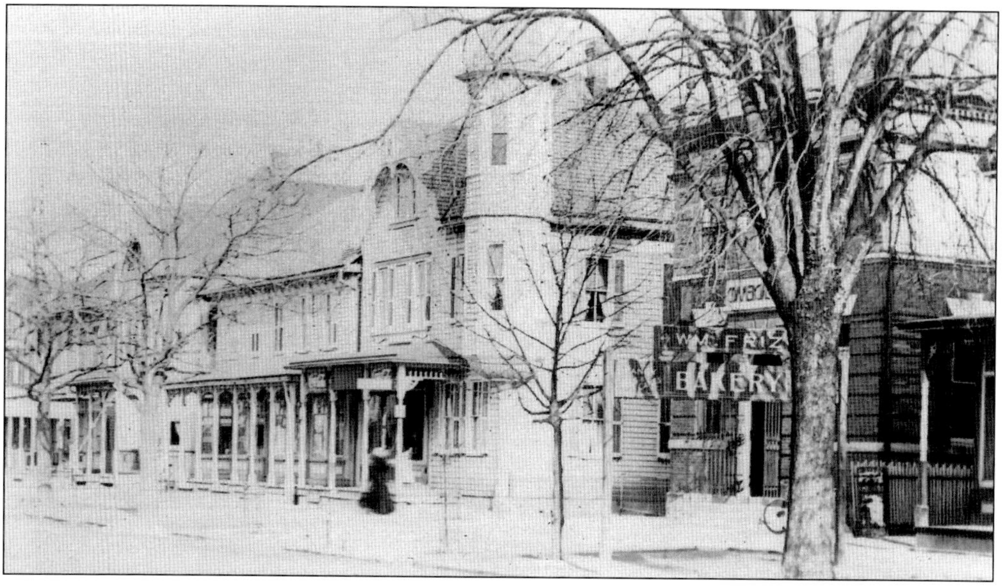

On July 1, 1854, the inaugural trip of the Camden & Atlantic Railroad left Coopers Ferry, Camden, for Atlantic City. Aboard that train were a number of prominent German Americans from Philadelphia. As the story goes, the train made a scheduled stop at Landing Creek to take on water, and the men got off to look over the Gloucester Tract, which was for sale. These gentlemen envisioned a German settlement, with an urban center, surrounded by a farming district. This would be a great agricultural and industrial community; a commercial hub served by direct railroad and maritime connections to Philadelphia and New York. Germans could own farms and businesses and walk along tree-lined streets. This would be a place where they could enjoy American freedom as well as preserve their German way of life. These two photographs show Philadelphia Avenue about 1915.

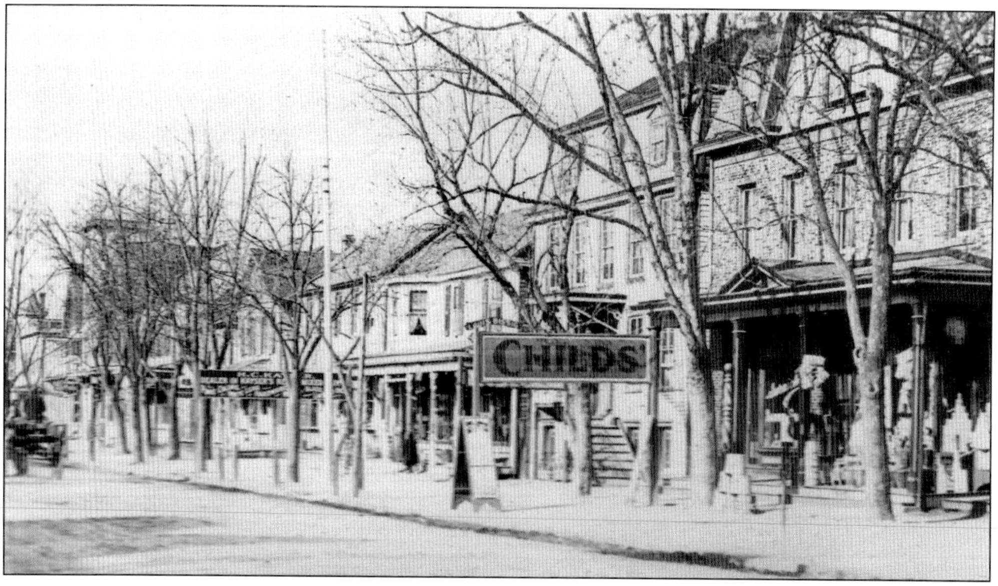

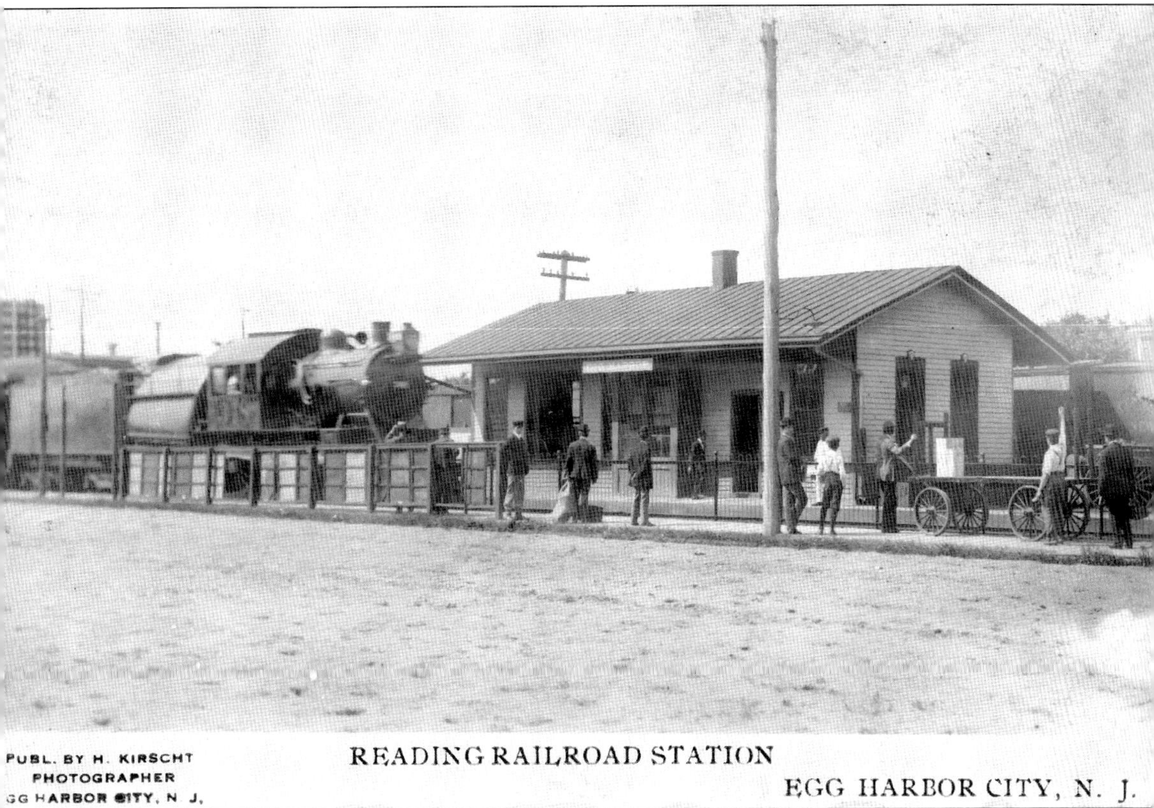

The Atlantic City Railroad (ACRR)'s Egg Harbor City station was located on Aloe Street, between Philadelphia and South Liverpool Avenues in Galloway Township. The Reading Company acquired control of the Philadelphia & Atlantic City Railway (P&AC) on September 20, 1883, and modernized the entire line. On March 26, 1889, the P&AC, along with other Reading-controlled lines in South Jersey, were consolidated into the Atlantic City Railroad.

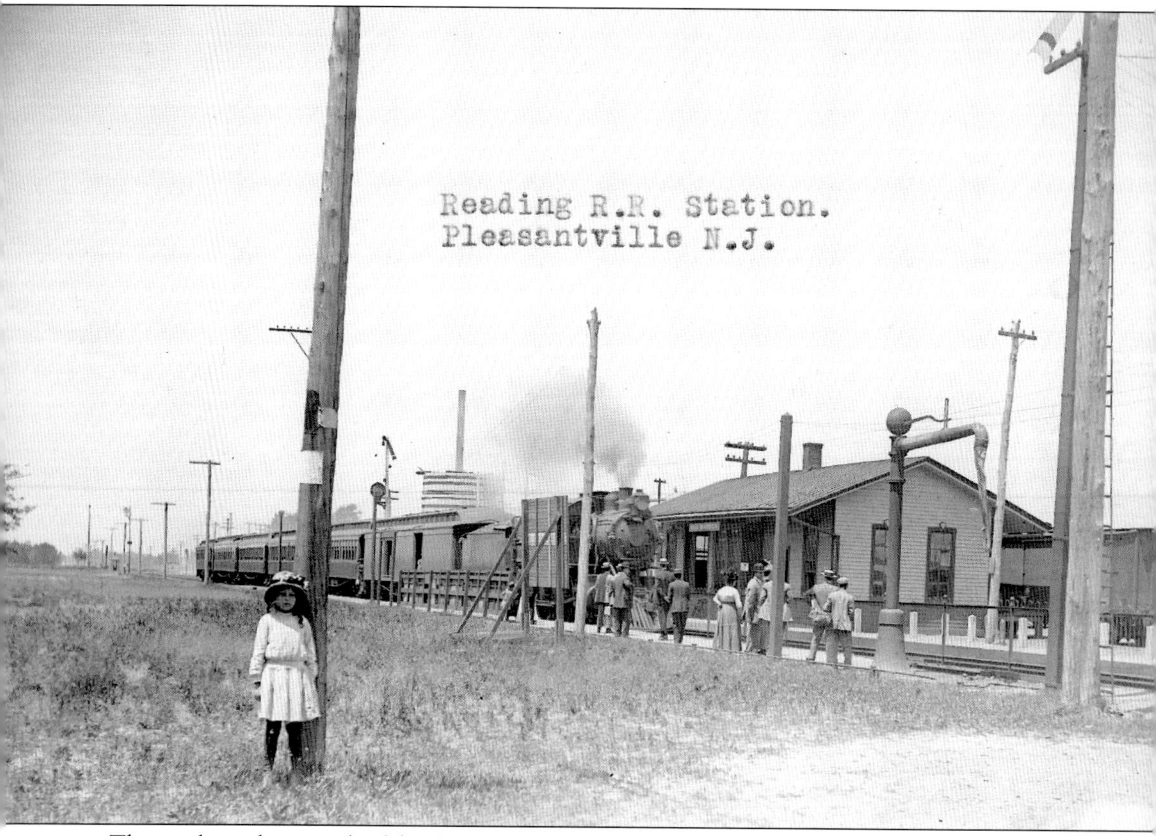

This is a later photograph of the ACRR's Egg Harbor City station. It is believed that this photograph was taken about 1903 by Herman Kirscht. The northbound waiting room, so prominently displayed in later photographs, was yet to be constructed. The ACRR provided a direct route between Egg Harbor City and Pleasantville. Today, much of this property is the site of the Senn Oil Company and ServPro.

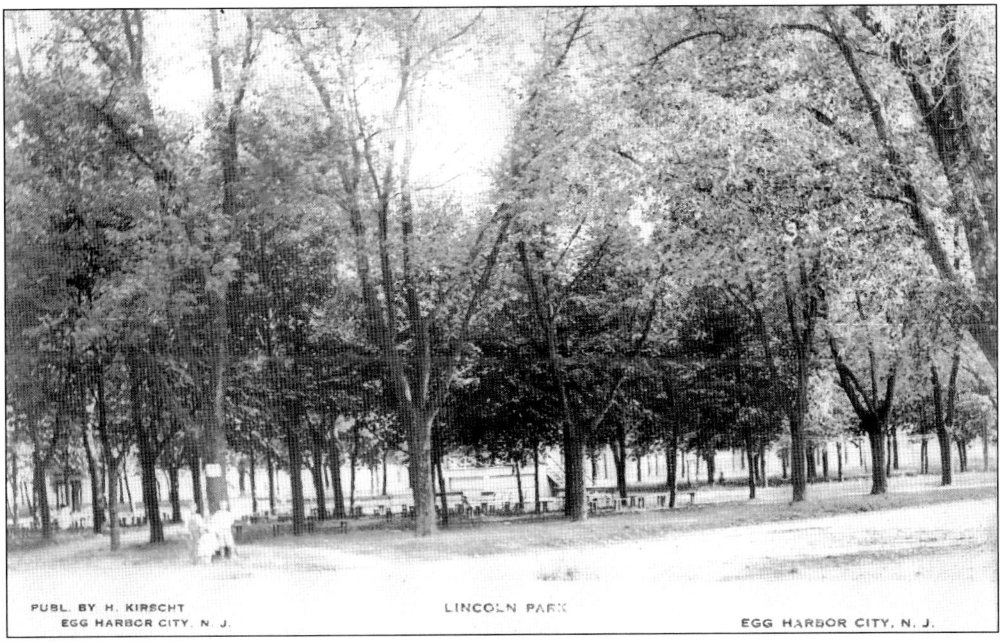

The founders of the Gloucester Farm and Town Association and Egg Harbor City considered parks and other public spaces important. Excursion Park has always been a public place. It was the location of the city's Excursion Hall, which not only served as a school and community center, but also as the municipal hall for many years. It was renamed Lincoln Park in 1905.

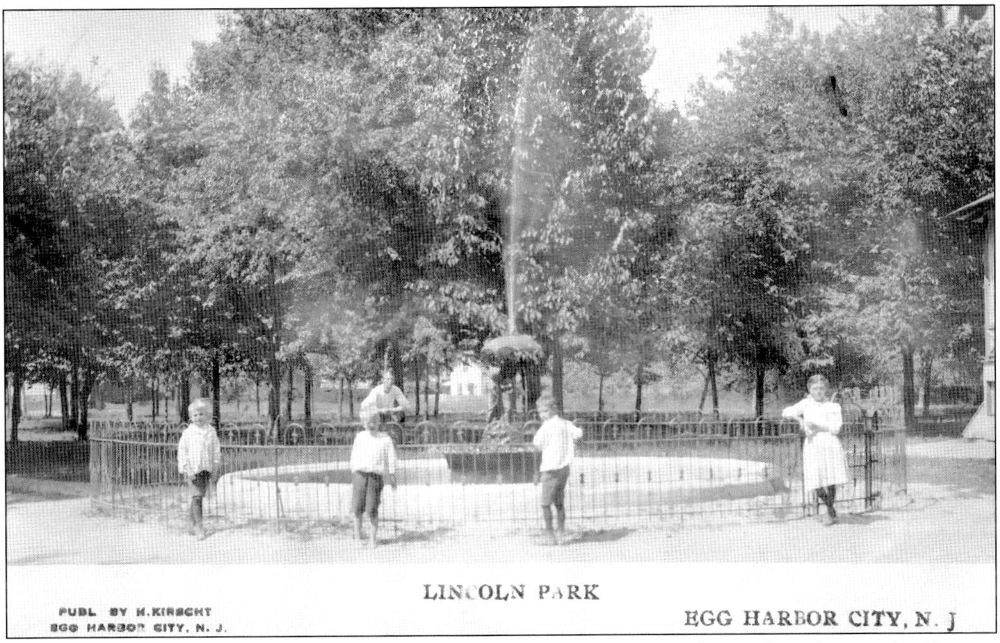

This fountain was once in Egg Harbor City's Lincoln Park. It was donated to the city by George Gerlach for the Golden Jubilee celebration in 1905. During the term of city clerk John Schuster Jr., the fountain was removed for safety reasons. It was donated to the Egg Harbor City Historical Society by Rosalie Schuster, his wife, in 1993. It is located next to the Roundhouse Museum and continues to operate today.

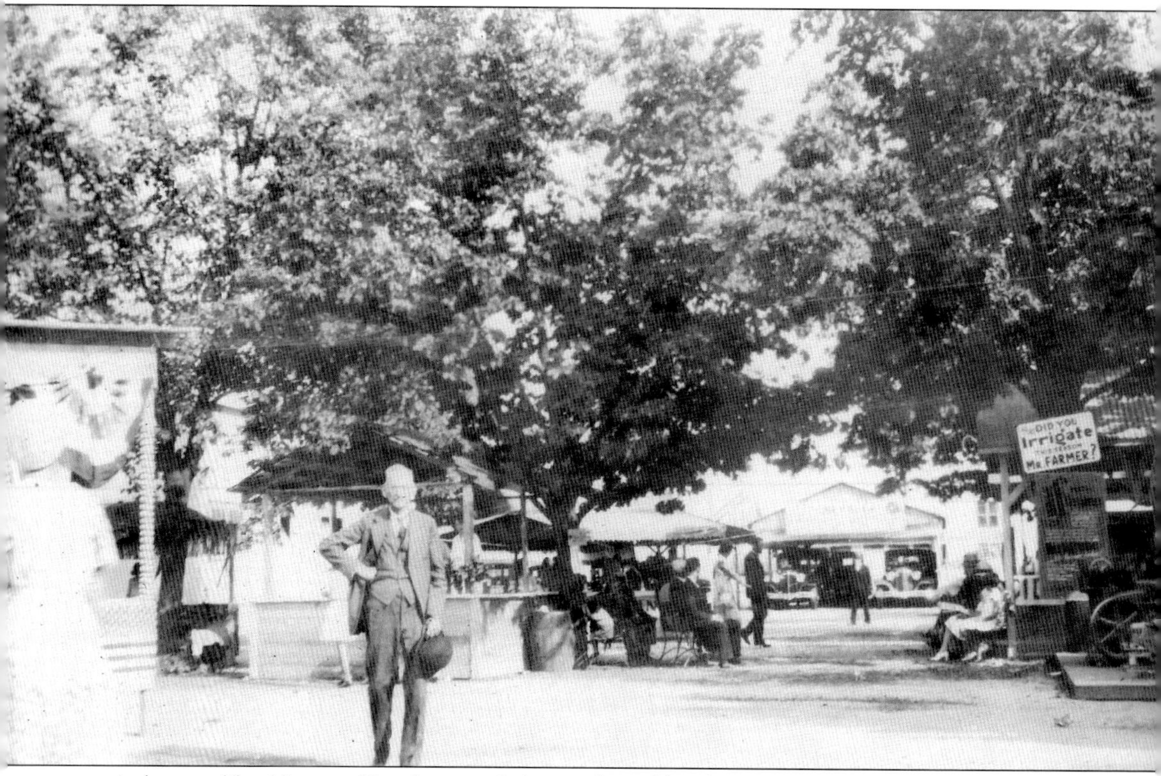

As he got older, Herman Kirscht recorded a number of family trips, especially their journeys to Egg Harbor City. In September 1930, they went to the 15th annual Atlantic County Agricultural Fair in Egg Harbor City. That year, the fair featured vaudeville actor "Paulus, The Nerveless," whose finale included a 200-foot slide down a slender line, which he held onto by his teeth.

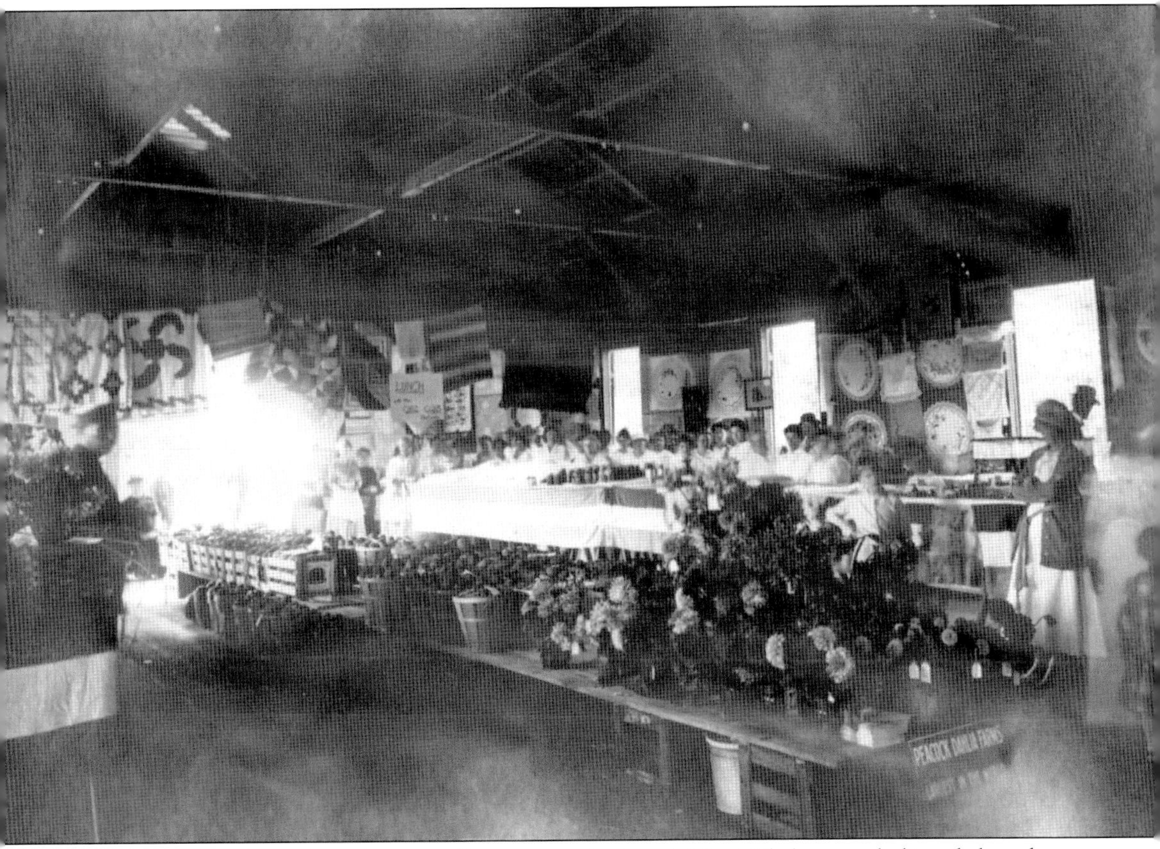

Egg Harbor City has a long history of hosting agricultural fairs. While some believed that the annual fairs lost much of their agricultural aspects through the years, they continued to be widely popular and functioned as major social affairs. World War II ended the fairs in the city. The Atlantic County 4-H continues this century-and-a-half tradition with an annual fair in nearby South Egg Harbor, Galloway Township.

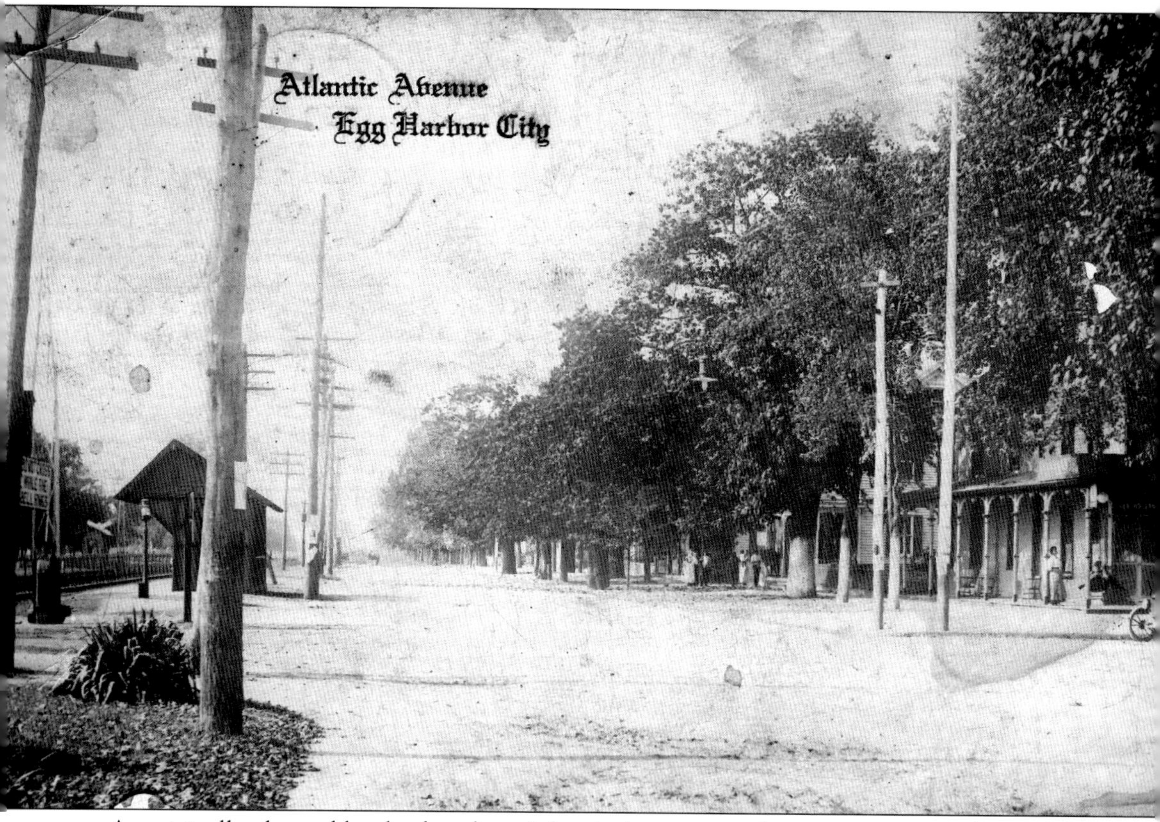

As originally planned by the founders, Atlantic Avenue was the major east-west thoroughfare through Egg Harbor City. The railroad station, the piano factory, the Gloucester Farm and Town Association offices and hotel, real estate offices, and some of the city's first hotels once lined this street. Many of the association officials lived in the immediate area.

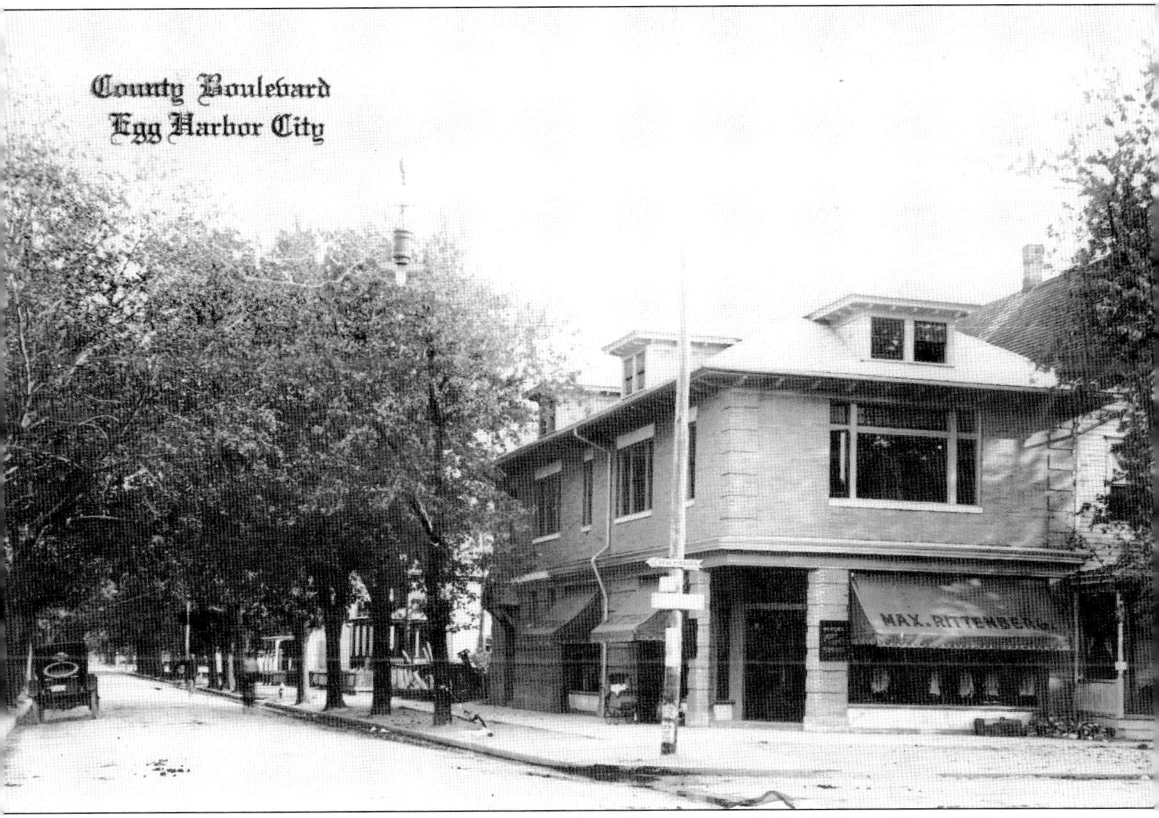

Max Rittenberg's Department Store was located at the corner of the White Horse Pike and Philadelphia Avenue. Rittenberg was the father of Fanny Rittenberg, a well-known Egg Harbor City educator and principal. In the late 1950s, this building was used as a clothing factory. Today, it is the site of an Exxon station.

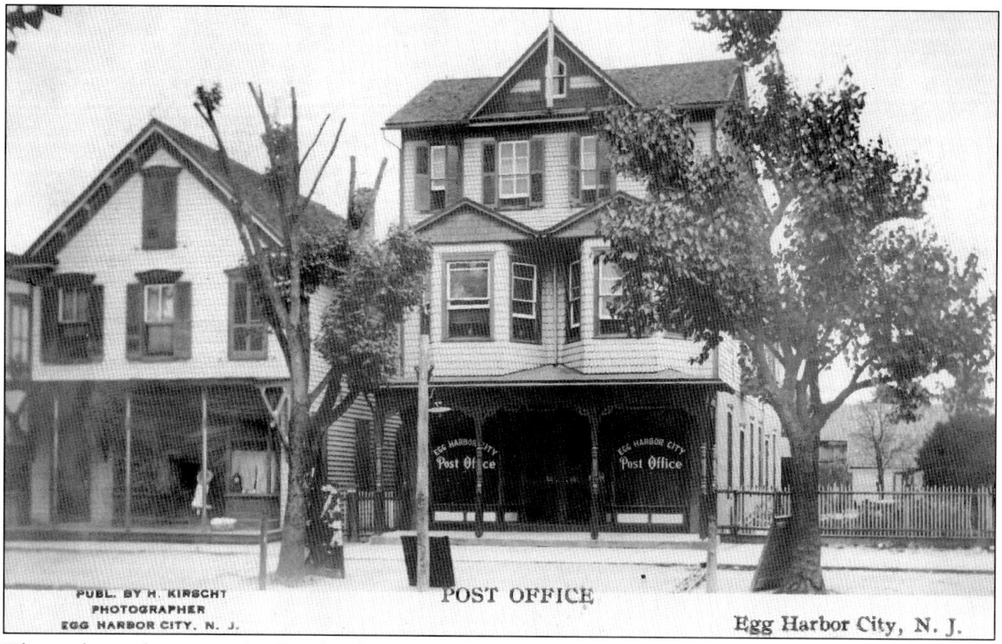

Throughout the years, the Egg Harbor City Post Office was in several locations, including in this building at 118 Philadelphia Avenue. In 1922, the post office moved into the recently constructed Broadway Building, across the street. Today, both of the buildings seen here are used by South Jersey Auto Supply.

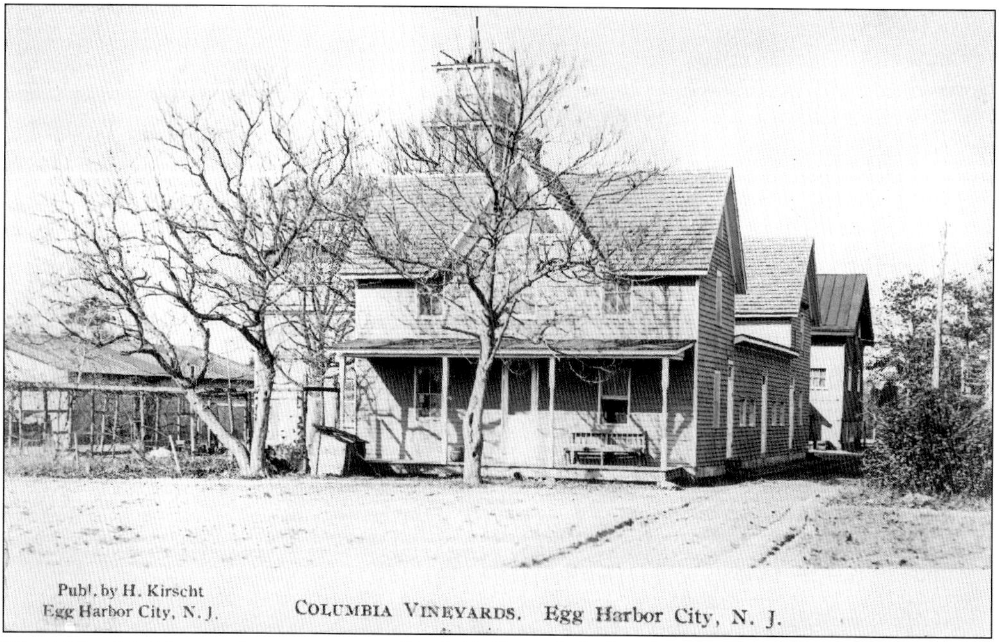

The Columbia Vineyard was once owned by L.N. Renault & Sons. Located on Philadelphia Avenue and Fichte Street, many of the buildings are now gone. More than any other commercial enterprise, Egg Harbor City's history was uniquely connected to the wine industry. That history and the size of the industry have earned the municipality the nickname "the Wine City." Renault Winery, which outlasted economic downturns and Prohibition, will celebrate its 150th anniversary in 2015.

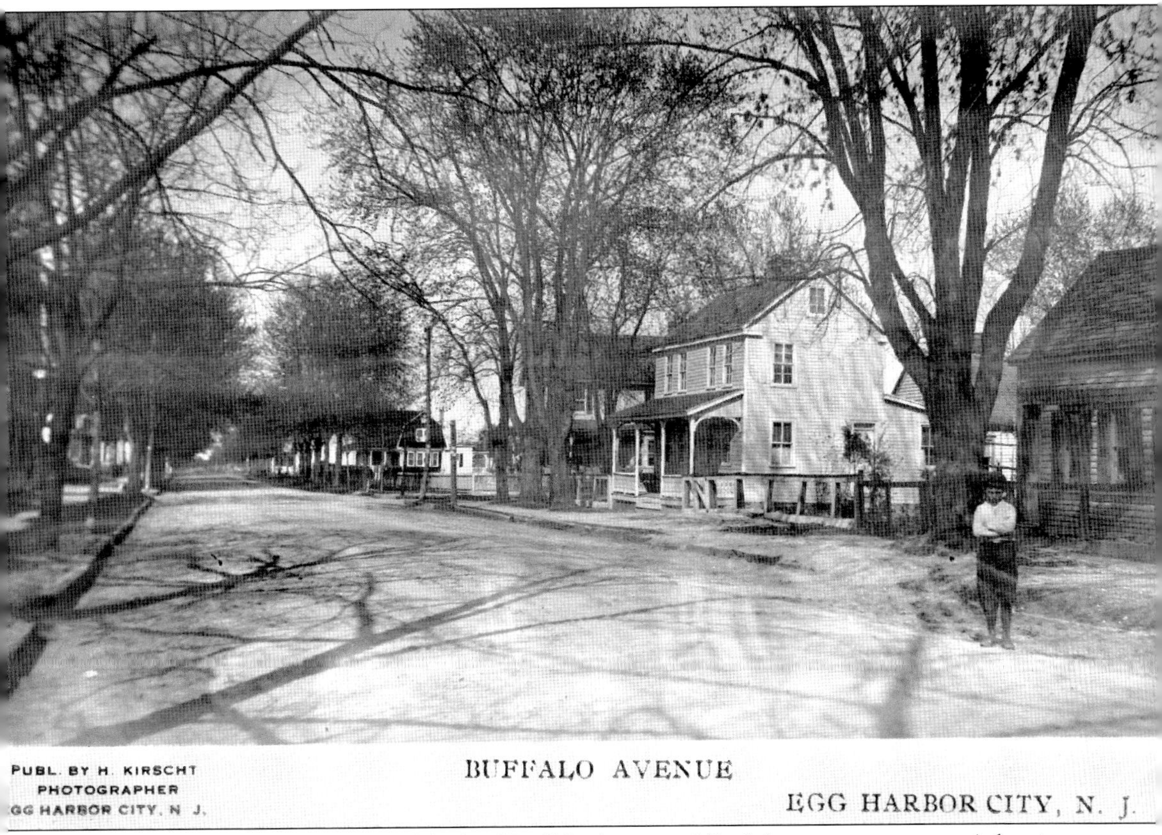

This is an early scene of the 200 block of Buffalo Avenue. All of the avenues, except Atlantic Avenue, were named after port cities. This was but one of the many marketing strategies used to entice Germans from throughout the country to settle in Egg Harbor City and the surrounding area. Some of the wider roadways, such as Philadelphia, Baltimore, and New York Avenues, were named to appeal to the residents of those cities with large German populations or wealthy benefactors.

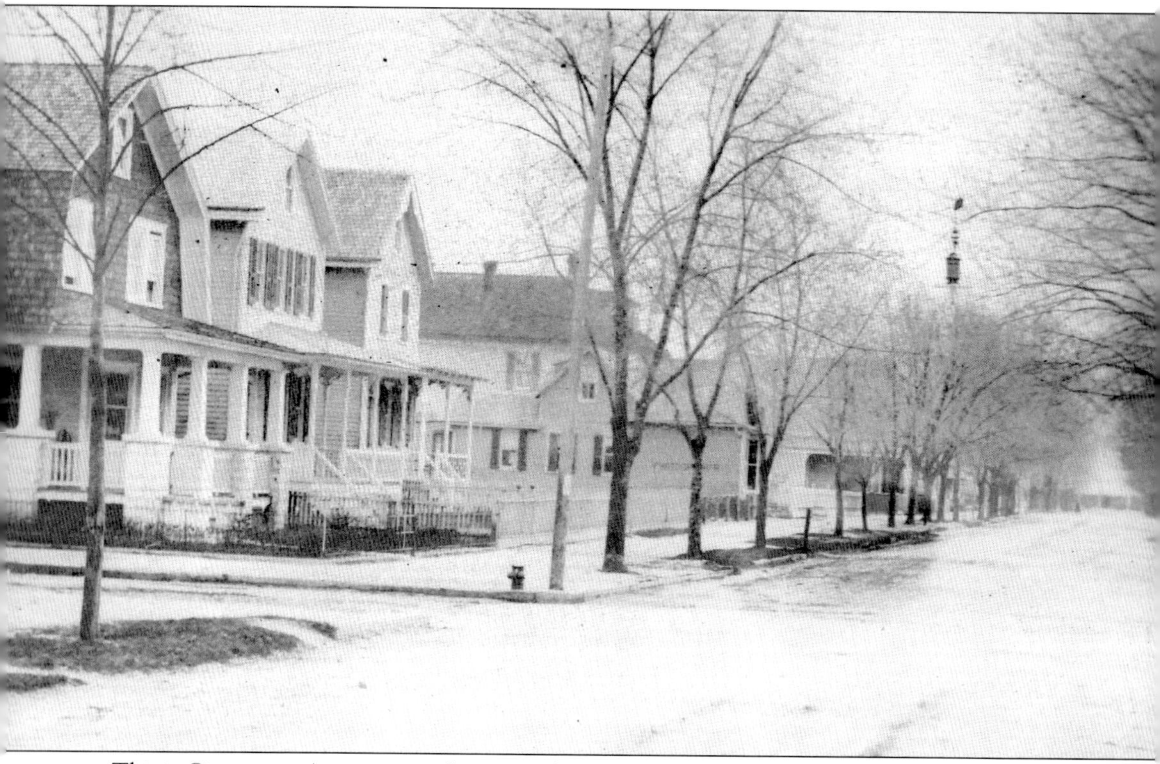

This is Cincinnati Avenue, seen from just above the intersection with Beethoven Street. Herman Kirscht's photography studio is on the left, while Arago Street and the White Horse Pike are in the distance. Like several other streets in the city, this thoroughfare still contains a number of commercial establishments mixed in with the residential community.

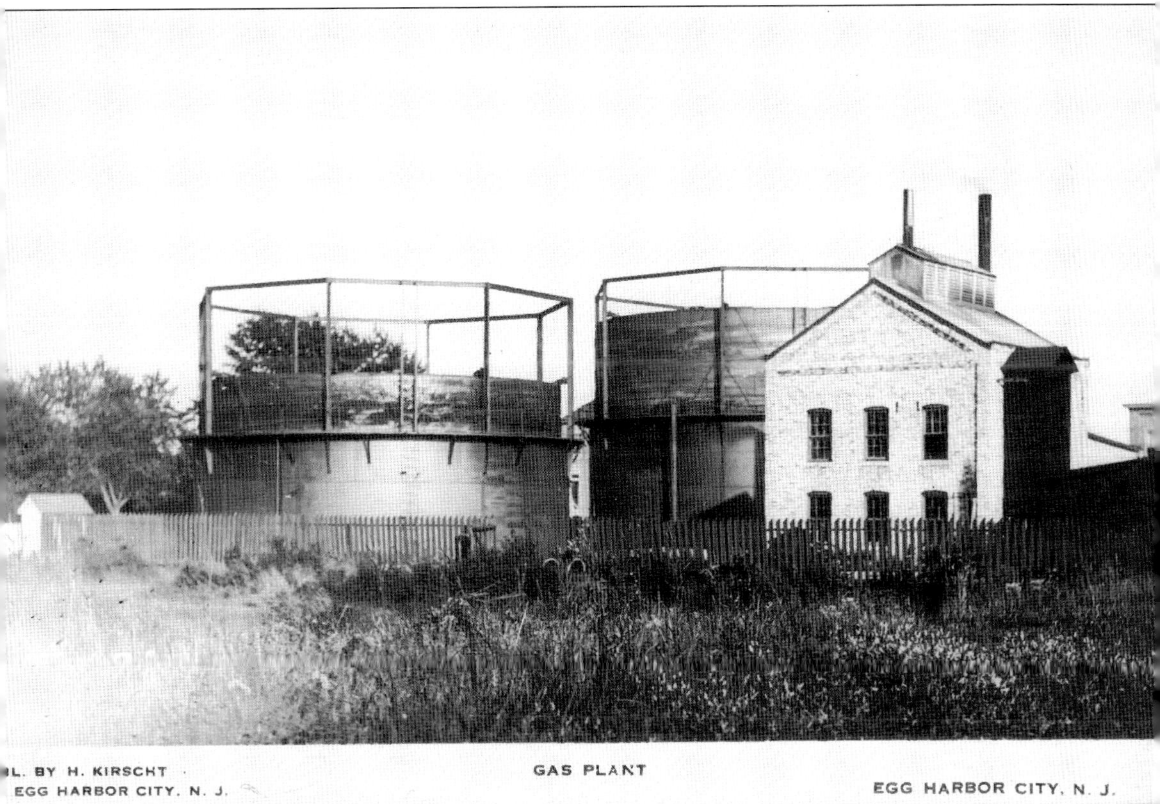

In 1902, the Egg Harbor City Common Council authorized Lorenz Krein, a local hotelier and businessman, to lay and maintain gas pipes in Egg Harbor City. The Enterprise Gas Company was organized that year and given the same authorization in February 1904. By 1905, the company had built a plant on Atlantic and Cincinnati Avenues, adjacent to Lincoln Park. The facility became a part of the Atlantic City Gas Company in 1927.

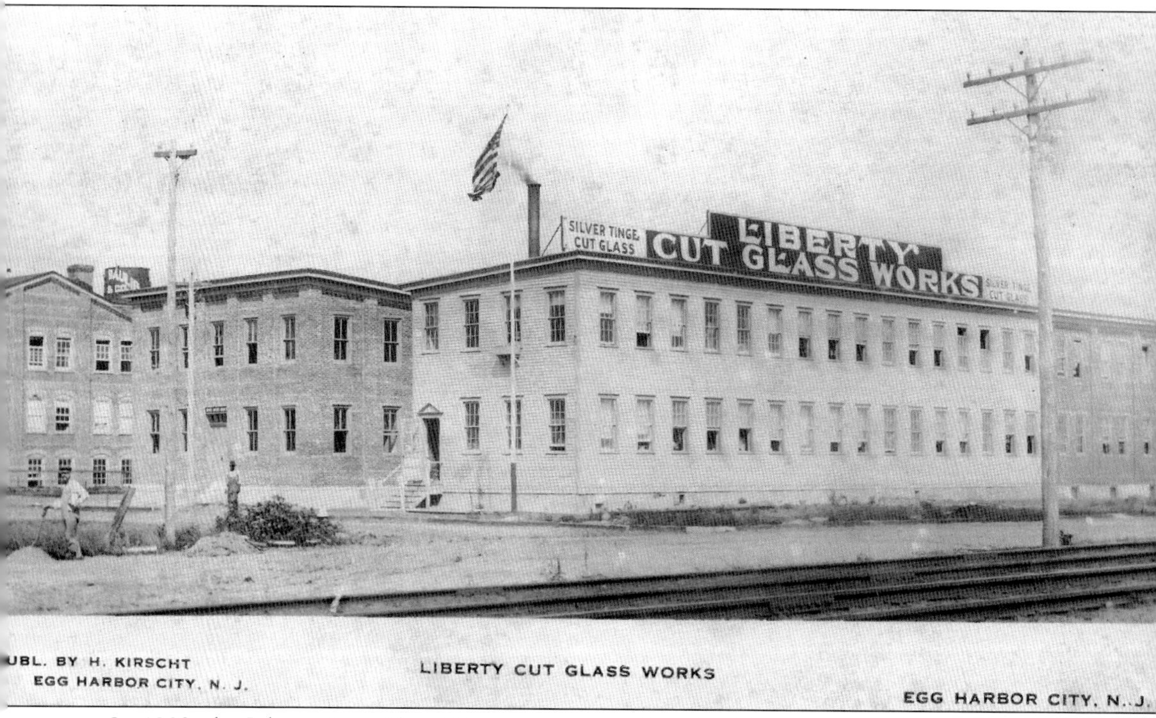

In 1903, the Liberty Cut Glass Works was founded in Egg Harbor City. It became one of the country's largest glass-cutting firms. Located at the corner of Atlantic and Buffalo Avenues, Liberty made a wide variety of tableware and ornamental objects from imported, hand-blown blanks. The company became well known for its wide variety of colors during the Depression. Over the years, fires damaged the property on several occasions.

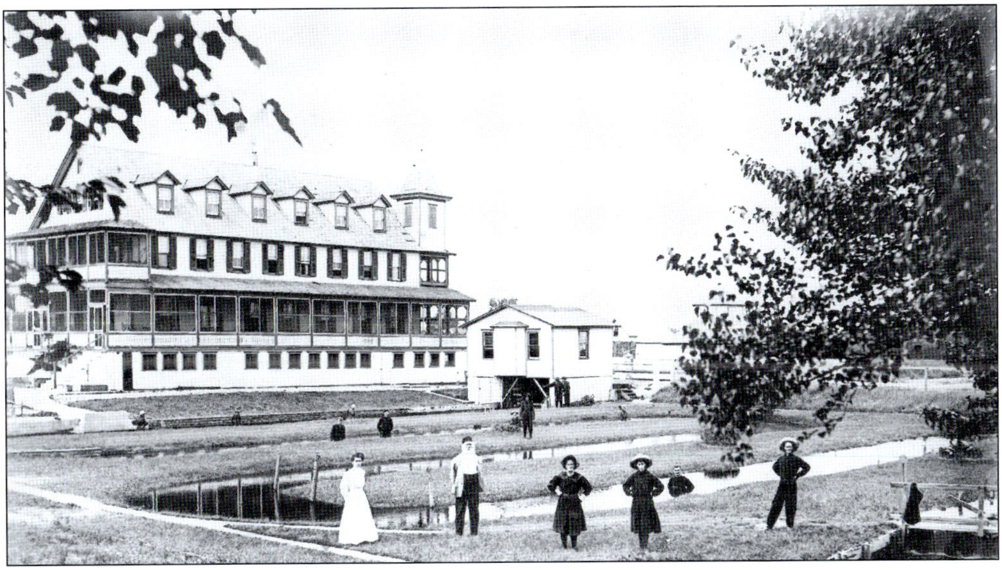

One of the stories surrounding the discovery of the area's "Fountain of Youth" claims that a hunting party found the stream in 1836. The group stopped and drank some of the water. After finding it palatable and refreshing, Dr. Charles Smith decided to get into the cedar-colored water. He claimed that he was reinvigorated by the bath. The other men also took baths and later claimed that they never felt tired on their walk to Salem. The stream was "lost" until 1858, when Dr. Smith found it on a map of the newly created Egg Harbor City. He claimed that the accumulation of minerals such as salt and phosphates in the body caused gases, which led to rheumatism and gout. According to him, other maladies, such as arthritis, apoplexy, insomnia, and "female diseases" could also be cured by subscribing to his strict course of treatment.

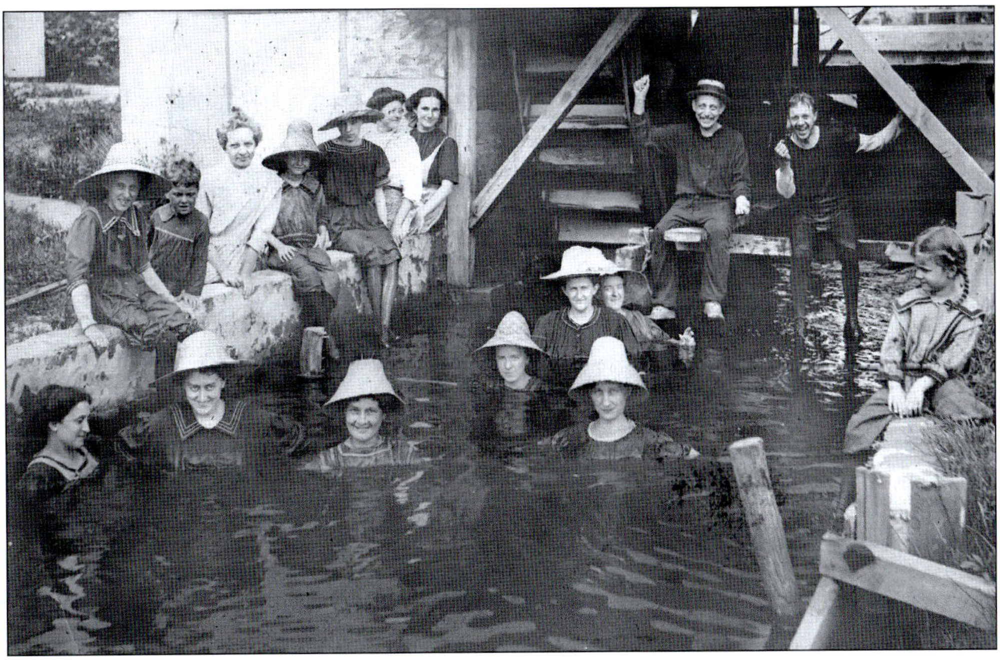

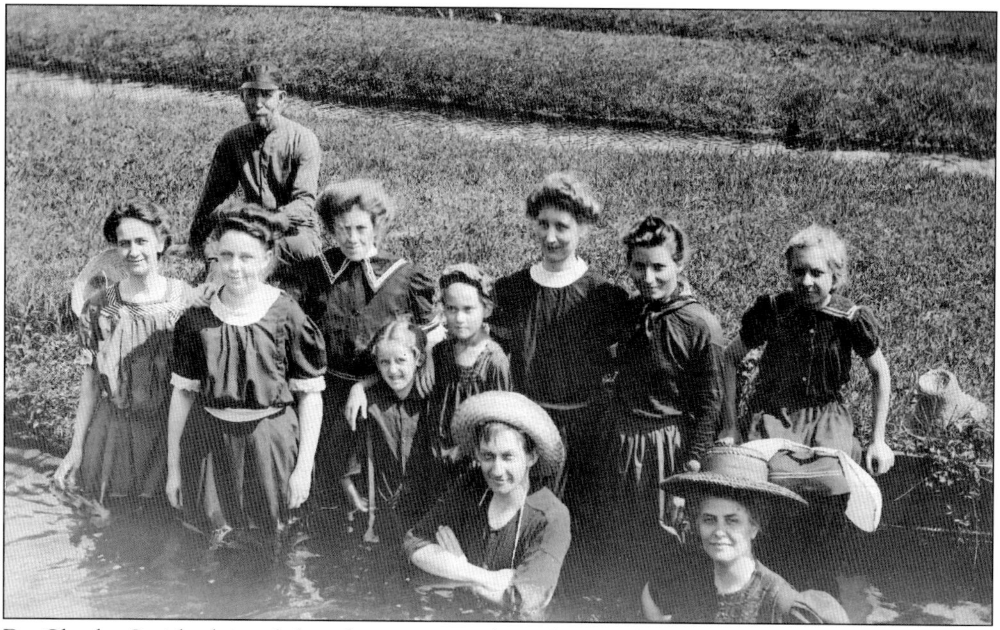

Dr. Charles Smith claimed that the water was free of minerals and able to "draw" the causes of disease out of the body. He also claimed it would "restore youth to the aged." He also prescribed medicines, mud packs, sunbathing, and special meals. Patients were to eat these meals, which had no gravy, sauces, or salt, one course at a time. He also believed in the antiseptic effects of pine trees, and he planted groves of them on his properties. Due to several circumstances, the doctor could not come to the city to open his sanitarium until 1897. In 1900, Dr. Smith appeared before the city council and presented his plan for a sanitarium. The council enthusiastically backed his proposal. Five years later, Dr. Smith and a number of local businessmen incorporated the Neutral Water Health Resort. By 1908, the sanitarium was thriving, with Dr. Smith sometimes joining his patients in the water.

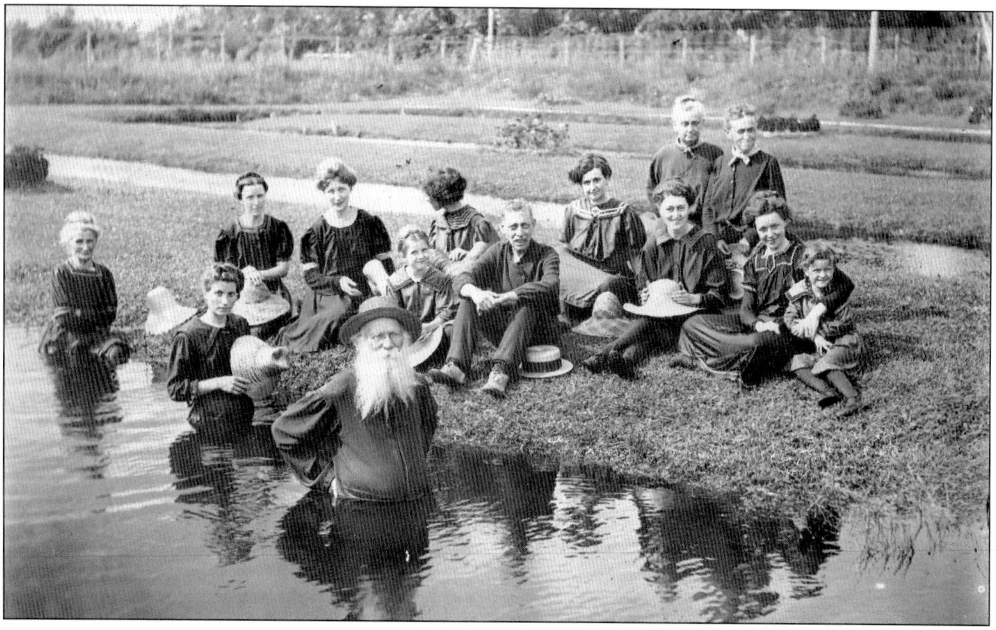

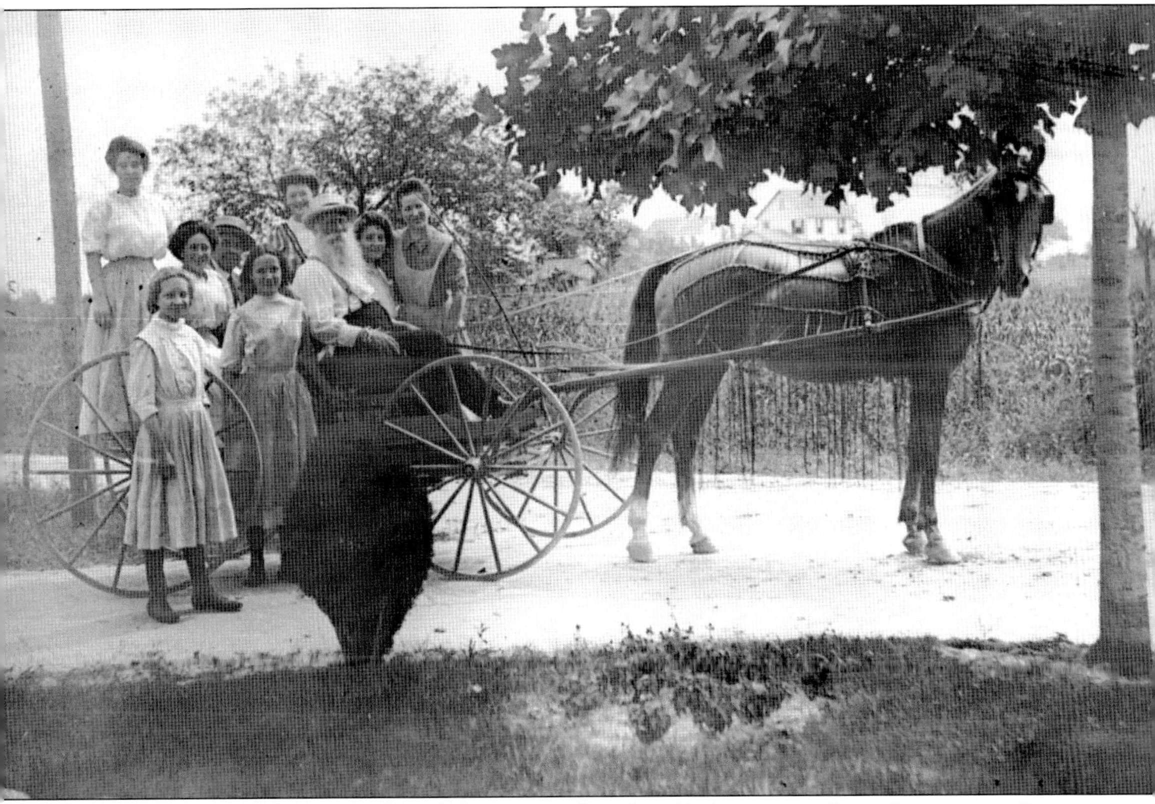

Beginning in 1913, Dr. Smith leased the Egg Harbor City Park property from the municipality for 50 years. He sponsored annual picnics for children at the City Park, transporting them in horse-drawn carriages. These highly anticipated events included refreshments, music, dancing, and games for children. While he was considered a respected member of the community and was liked by many, local residents thought his treatments odd. Dr. Smith is seen here at the reins.

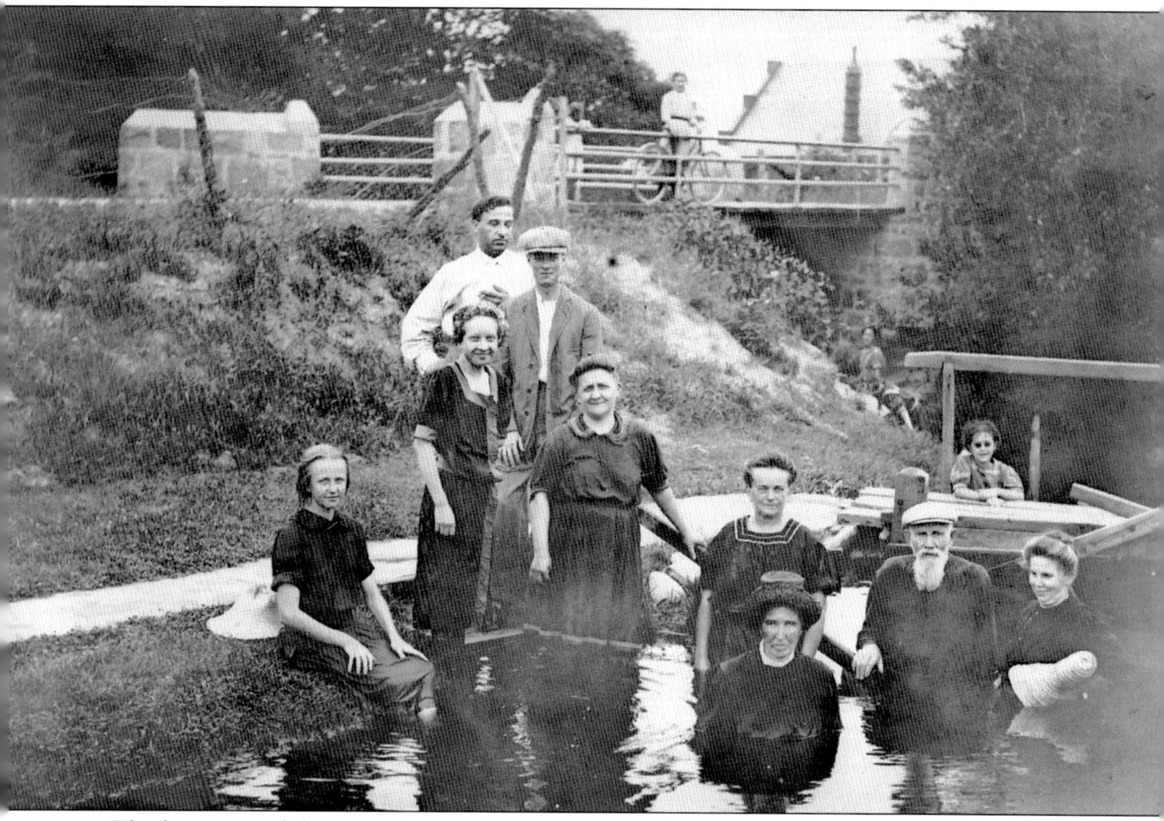

The last years of the sanitarium were punctuated with questions about the validity of mineral water treatments and lawsuits over ownership of the property. After the doctor passed away on March 30, 1923, the sanitarium was reopened briefly. It then became the Egg Harbor Hospital and a hotel. Eventually, the property was converted to the Atlantic County House of Detention. This view of the serpentine is near Claudius Avenue and shows the old waterworks building, which was scheduled to be demolished in early 2014. Clara and her mother can be seen standing in the center of this image.

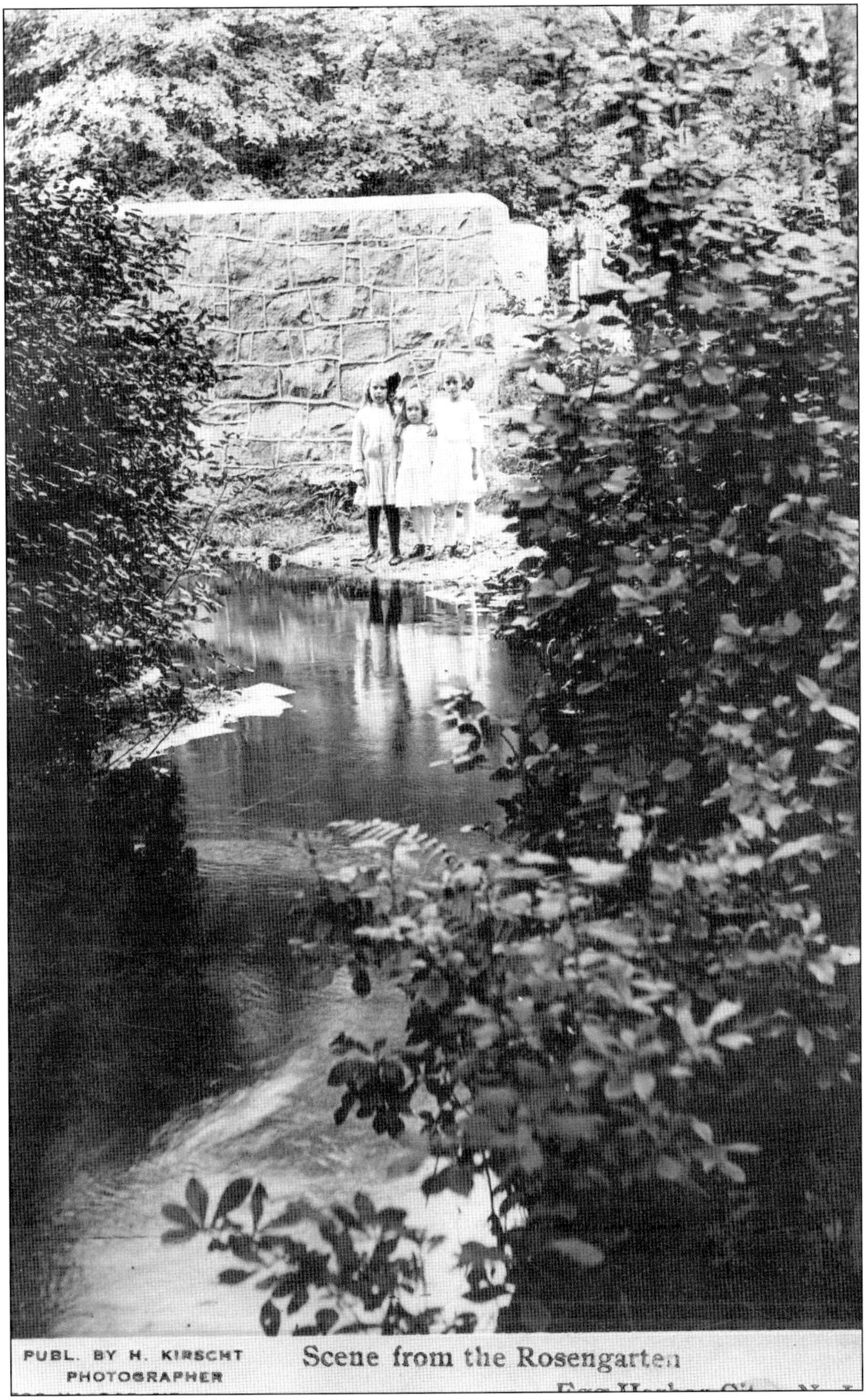

The name "Rosengarten," which is German for rose garden, was commonly used to describe various places throughout Egg Harbor City's early history. Very little is known about this place, or even if it was located in the city or area. However, the little girl in the center appears to be Clara Kirscht, which dates this photograph to about 1902.

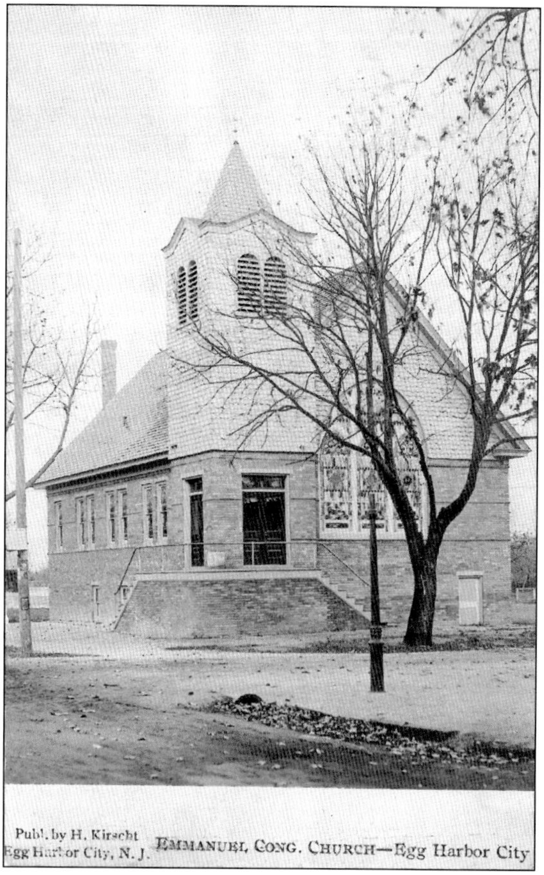

Taken by Herman Kirscht a short time after the building was completed in 1909, this photograph shows Emmanuel Congregational Church, located at the corner of the White Horse Pike and Liverpool Avenue.

The fisherman below the bridge appears to be a young Max Kirscht. Scenes like this were common in Egg Harbor City in the early 1900s, around the time the municipality was celebrating its 50th anniversary.

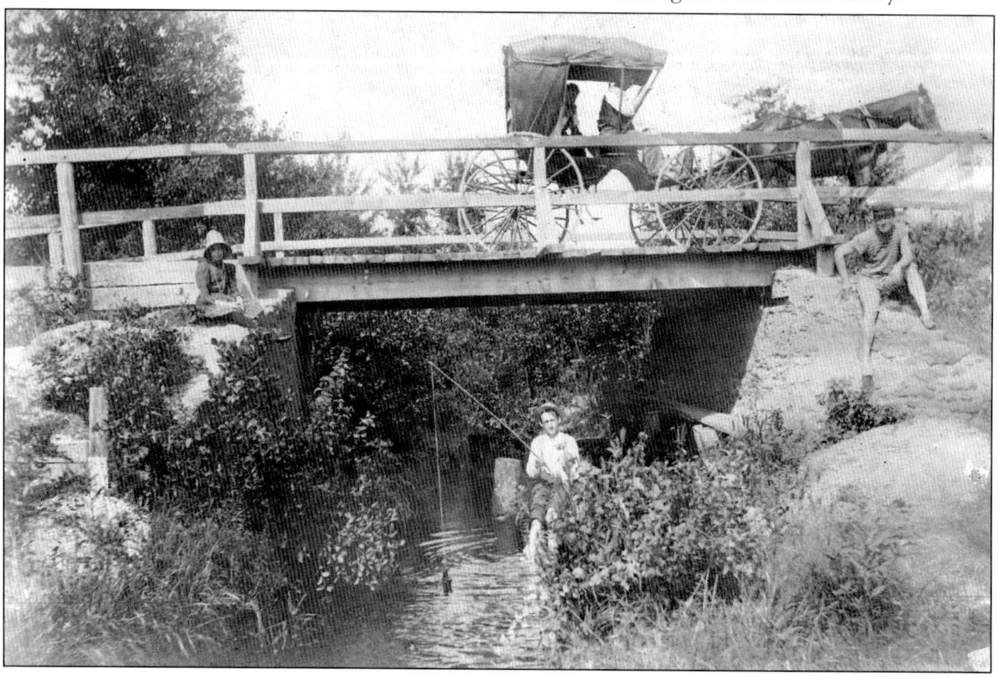

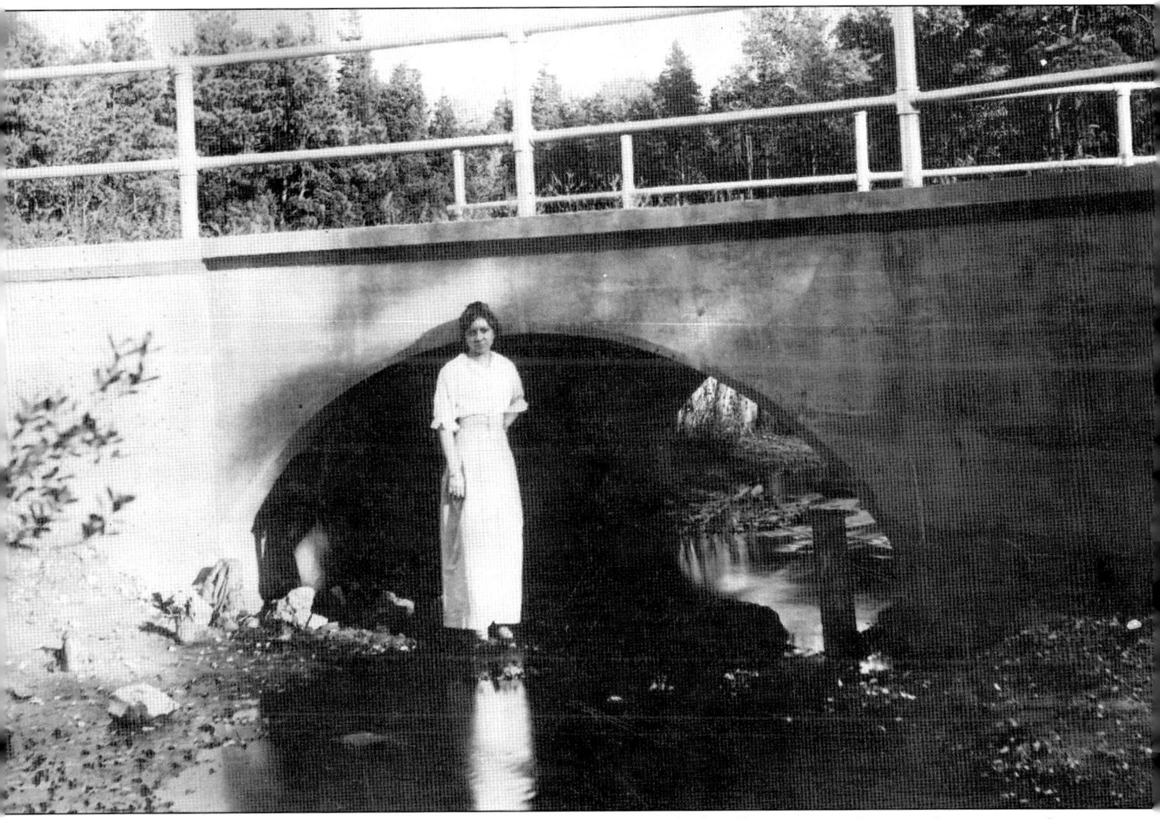

An example of Herman Kirscht's later work, the photograph for this postcard was taken around 1921 at the Duttke Bridge on Hamburg Avenue in Egg Harbor City. Kirscht's daughter Clara is the young lady standing precariously on the stone in the middle of the creek.

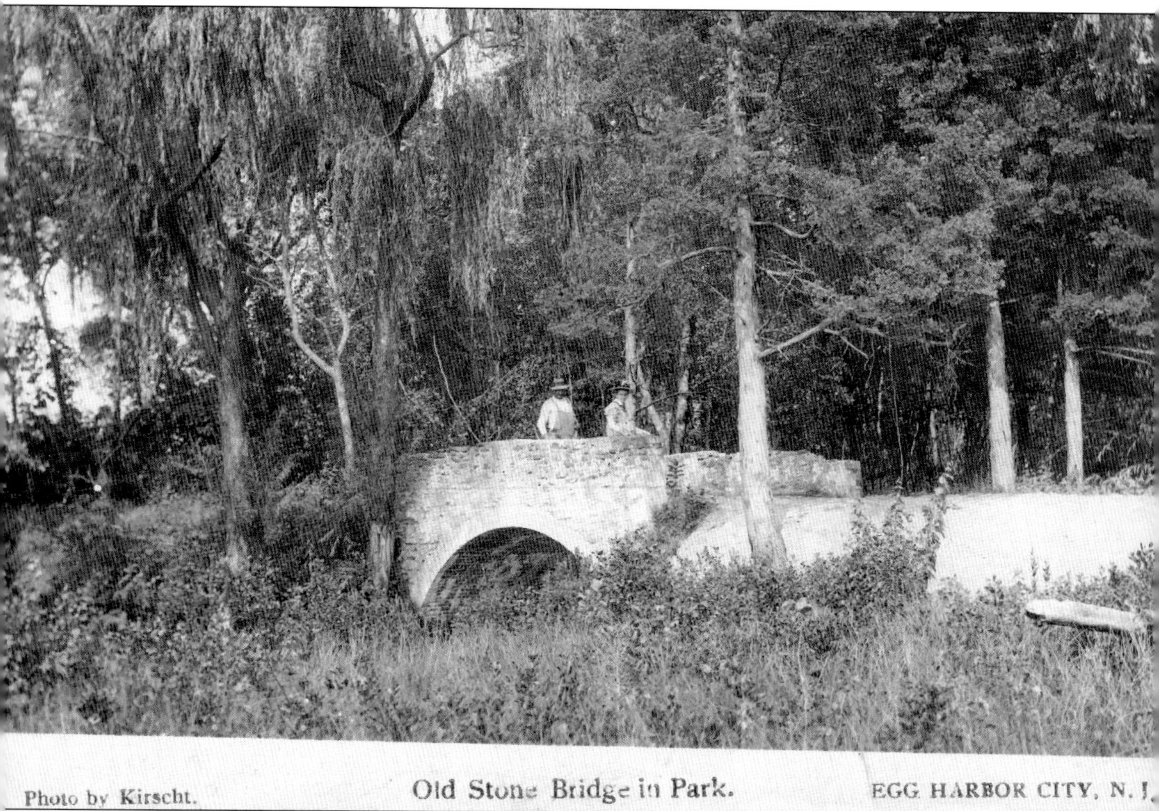

From the beginning, the founders proposed a park in the center of Egg Harbor City, complete with a botanical garden and a model farm. While the model farm was started, the botanical garden never became a reality. Eventually, the park became known simply as the City Park. The bridge is long gone, but the park still serves as a respite for many area residents and tourists.

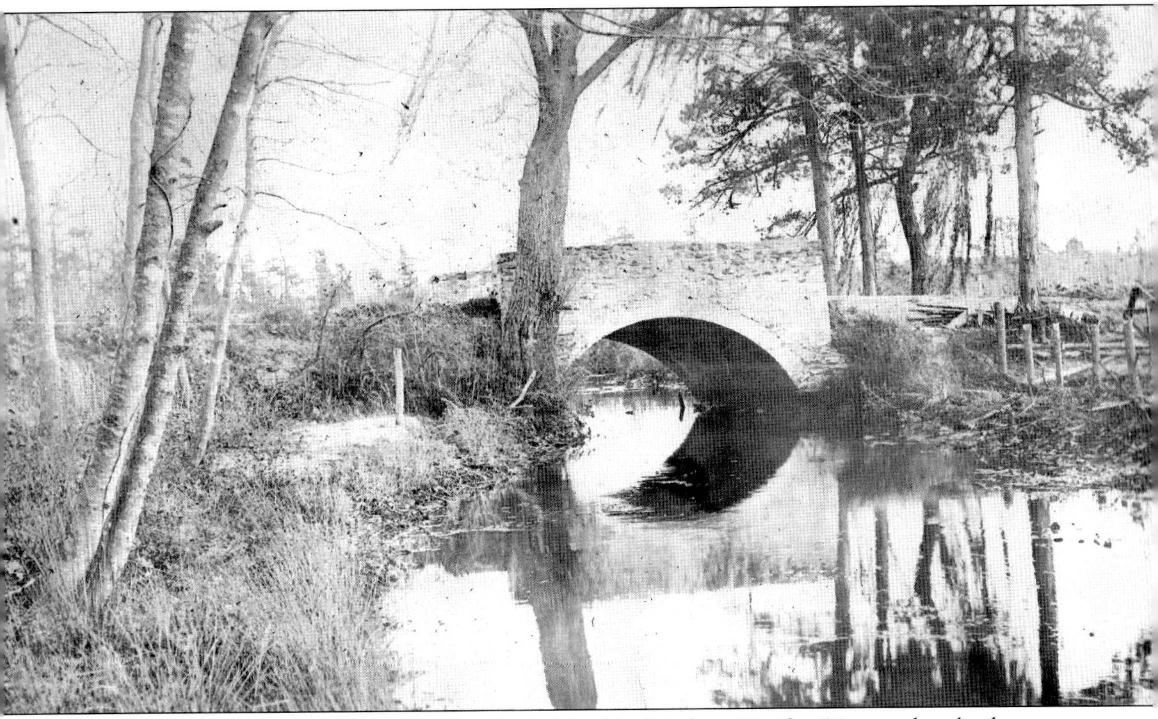

While Dr. Charles Smith leased the City Park from Egg Harbor City for 50 years, he also began obtaining surrounding property in 1913. The reasons behind Dr. Smith's decision are unclear. However, he did sublet the Bungalow Inn, and he utilized the rest of the property for a variety of events, including his famous picnics. The view of the old stone bridge is from the opposite side.

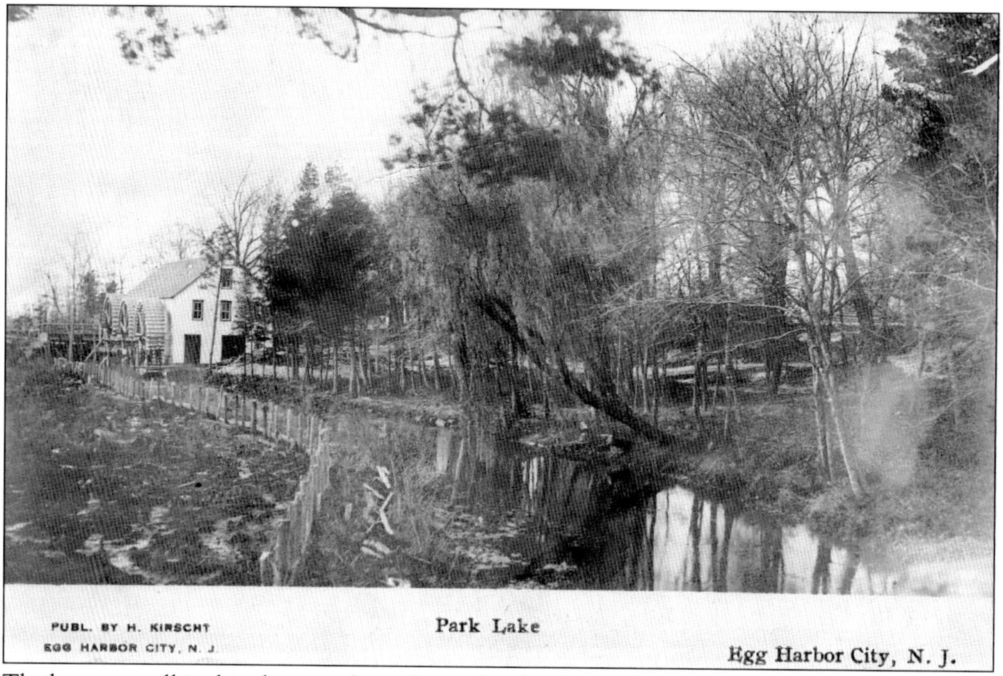

The large sawmill in this photograph was located at the City Park, near the dam. This three-wheeled mill was a popular place for visitors to have their picture taken and was featured prominently in many photographs and postcards. The building is long gone, and its exact fate is still unknown. The mill raceway still exists.

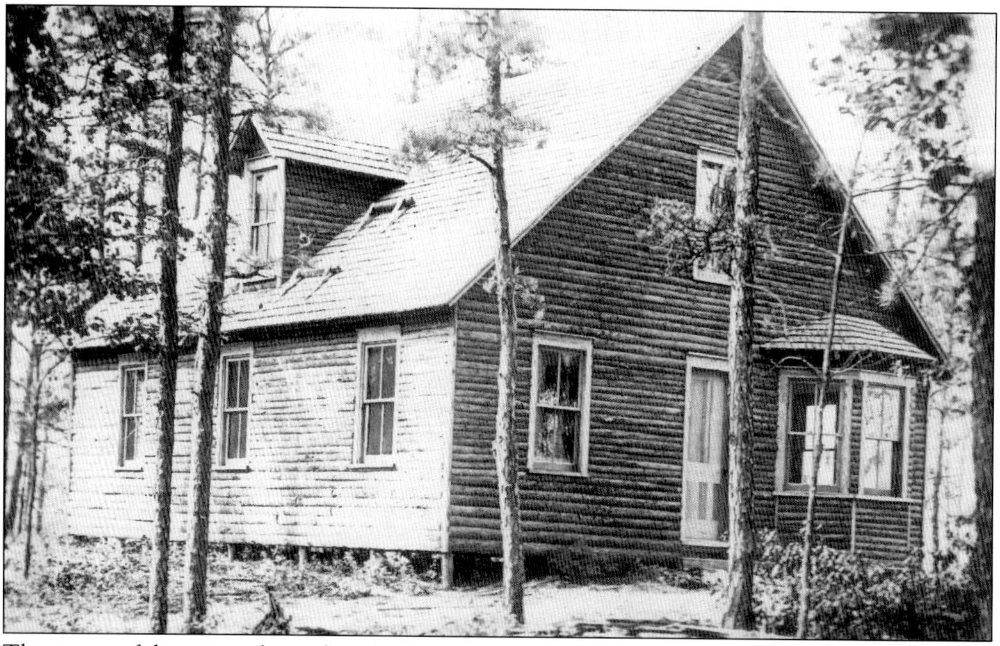

This is one of the private bungalows built at the City Park, near where the campground is located today. Once known as the City Park, much of this area was leased by Dr. Charles Smith, who rebuilt the dam and did other improvements to the site. Today, it is known as Egg Harbor City Lake Park.

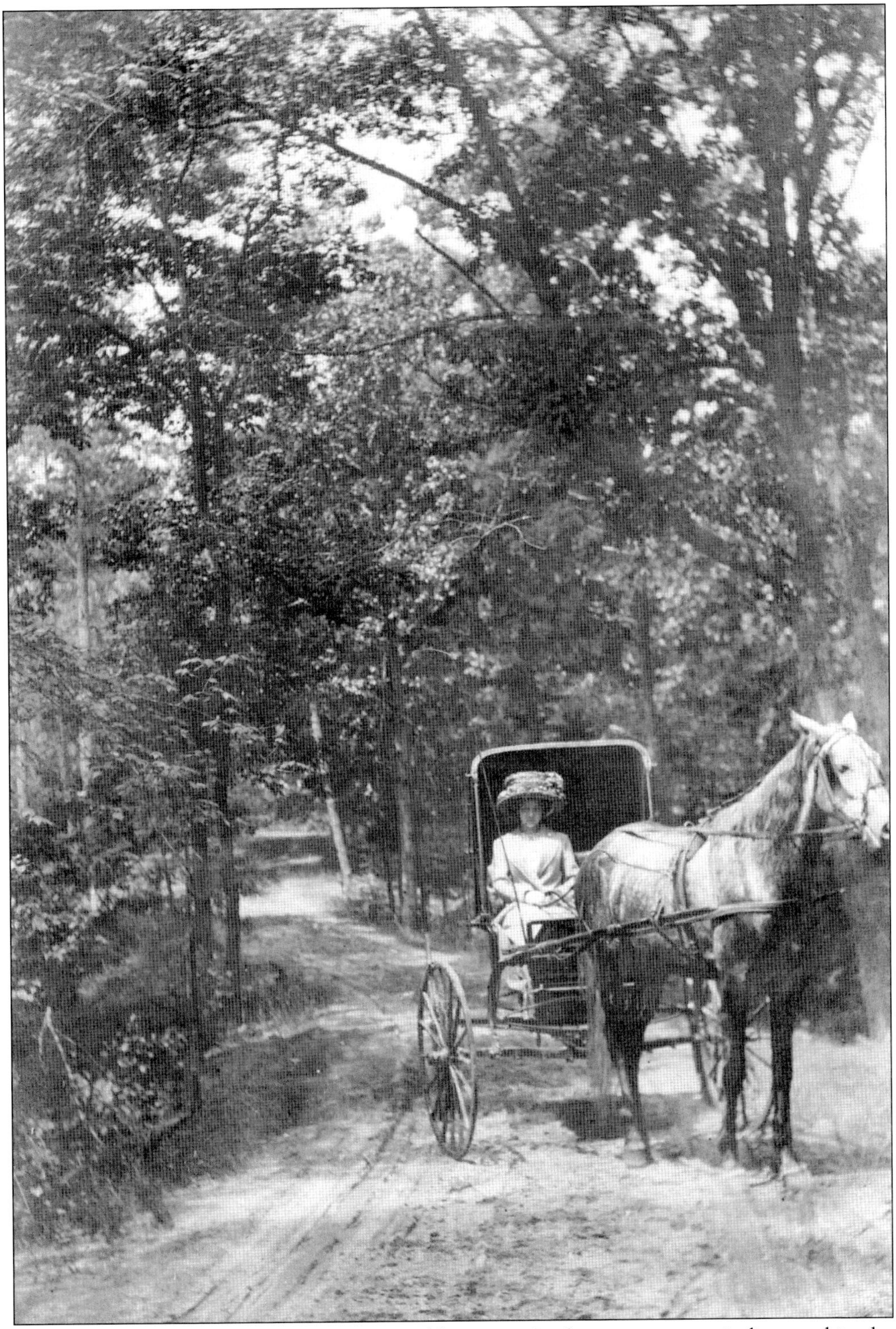

Mabel Heinzer is seen here after she stopped her two-wheel carriage on a winding road in the City Park in 1911. She was a favorite subject of Max Kirscht.

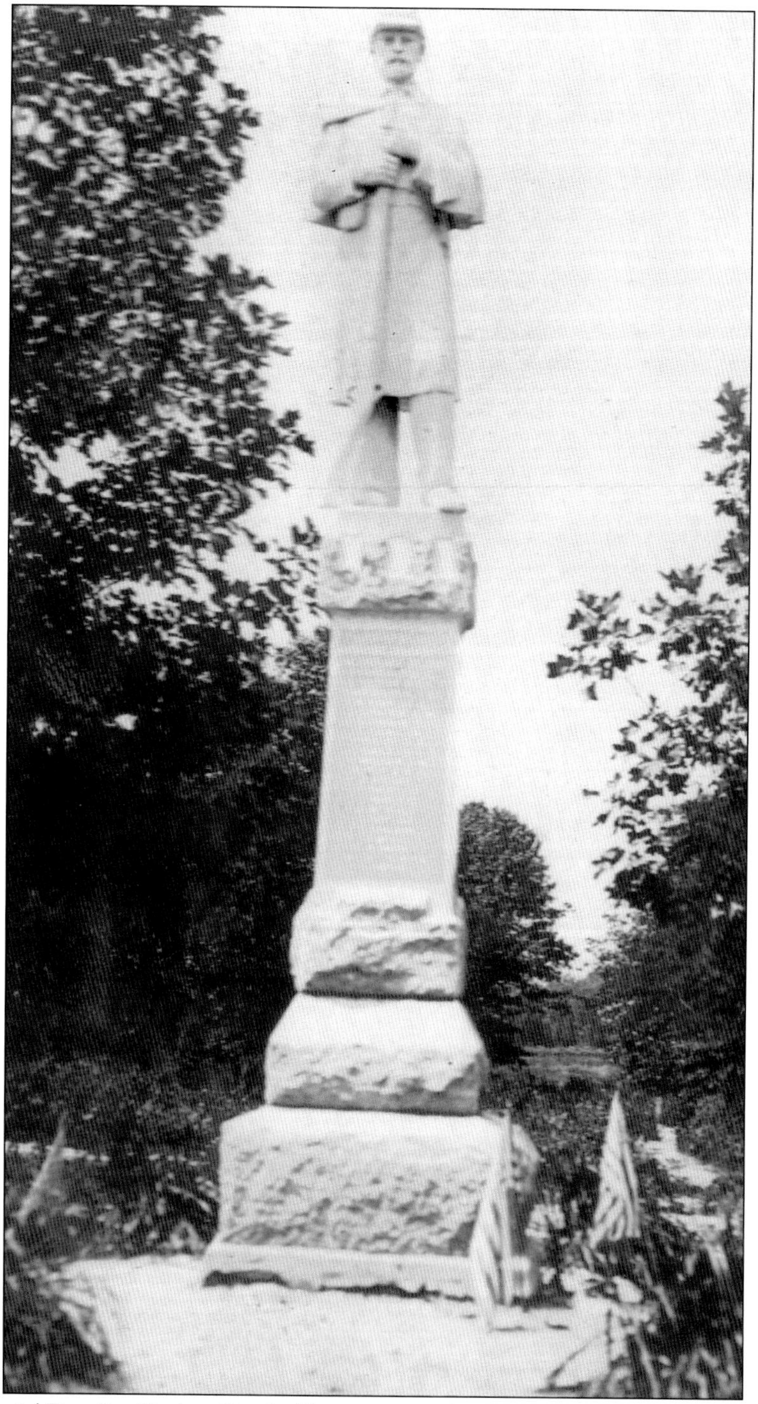

Every Memorial Day, Egg Harbor City holds services at the Veterans Commemorative Memorials in Lincoln Park and, later, at the Civil War monument in the Egg Harbor City Cemetery, which is pictured here. This photograph was taken by Herman Kirscht. The city was home to the General Stahel Post No. 62 of the Grand Army of the Republic. For many years, members of this organization were active in the community.

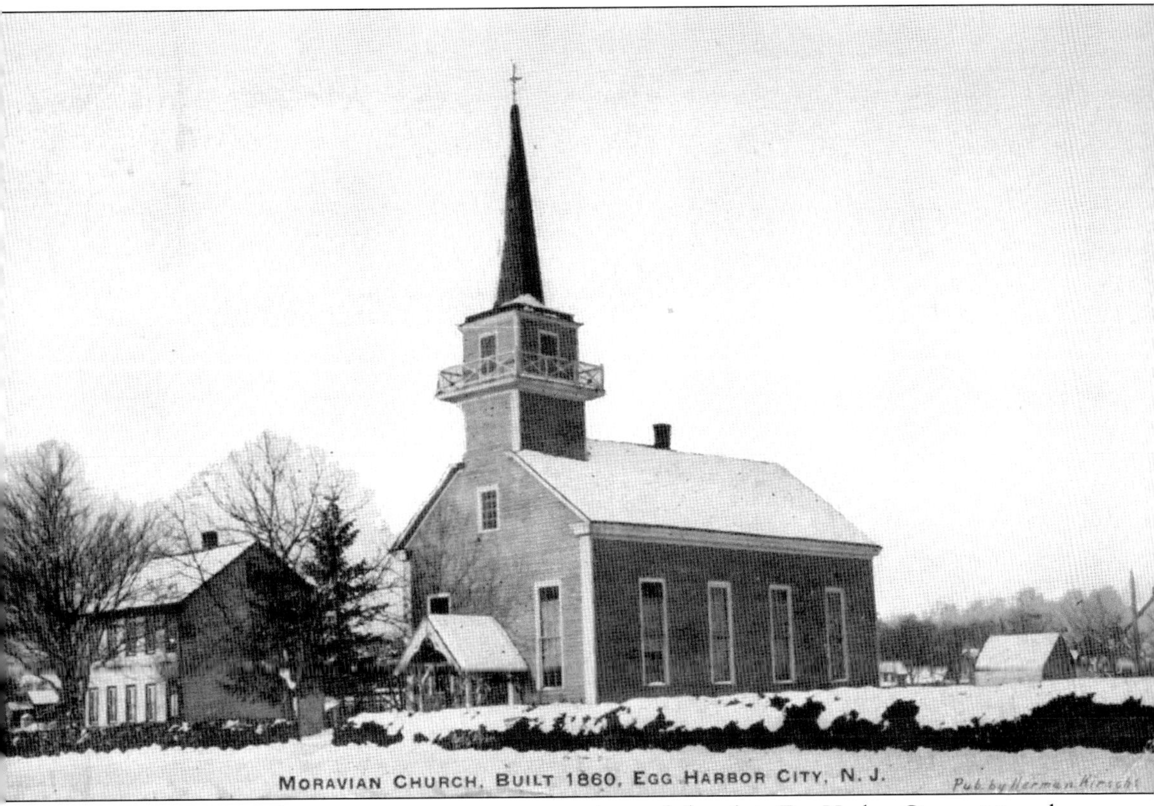

A small community desiring a permanent congregation and church in Egg Harbor City petitioned two religious denominations for regular preachers. When no action was forthcoming, they approached the Home Mission Board of the Moravian Church in Bethlehem, Pennsylvania. In March 1859, the board sent Rev. Christian Israel to Egg Harbor City. He eventually organized a Moravian congregation of 63 adults and 63 children.

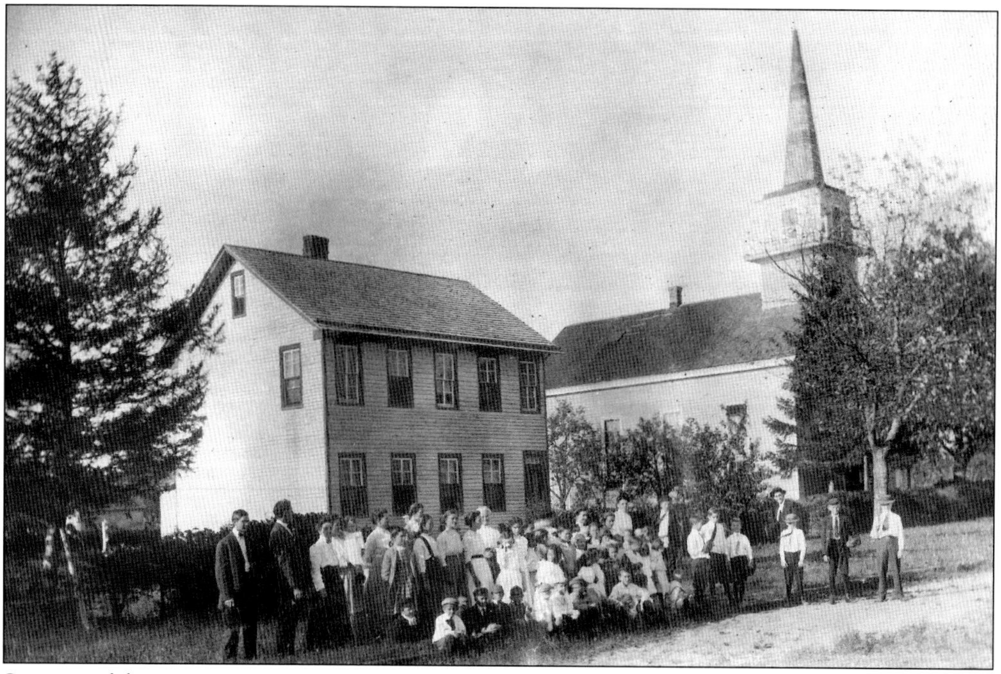

Services of the Moravian congregation were initially held in Excursion Hall, which was in Lincoln Park, and in the home of one of the members. In February 1860, the congregation decided to erect a church. The project was aided by an offer of free building lots by the Gloucester Farm and Town Association—if the church was completed within the year. The structure was completed during that time and dedicated on December 16, 1860.

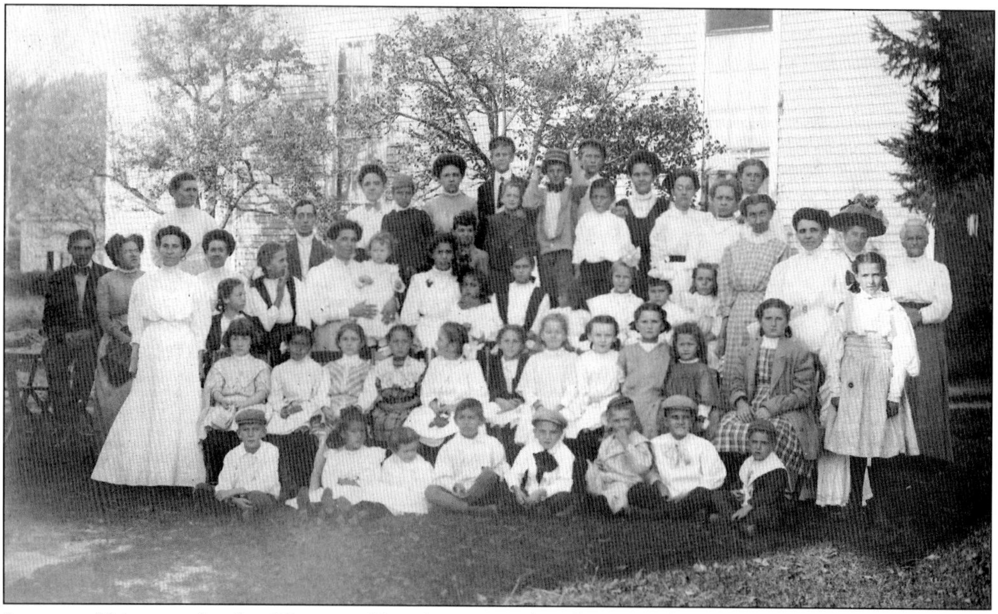

In one of his scrapbooks, Herman Kirscht wrote that he attended the Moravian church with his parents when he was a child. In this photograph, believed to have been taken in 1910, the participants in this Sunday school picnic do their best to stay still for Kirscht while he takes their photograph.

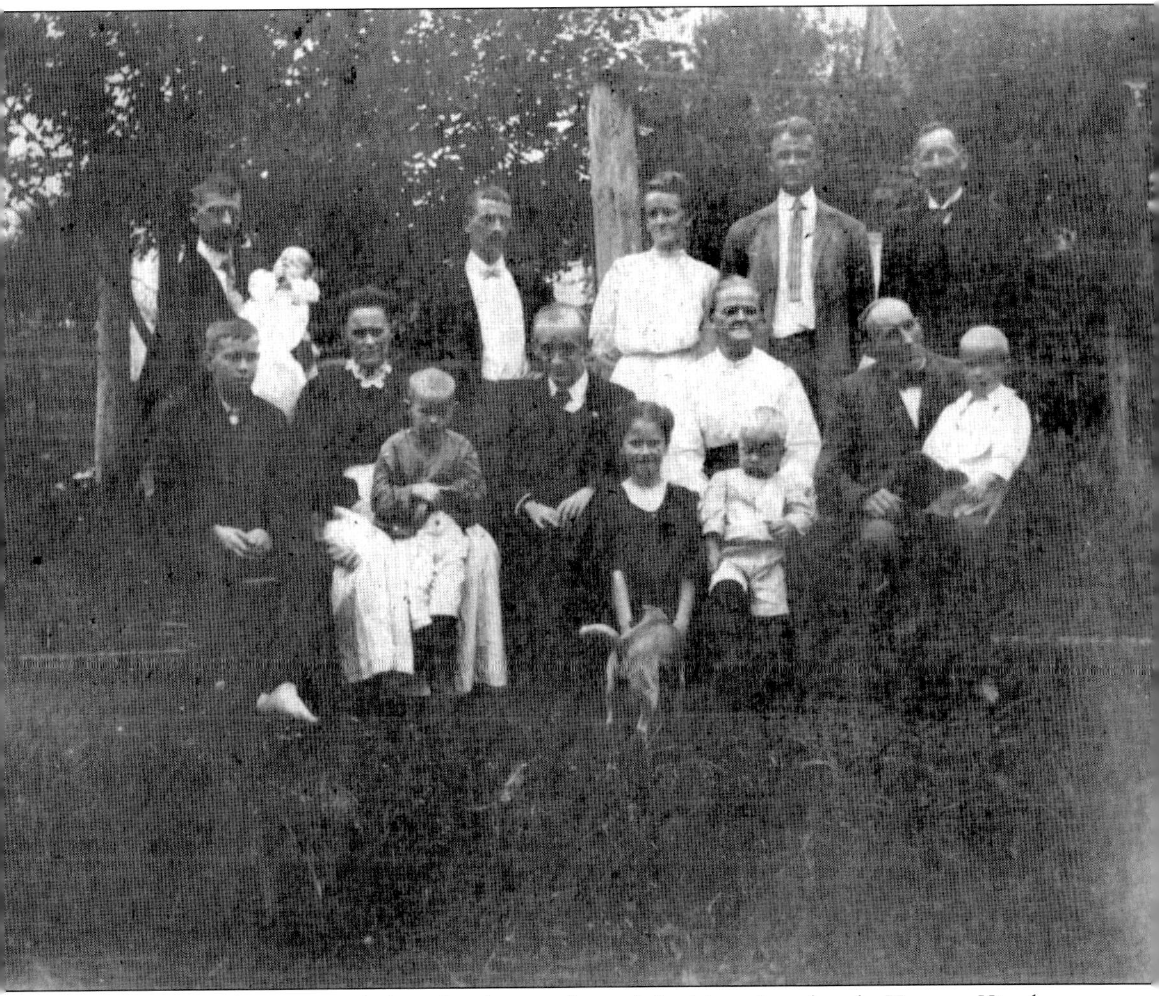

Taken in 1912, this group is believed to be members of the Moravian church. Herman Kirscht appears to be in the back row on the far right. In 1927, the classical portico and other improvements were added to the church. It is one of three old Moravian churches in New Jersey, and it is the only one that still holds services.

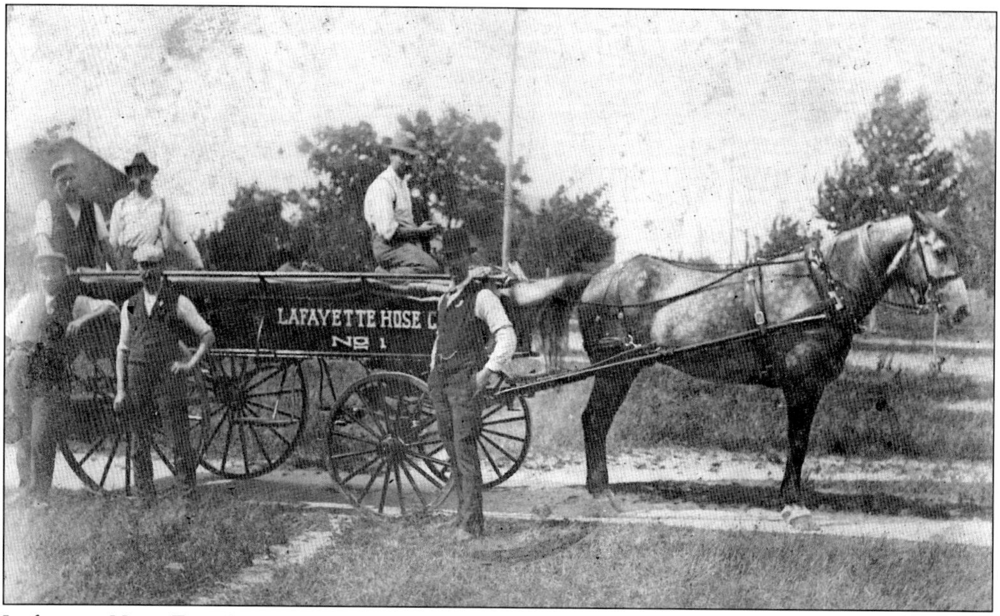

Lafayette Hose Fire Company No. 1, Egg Harbor City's first fire company, was founded on November 14, 1880. The company later erected a two-story brick station at Cincinnati Avenue and Buerger Street, which still stands. Much of the early equipment was pulled by the firemen, except for this horse-drawn hose cart. This photograph is an example of Herman Kirscht's early work. (Courtesy of the Egg Harbor City Historical Society.)

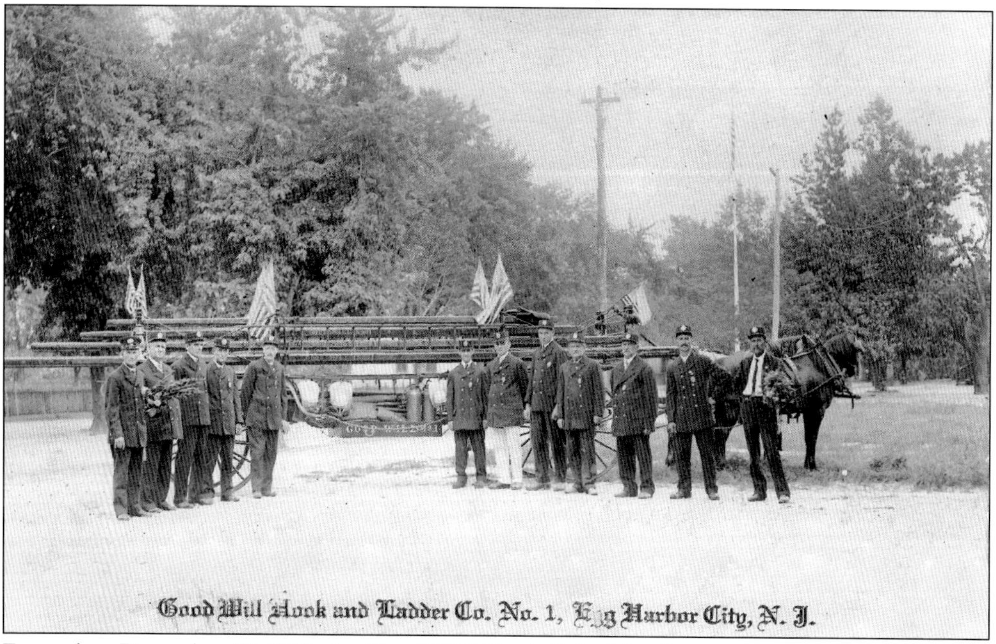

Formed on December 15, 1887, the Good Will Hook & Ladder Company was Egg Harbor City's second fire company. The company purchased a used ladder truck from an Atlantic City fire company with the same name. Owing to their "frugal and thrifty" ways, the new company decided not to repaint the equipment, keeping the old name. They eventually built a station at the White Horse Pike and Buffalo Avenue. (Courtesy of the Egg Harbor City Historical Society.)

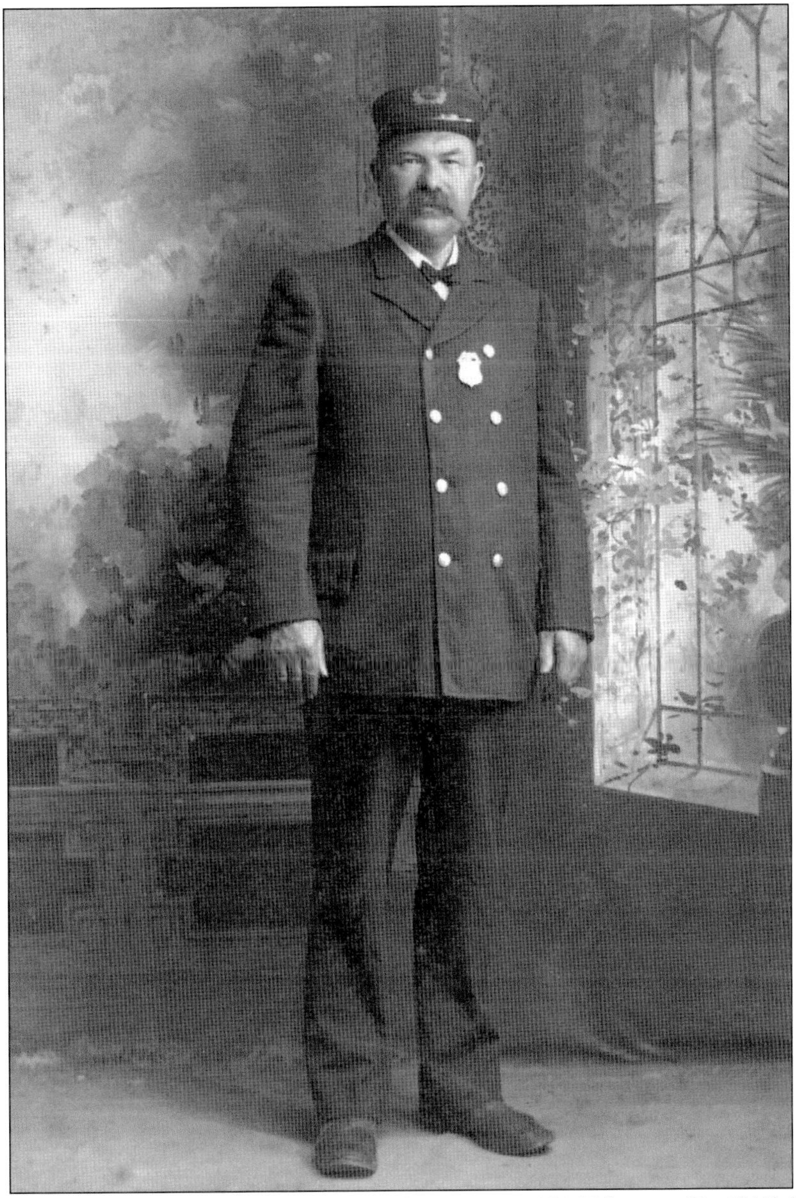

While still in Germany, Henry Wimberg Sr. (August 4, 1851–February 22, 1912) became a carpenter's apprentice. After coming to the United States at age 24, Wimberg married Anna Jacoby and settled in Williamsburg, Brooklyn, where he manufactured humidors and cigar boxes. The family eventually moved to Egg Harbor City, possibly to take advantage of the thriving cigar manufacturing industry that had developed there in recent years. As in many small towns at the time, carpenters often received orders to construct coffins for the recently departed, which is probably how Wimberg entered into the undertaking profession. Family tradition has it that he owned a horse and wagon and was once asked to transport a casket to a local cemetery. In 1881, Wimberg entered the profession, taking over for Jacob Natter, who served the Catholic community. Wimberg was chief of the Lafayette Hose Fire Company and later became fire marshal for the city's two fire companies. He is seen here in his fire marshal uniform around 1905. (Courtesy of the Egg Harbor City Historical Society.)

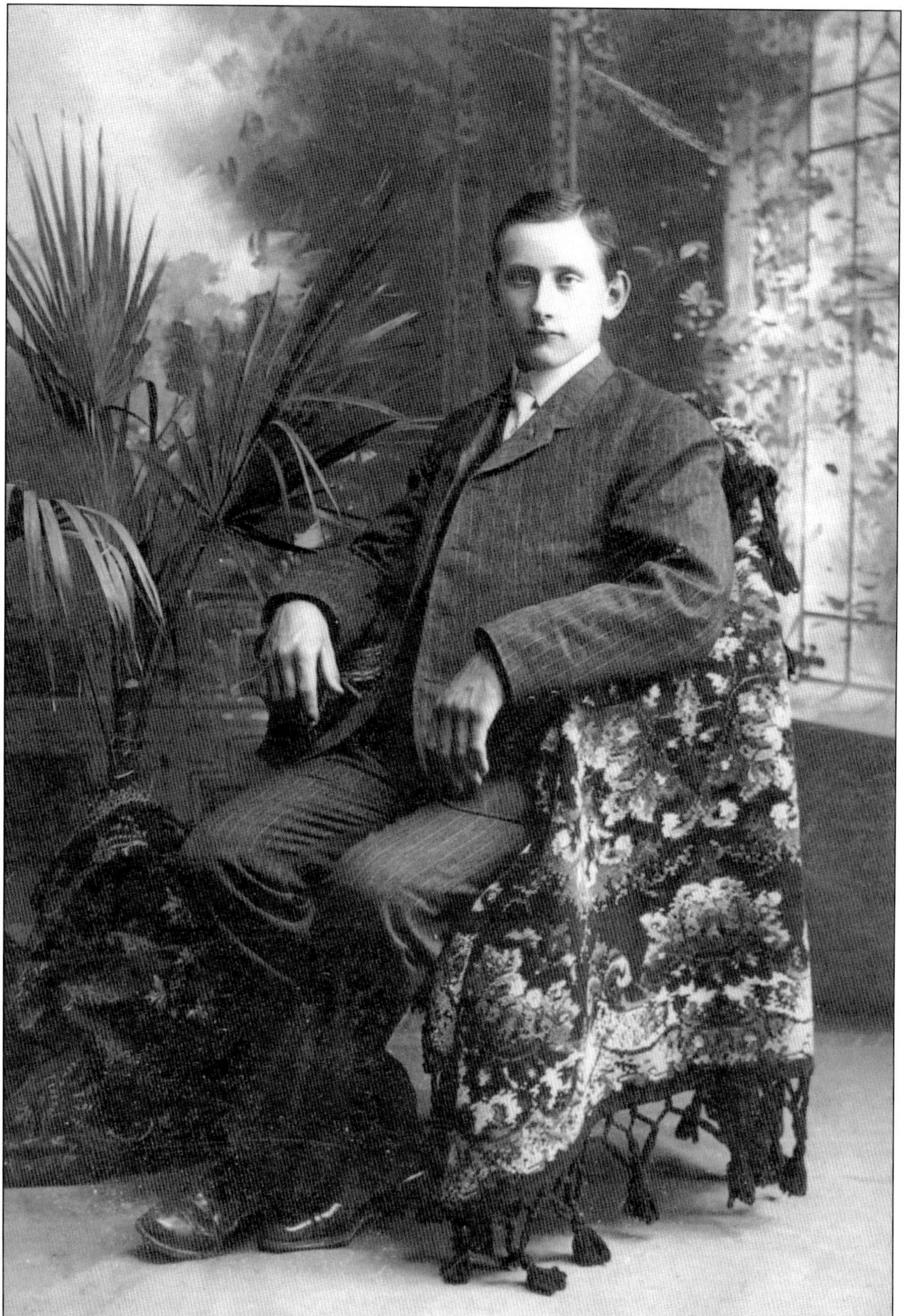

Herman Kirscht took this photograph of William George Huenke (September 27, 1887–July 26, 1958). Huenke was born and raised in Galloway Township, where his grandfather John Huenke, a pioneer German settler, had purchased a farm. (Courtesy of Joan Miles.)

This photograph of Gertrude Pauline and Paul Emil Kroekel was also taken by Herman Kirscht about 1902. Their parents were Charles and Rudolphine (Daetwyler) Kroekel. Charles was the longtime treasurer of Egg Harbor City. (Courtesy of Joan Miles.)

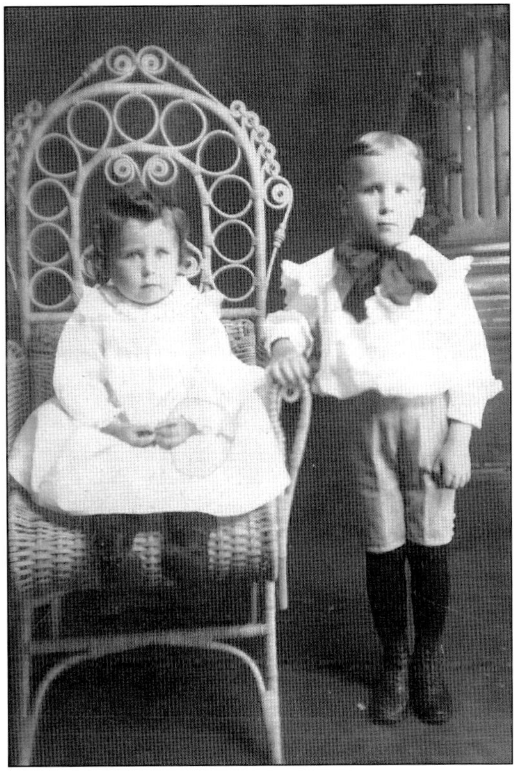

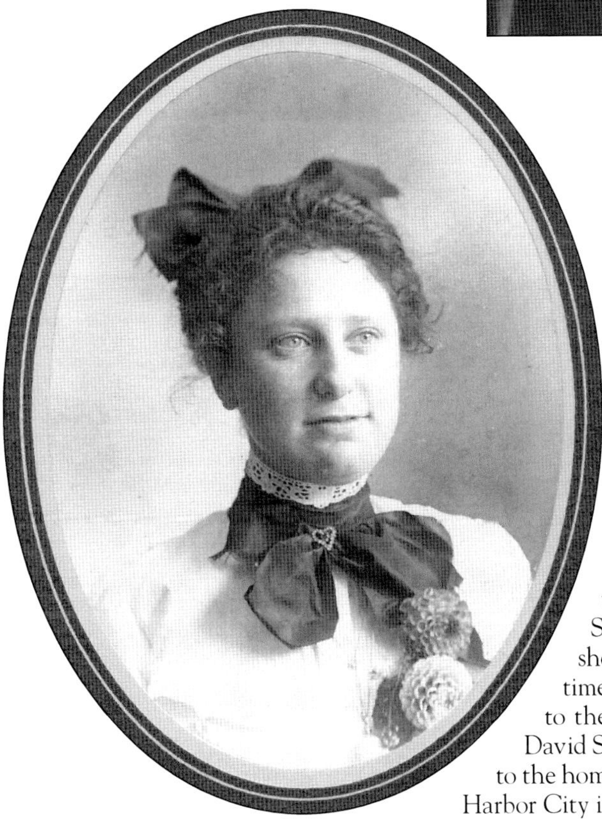

Anna Kreig (May 22, 1884–May 3, 1965) worked as a domestic servant for several prominent families in the Philadelphia area, including the Schmidt family. Between 1905 and 1930, she traveled to Europe with them several times. Among the notable people who came to the Schmidt home were Enrico Caruso, David Sarnoff, and Helen Keller. Kreig retired to the home of her sister Louisa Townsend in Egg Harbor City in 1955. (Courtesy of Mark Maxwell.)

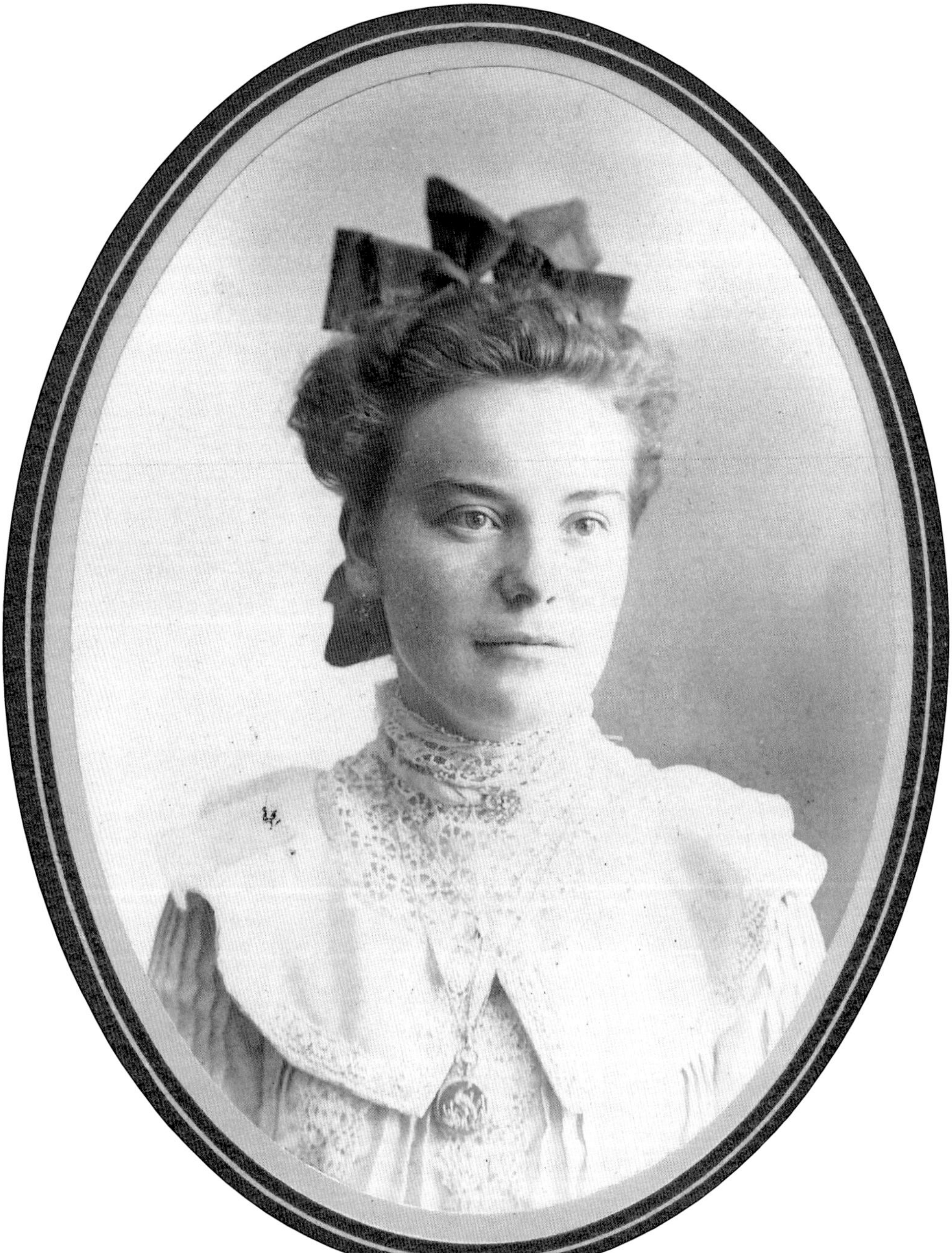

Lena Kranz was also a domestic servant in the Philadelphia area. Kranz and Anna Kreig, both from Galloway Township, were close friends their entire lives. Both this image and the one of Kreig on the previous page are from cabinet cards by Herman Kirscht. Mark Maxwell, president of the Egg Harbor City Historical Society and great-nephew of Anna Kreig, came across both the images of his aunt and her friend in an antique store in Pennsylvania in 2013. (Courtesy of Mark Maxwell.)

Three

PLEASANTVILLE

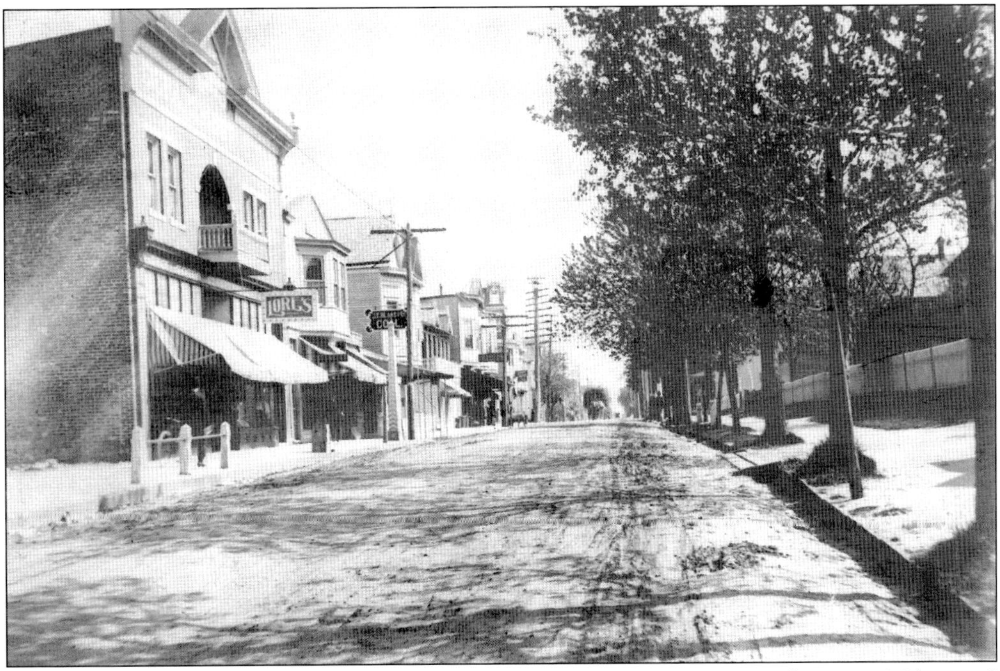

This photograph shows what is now the west side of South Main Street between Milan and Washington Avenues. On the left is Lore's Department Store, which was built in 1905. When Theodore Lore, a popular businessman in the city, moved to his second store at North Main Street and Washington Avenue, this became Weaver's Department Store. The photograph was taken about 1907.

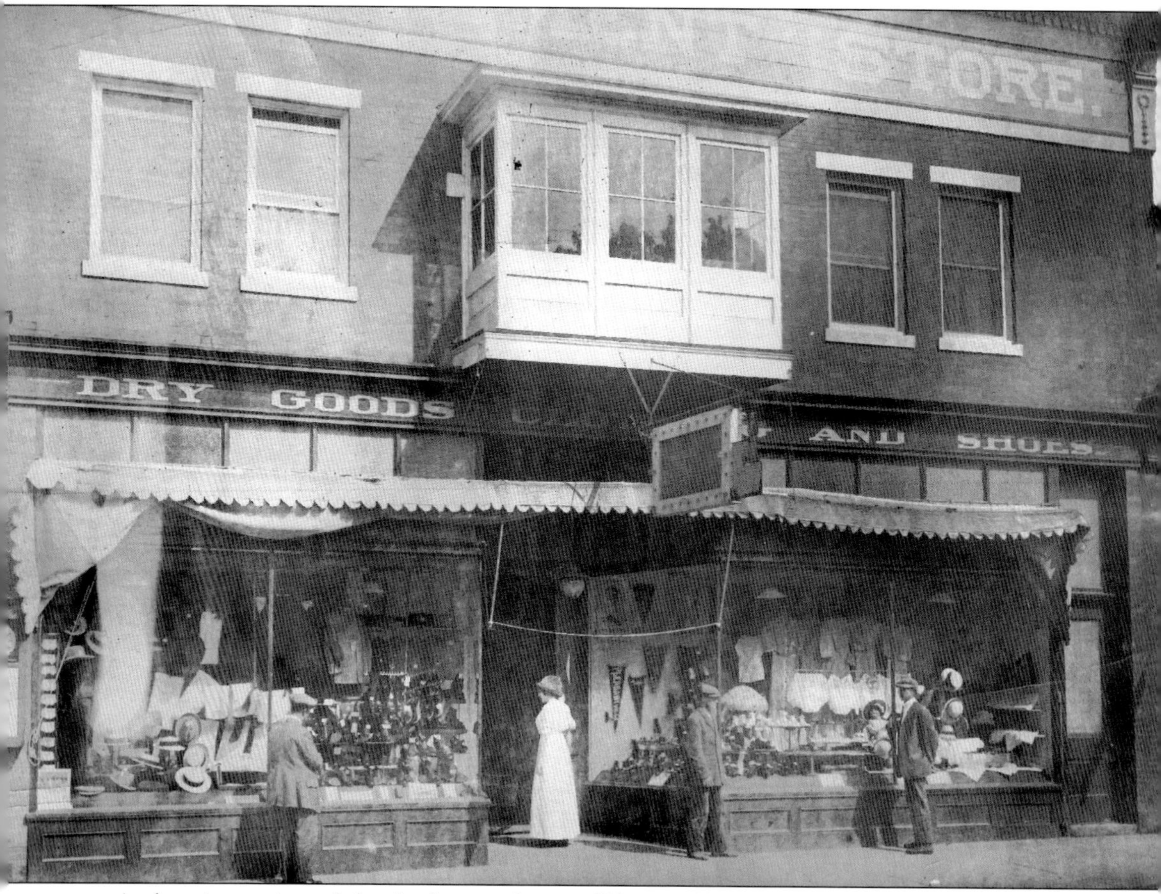

A close inspection of the display windows at Weaver's Department Store shows that it sold a wide variety of goods, including dresses, pennants, hats, shoes, shirts, and other clothing. Since the original Lore name is missing from the lighted sign over the sidewalk, it is believed that this photograph was taken after Lore's Department Store became Weaver's.

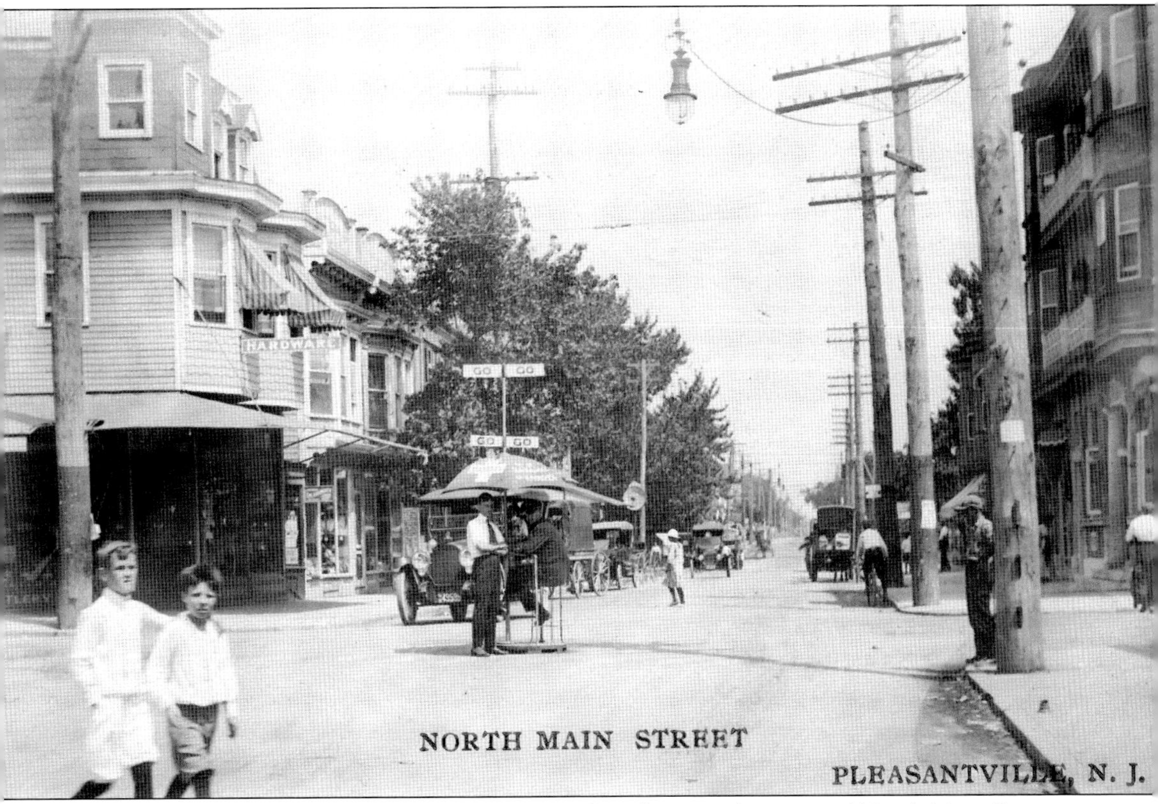

This photograph was taken from the intersection of Washington Avenue and North Main Street sometime after Lore's Department Store had moved out of the building on the left. By the time this photograph was taken, Blake's Hardware was operating from the site. For many years, Washington Avenue was known as "the clam road." Before the railroads, this was the start of the route many fishermen took to Philadelphia to sell their clams and shellfish.

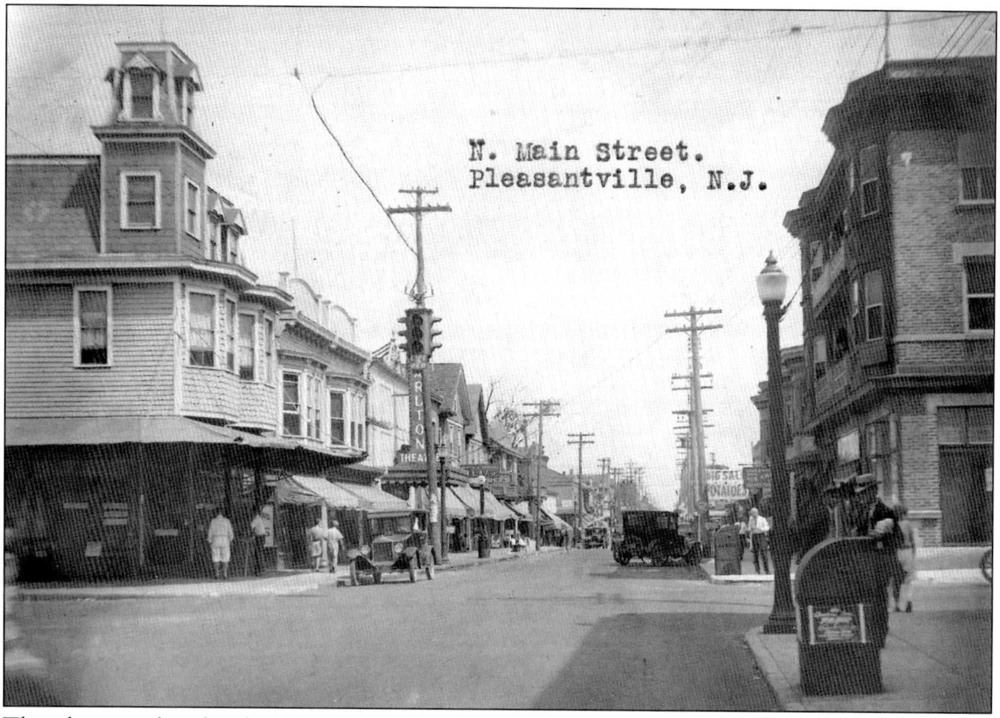

This photograph, taken by Herman Kirscht, shows an ever-changing North Main Street, complete with a four-way stoplight.

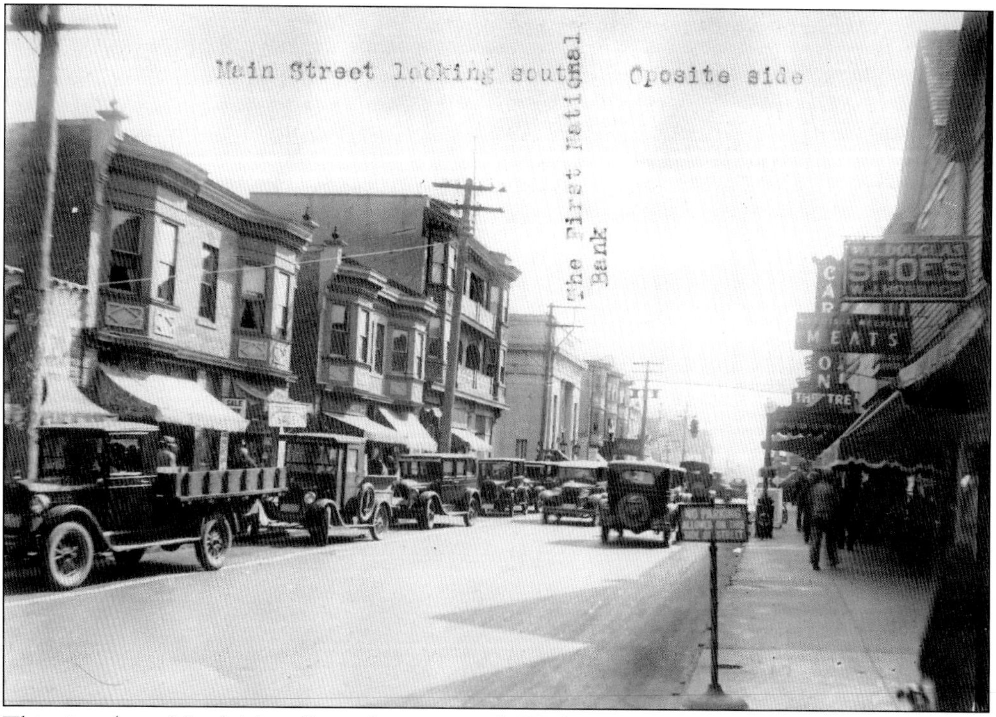

This view shows North Main Street facing towards Washington Avenue, with the Leech Building and the First National Bank in the distance. This was a busy intersection in the 1920s.

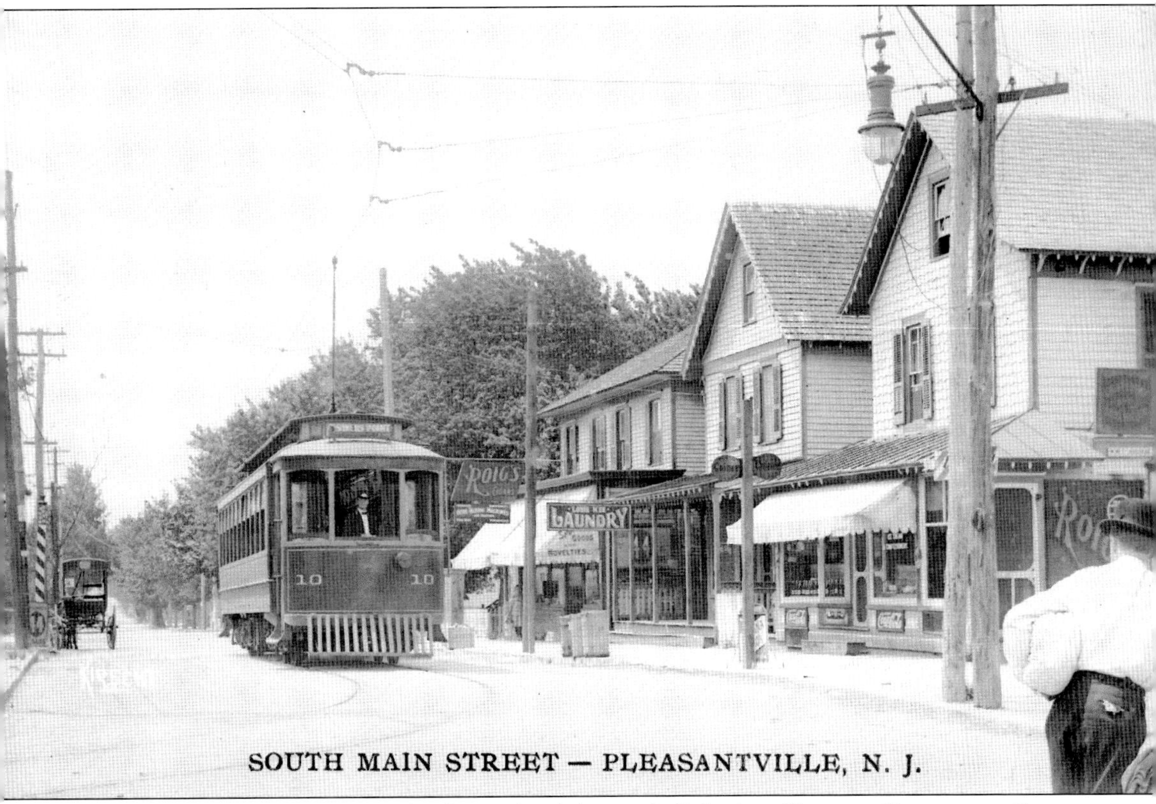

This early postcard by Max Kirscht shows the Atlantic & Suburban Traction Company trolley turning in front of the New Rodney Hotel. The trolley has probably just arrived from Absecon and is bound for Somers Point. This trolley line was first incorporated on July 16, 1902, and was completed in 1904. The terminal was in Atlantic City, situated at Florida Avenue and the boardwalk.

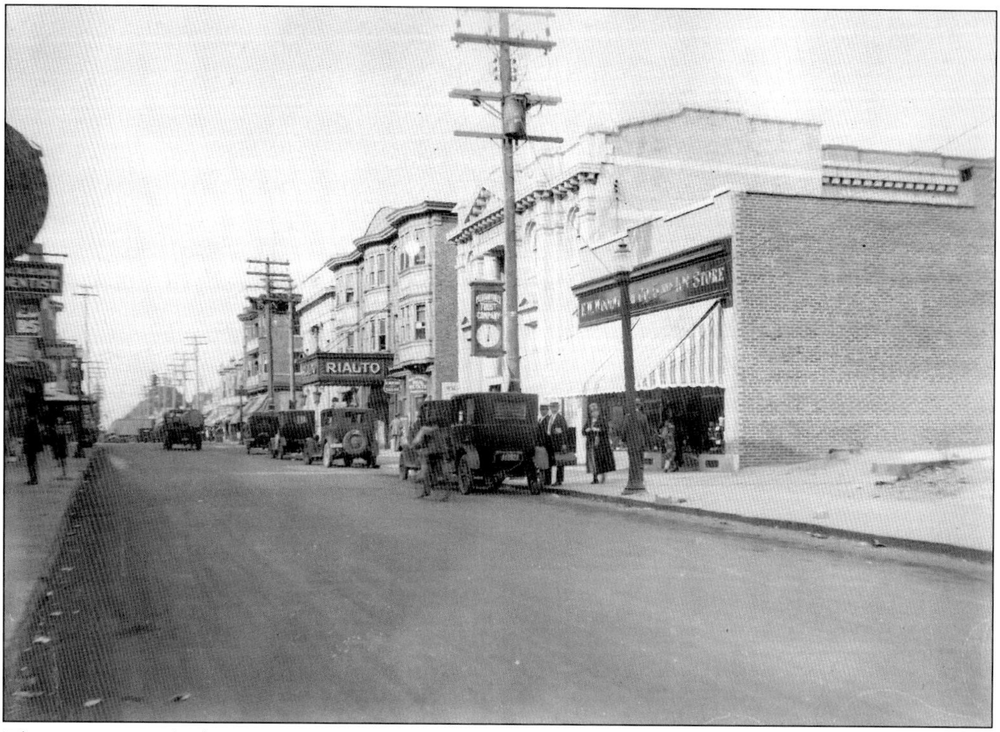

This great view looking up South Main Street shows the original location of the Woolworth's, the Pleasantville Trust Company building, and the Rialto Theater.

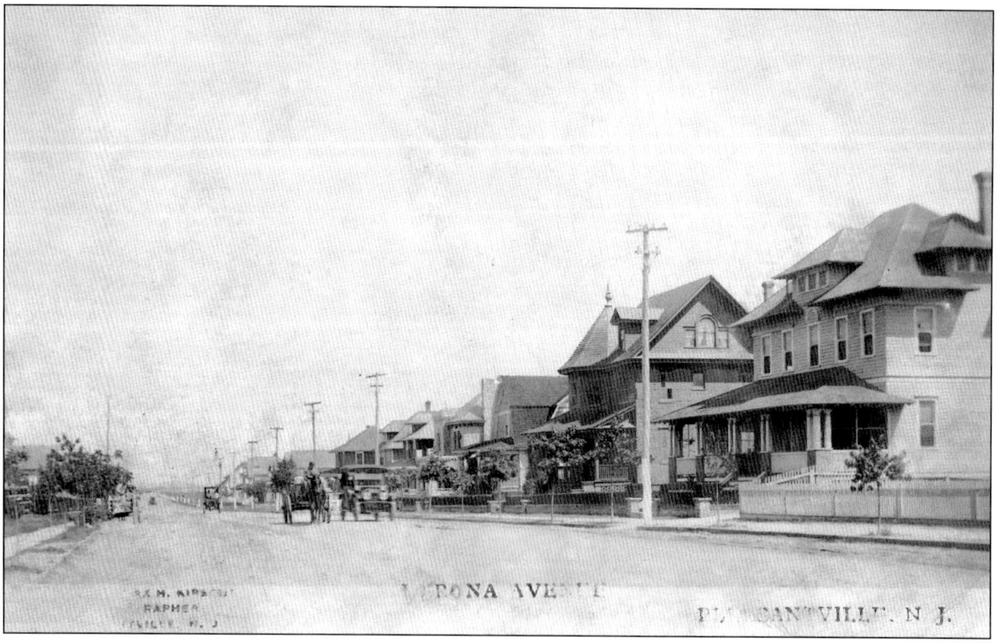

For some time, Old Turnpike and the Black Horse Pike were the only roads from the mainland to Atlantic City. Even after the extension and upgrade of the White Horse Pike from Absecon, reports in the late 1920s note that Verona Boulevard was frequently a "parking lot" during Sunday afternoons in the summer. This postcard shows the boulevard in a less-congested state.

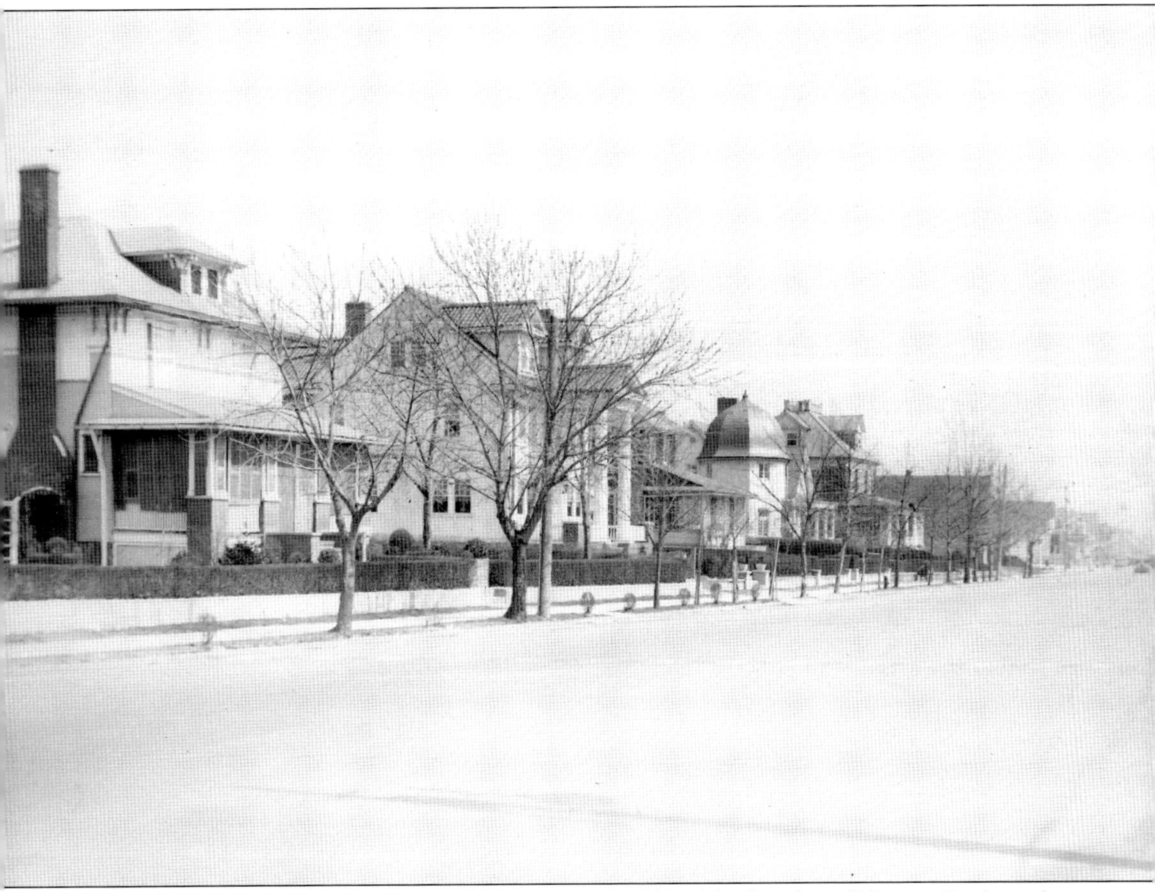

This view shows some of the opulent homes that once lined both sides of Verona Boulevard. Art Handler's Appliance Center now occupies a portion of the area on the left. Several of these homes are still standing.

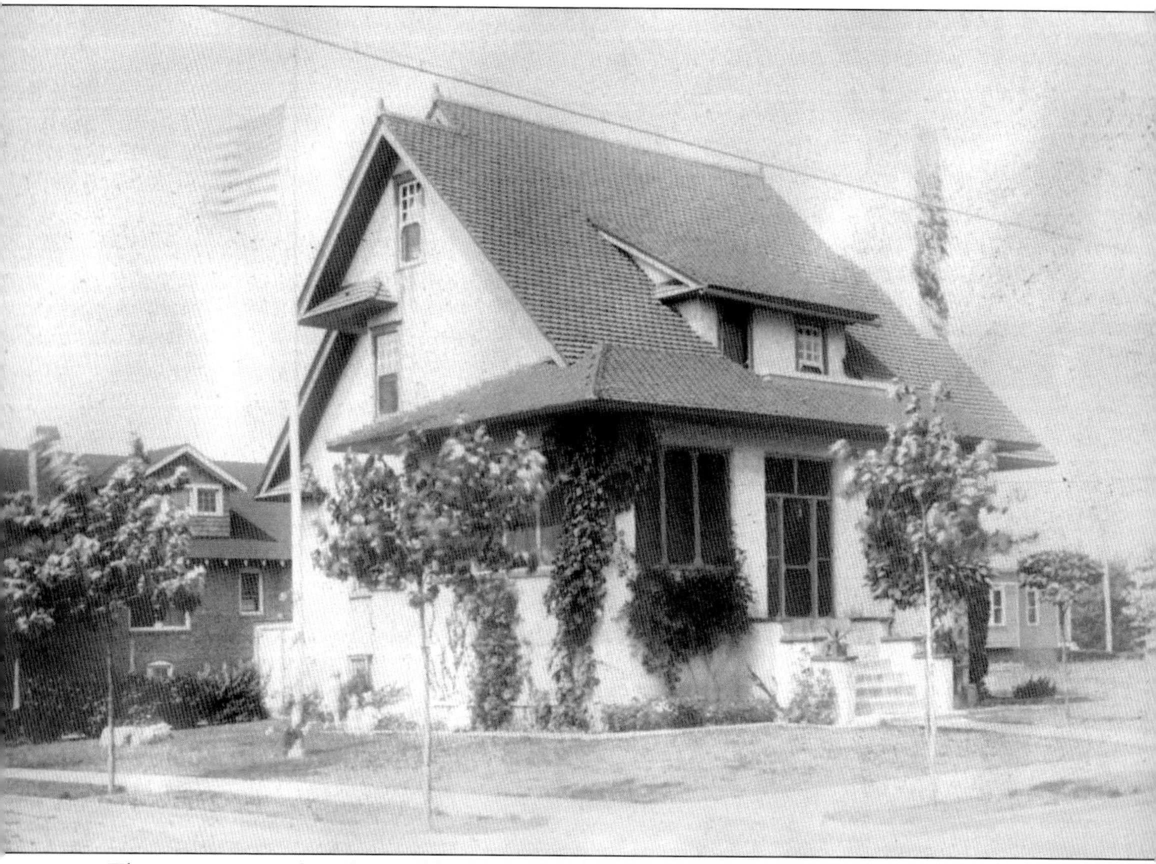

This image was referred to as "the Homestead on Verona Avenue" by Max Kirscht. This is one of the many new homes that began to be built along Verona Boulevard in Pleasantville and the West Atlantic City section of Egg Harbor Township in the late 1910s and 1920s.

This photograph faces west at the intersection of Franklin Avenue and Verona Boulevard. St. Mark's Episcopal Church is on the right, and South Main Street is in the distance.

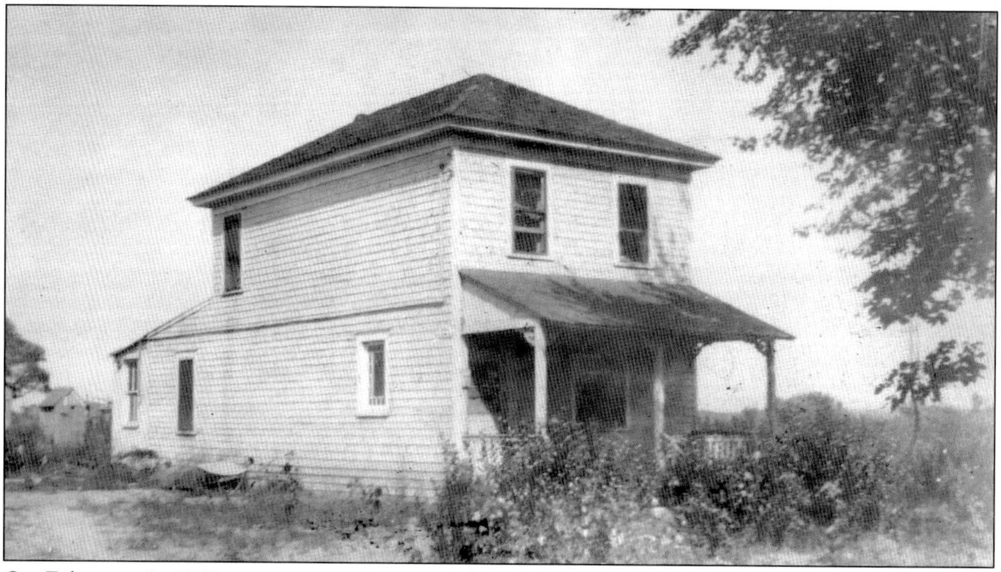

On February 3, 1853, an act to incorporate the Pleasantville and Atlantic Turnpike Company was approved by the New Jersey Legislature. The founders of the company, all local residents, did not complete the turnpike until many years later. It was the only roadway to Atlantic City for some time afterwards. With the rise in popularity of the bicycle in the 1890s, thousands of cyclists passed this tollhouse throughout the summer.

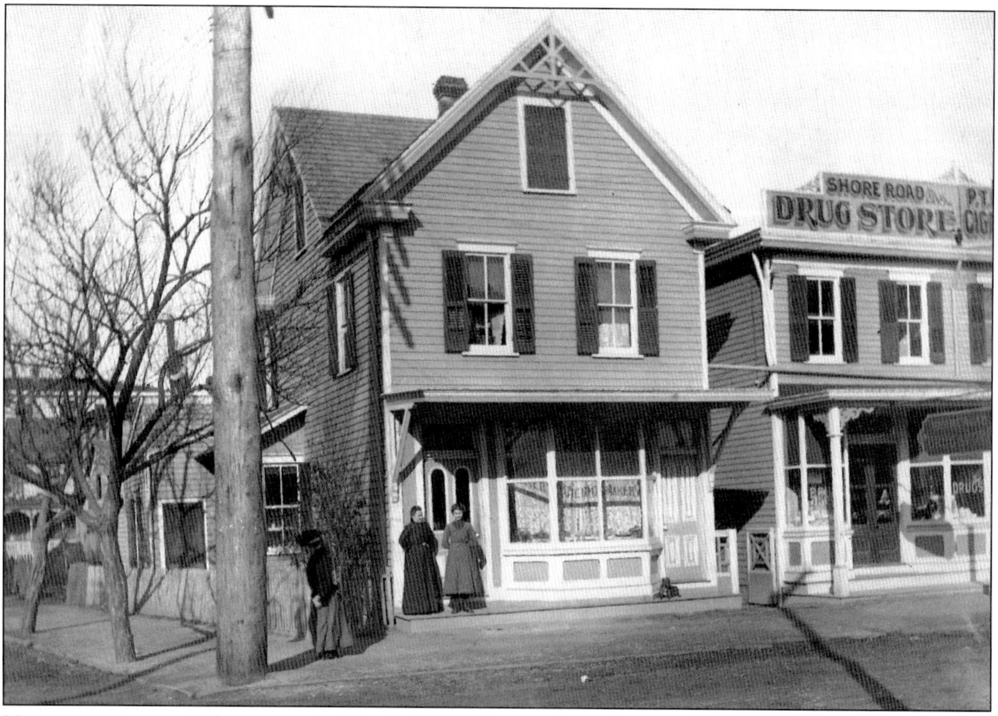

Heinzer's Vienna Bakery was in this building, located on the northwest corner of North Main Street and Washington Avenue. This building was later moved a short distance to 10 West Washington Avenue, where it was used as a candy store. Over the years, it has been utilized for a variety of purposes and still stands today.

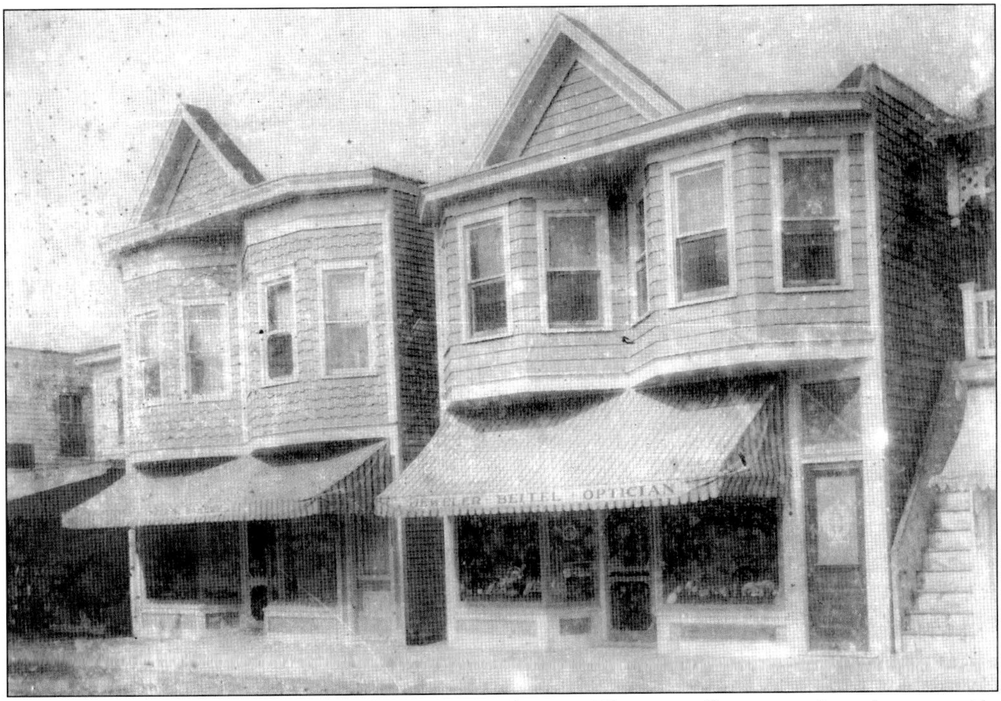

Seen here on the left is the second Heinzer's Bakery in Pleasantville, situated on the west side of South Main Street. Kay Heinzer started the business in 1896, and it steadily grew to include additional two bakers and three wagons to serve his customers. By 1906, he had moved to the new location and was enjoying a brisk business.

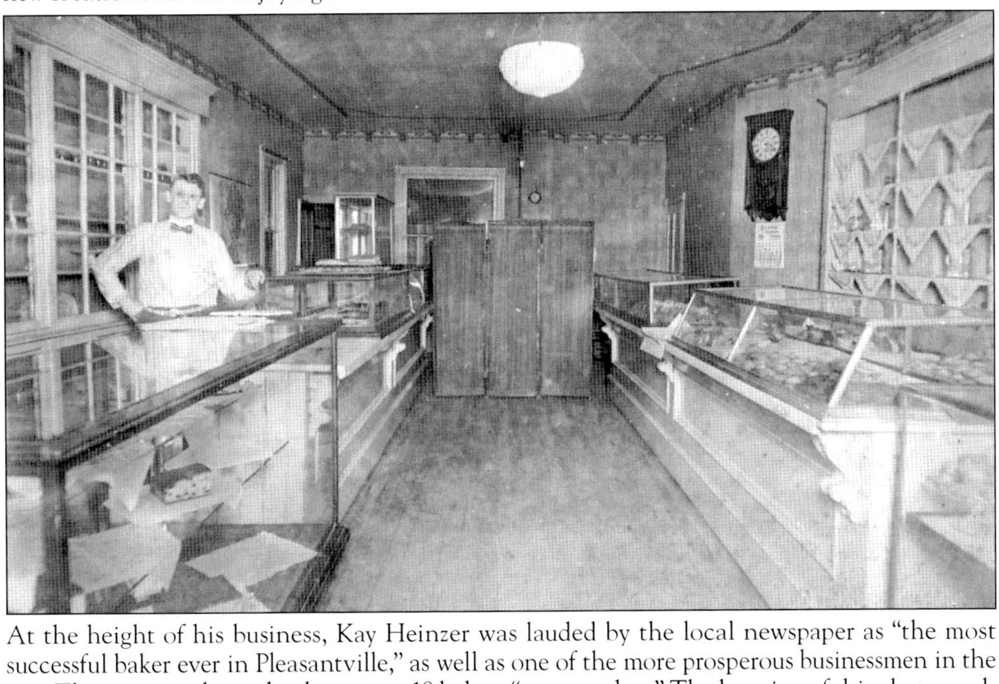

At the height of his business, Kay Heinzer was lauded by the local newspaper as "the most successful baker ever in Pleasantville," as well as one of the more prosperous businessmen in the city. The reporter claimed to have seen 18 bakers "come and go." The location of this photograph is unknown, but it may be Heinzer's South Main Street bakery.

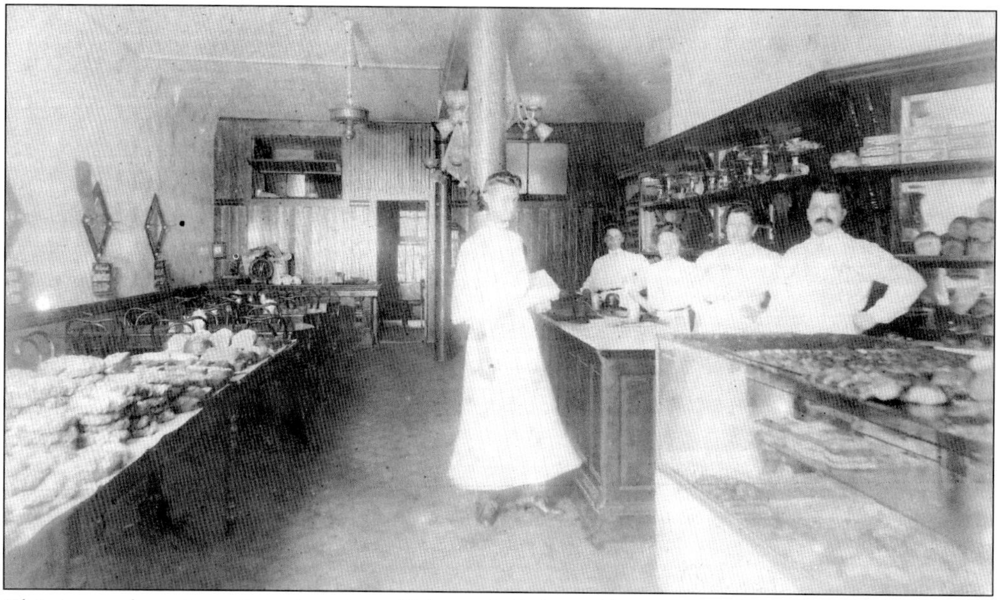

This is another view of the interior of Heinzer's Bakery. However, it is unknown when and in which store the photograph was taken.

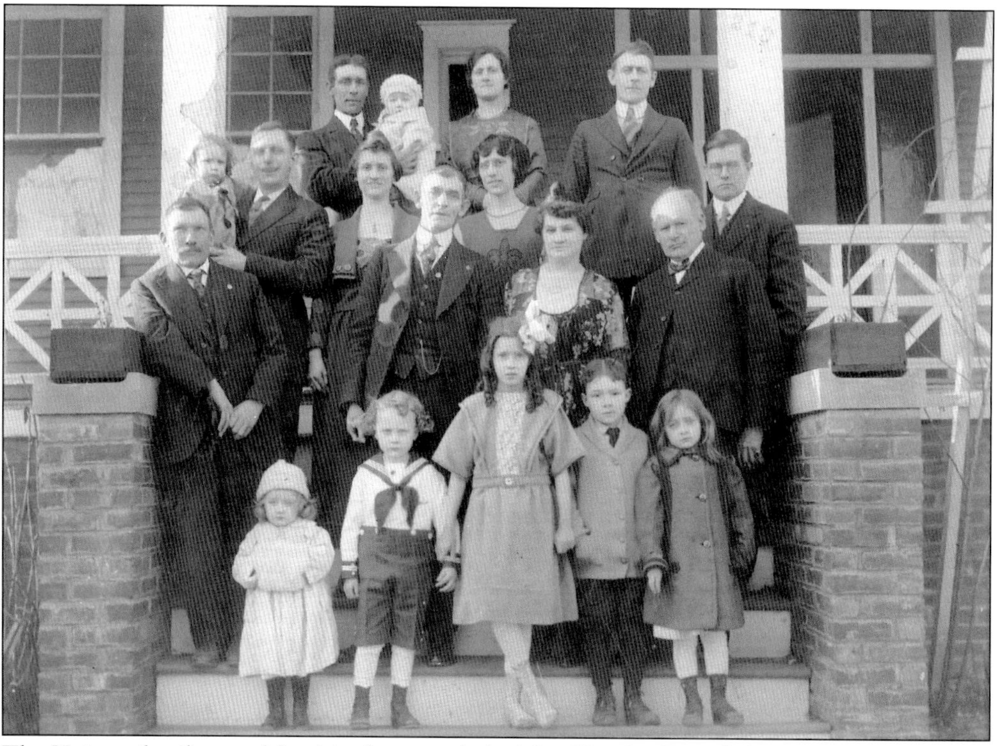

The Heinzer family posed for this photograph for Max Kirscht. From left to right are (first row) Helen Heinzer, George Bruminger, Margaret Steckle, Milton Heinzer, and Katherine Heinzer; (second row) Theodore Heinzer, Jake Walters, Katie Heinzer, and Melton Heinzer; (third row) Carol Bruminger, Chris Bruminger, Mabel Bruminger, Ida Steckle, and Fred Steckle; (fourth row) Edward Heinzer, Francis Heinzer, Hannah Heinzer, and Howard Heinzer.

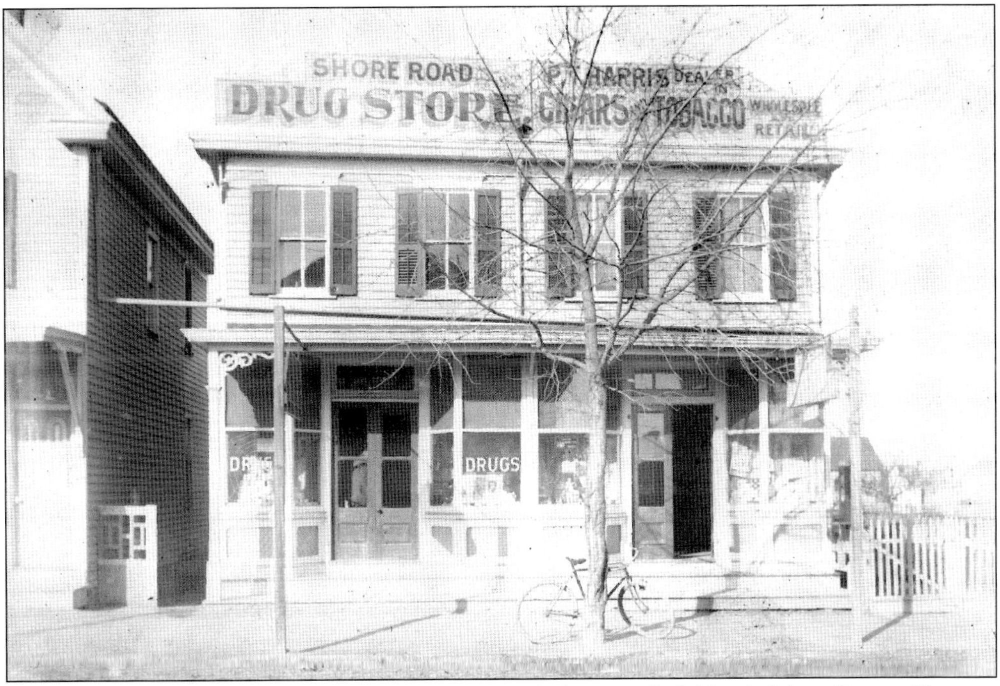

This building stood adjacent to Heinzer's Vienna Bakery, at 3–5 North Main Street. Herman Kirscht later purchased the structure, which eventually became his son's photograph studio.

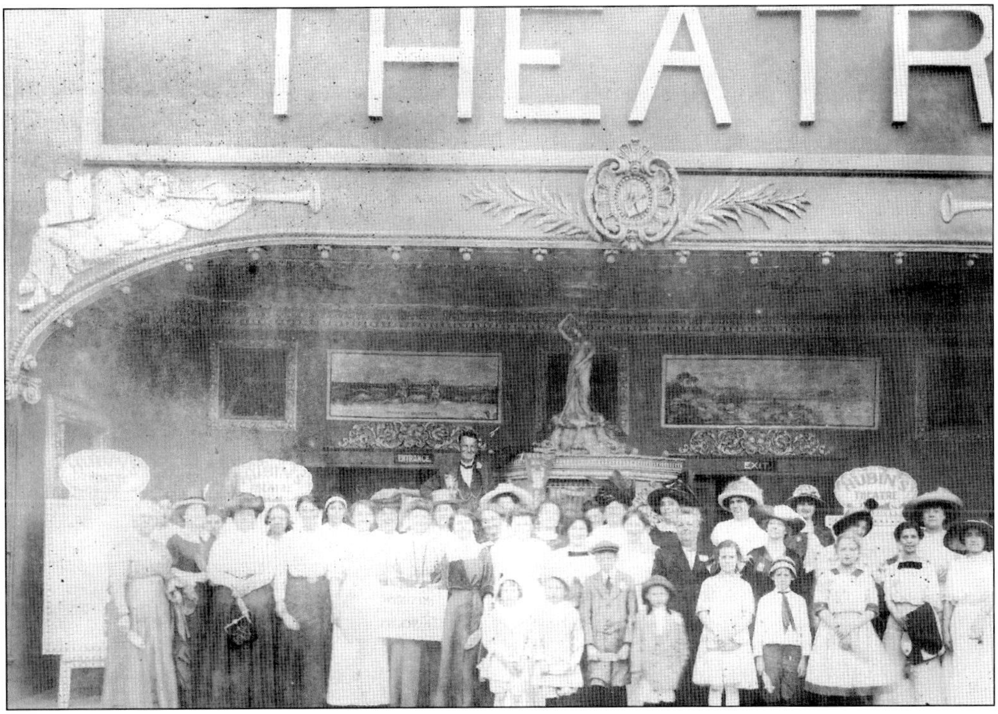

The Hubins Theatre advertised, "Always a Fine Program of the Latest and Best Moving Pictures Shown on the Day and Night Screen. Pictures changed daily. A nice place to go." Admission was 15¢ for adults and 10¢ for children. The Hubins Theatre eventually became the Carlton Theater.

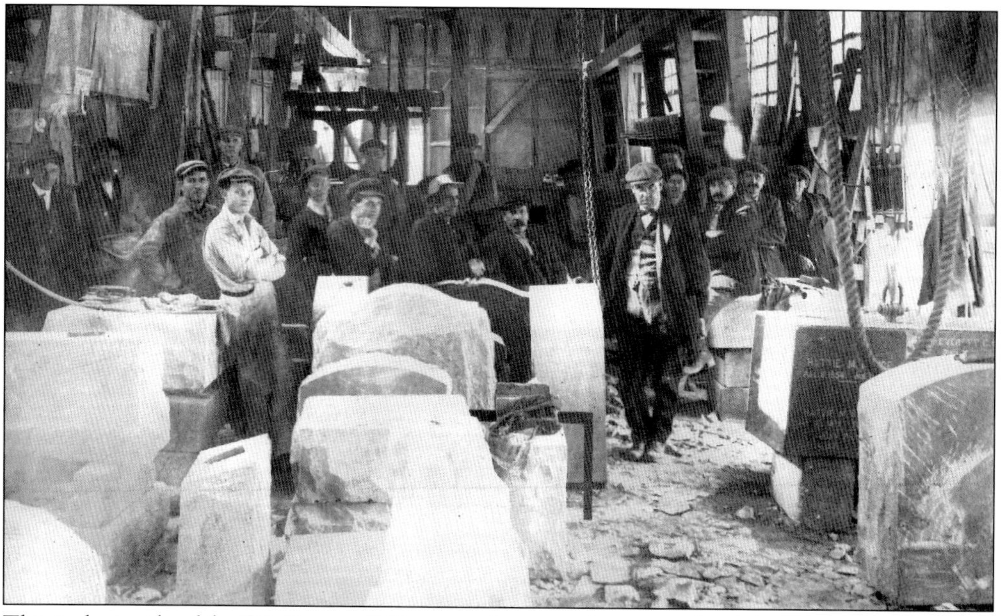

This is the inside of the O.J. Hammell Company factory, adjacent to the Atlantic City Cemetery in Pleasantville, where the company moved in 1902. The company produced headstones, mausoleums, and public memorials, including the monuments for the Greenwich Tea Burners and the Battle of Chestnut Neck. At one time, the company had sales offices in 58 cities in the eastern United States. This photograph was taken by Max Kirscht about 1914.

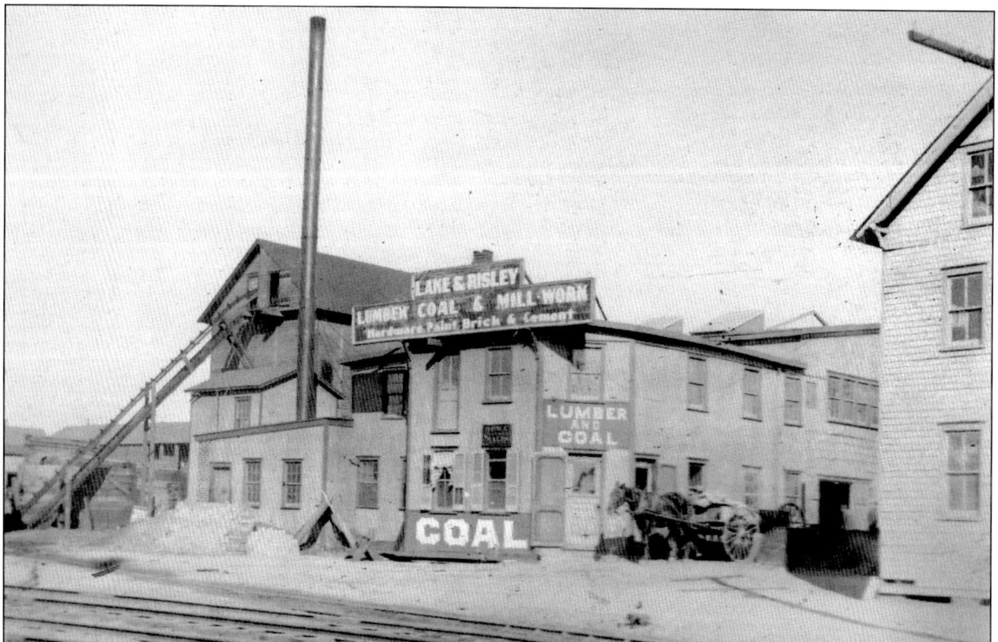

Shortly after daybreak on June 18, 1909, one of the largest fires in Pleasantville history struck the Lake & Risley lumberyard. This huge facility, located on the former Tri-County Building Supply site, was burned to the ground, hurting dozens of volunteers who tried to stop the fire and save adjacent buildings. At the time, it was estimated that there was $100,000 in damage.

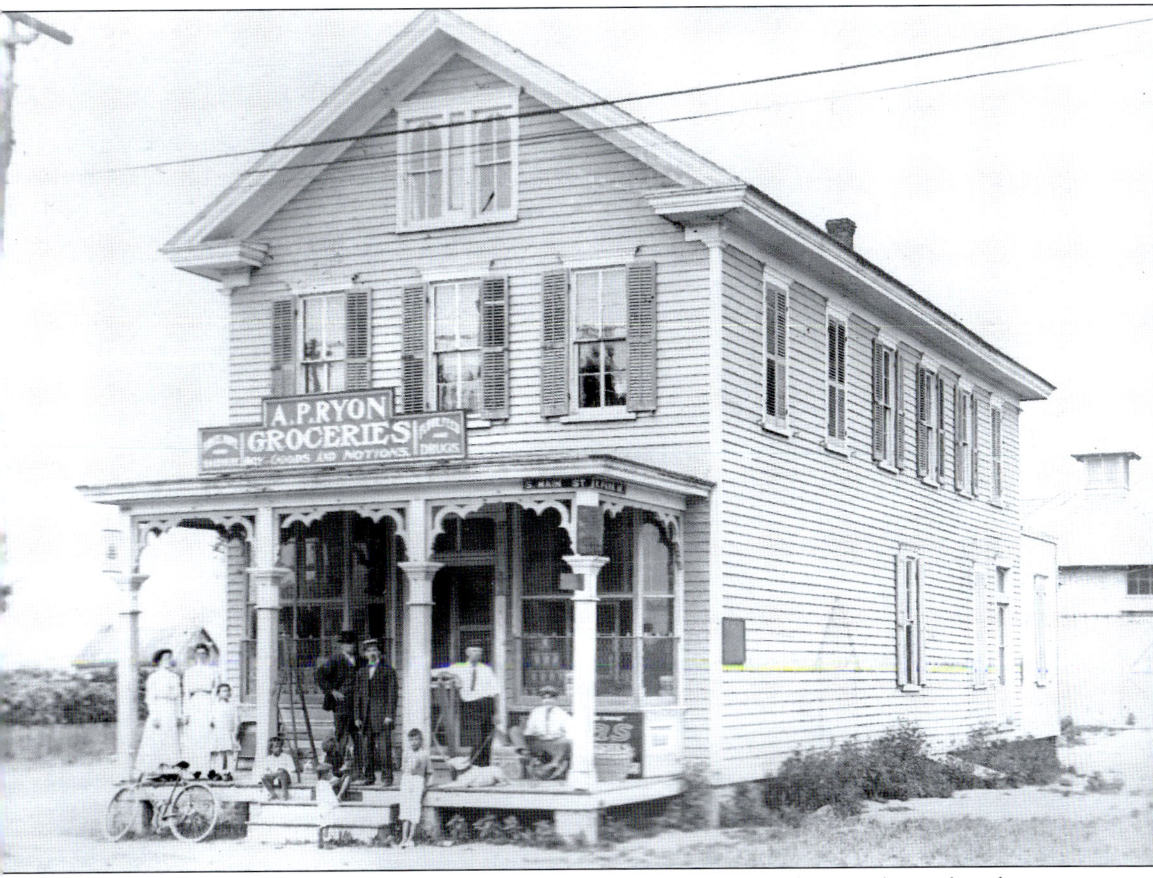

Built in 1889 by Pardon Ryon Jr., A.P. Ryon Groceries was a typical general merchandising establishment that catered to the Smith's Landing area. The second floor was used for meetings and other functions. In 1909, the structure was moved to its present location on the southeast corner of East Park Avenue and South Main Street and then sold. The building is still used today as a business establishment, currently housing a dry-cleaning business.

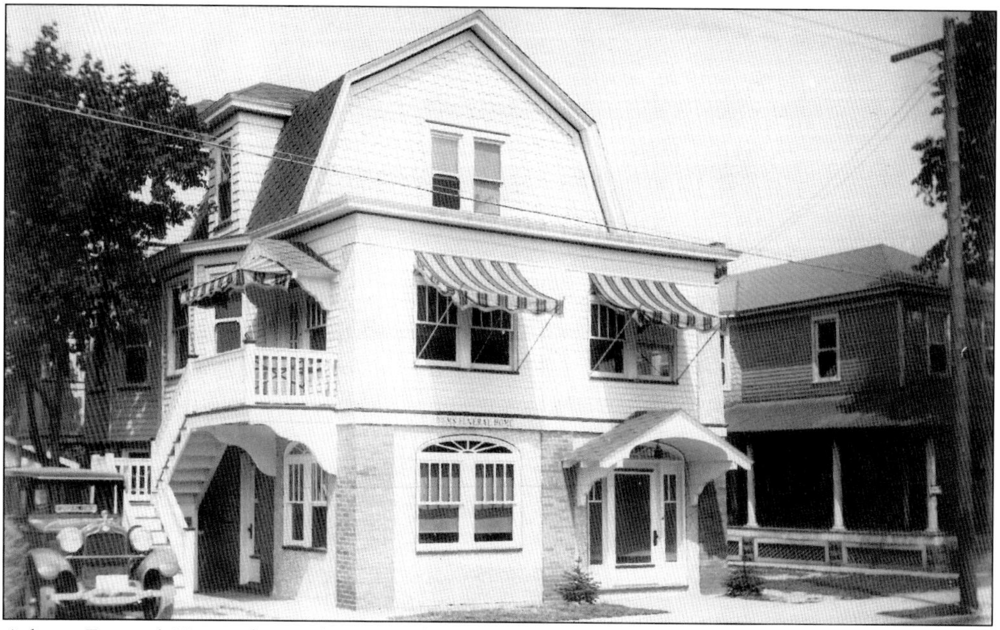

Adams Funeral Home, located on North Second Street in Pleasantville, was just around the corner from the homes of both Herman and Max Kirscht. Like many carpenters in the late 1800s, Elisha Adams also became an undertaker. He started directing funerals from his home in 1902, moving to the North Second Street location about five years later. The business was sold to Frank Perfect in 1957 and is still known today as the Adams-Perfect Funeral Home.

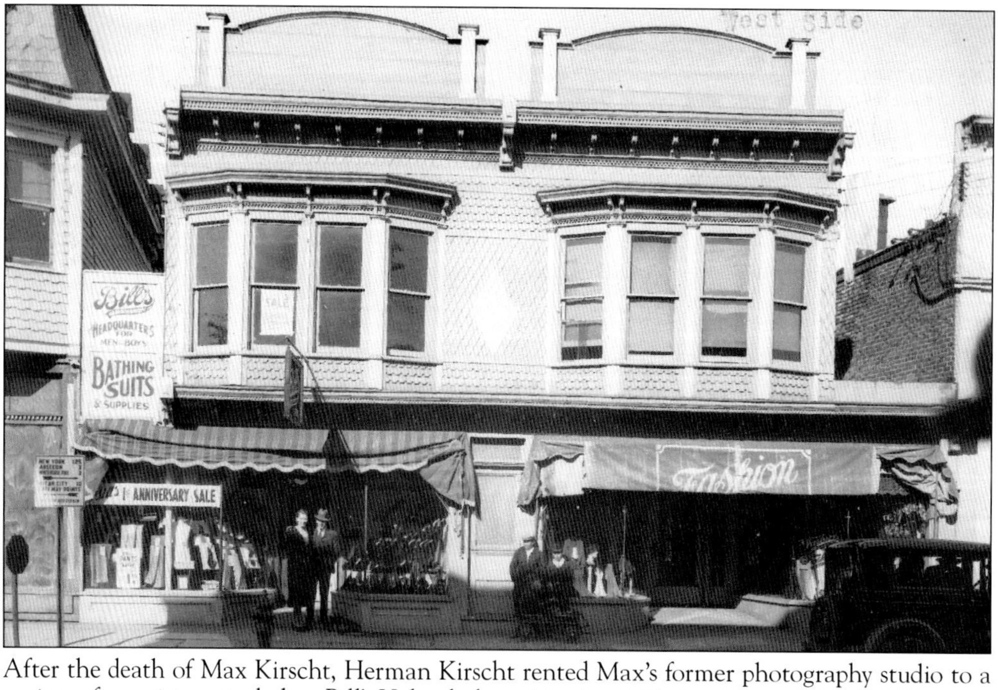

After the death of Max Kirscht, Herman Kirscht rented Max's former photography studio to a variety of proprietors, including Bill's Haberdashery, Mattison's Variety Shop, and Polly's Shoppes. He also tried to sell the property, as evidenced by the sign in the second-floor window. Note that the wooden Lore's Department Store building still occupies the site to the left.

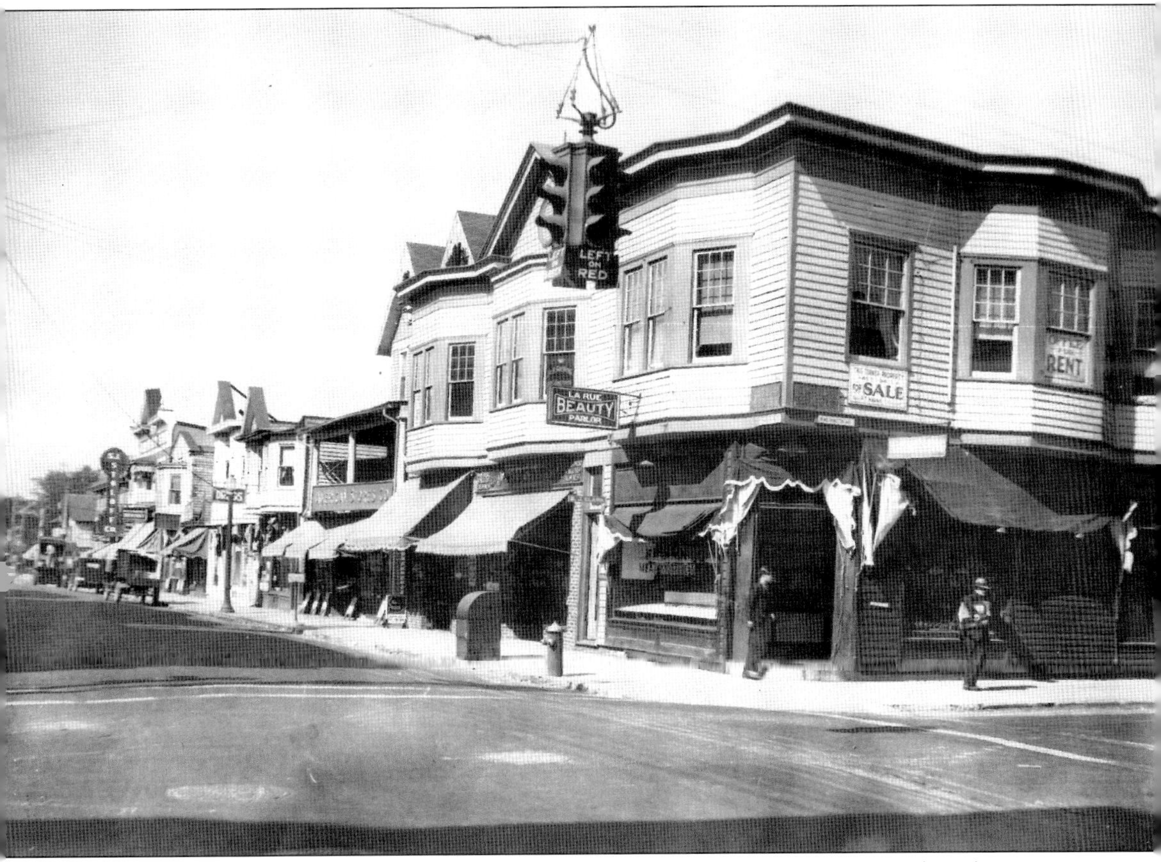

In 1903, the southwest corner of the Burkard Building, located at South Main Street and Washington Avenue, was occupied by Crawford's Pharmacy. Thomas F. Crawford operated what was described as a "modern drug store with a splendid fountain" at this location for 24 years. He was also the mayor of Pleasantville for 10 years, over three separate terms. He moved his pharmacy to Absecon in 1927.

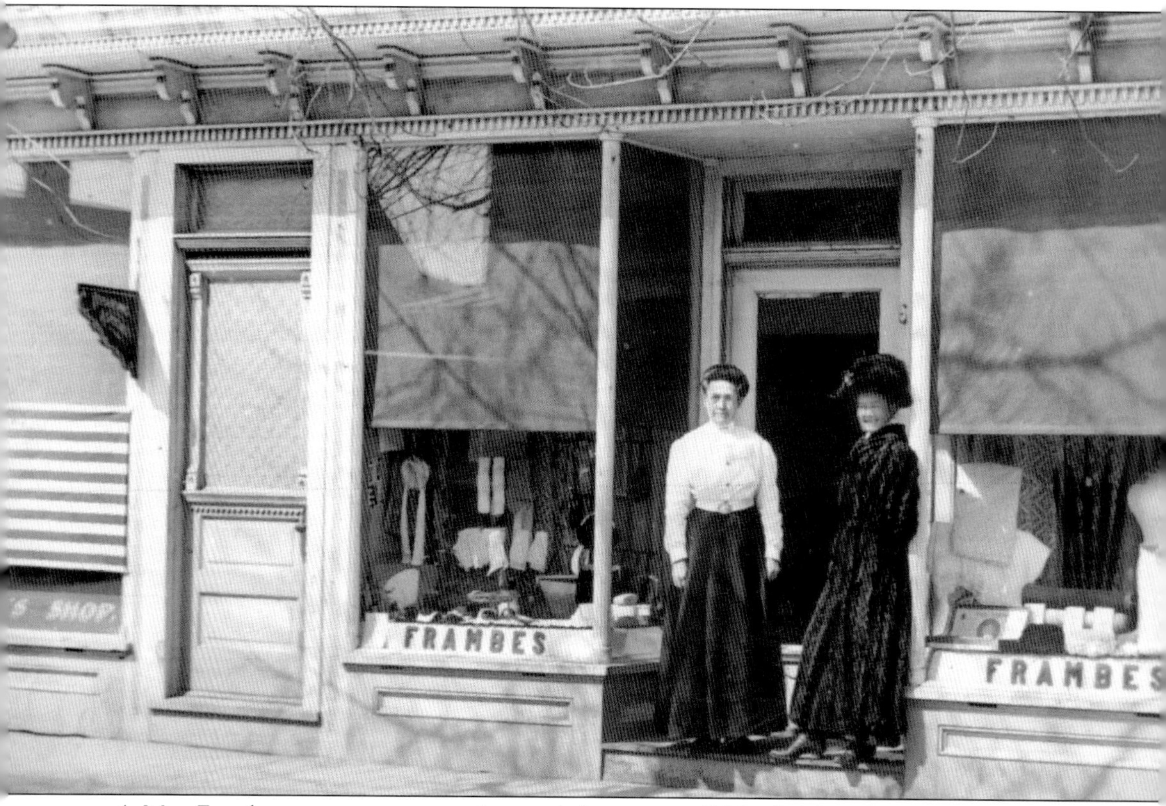

A Mrs. Frambes ran a prosperous dry goods business at 7 North Main Street in Pleasantville, which was owned by Herman Kirscht. Max Kirscht later operated his photography studio from the shop next door. This photograph is believed to have been taken in 1903.

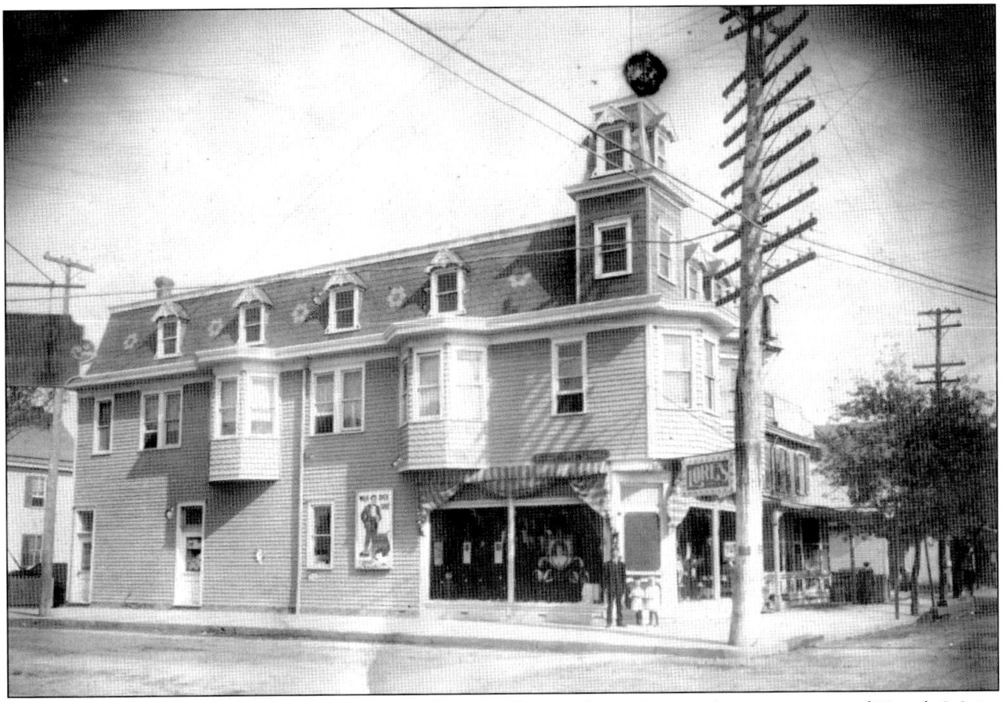

This was Theodore Lore's second dry goods store, located on the northwest corner of North Main Street and Washington Avenue.

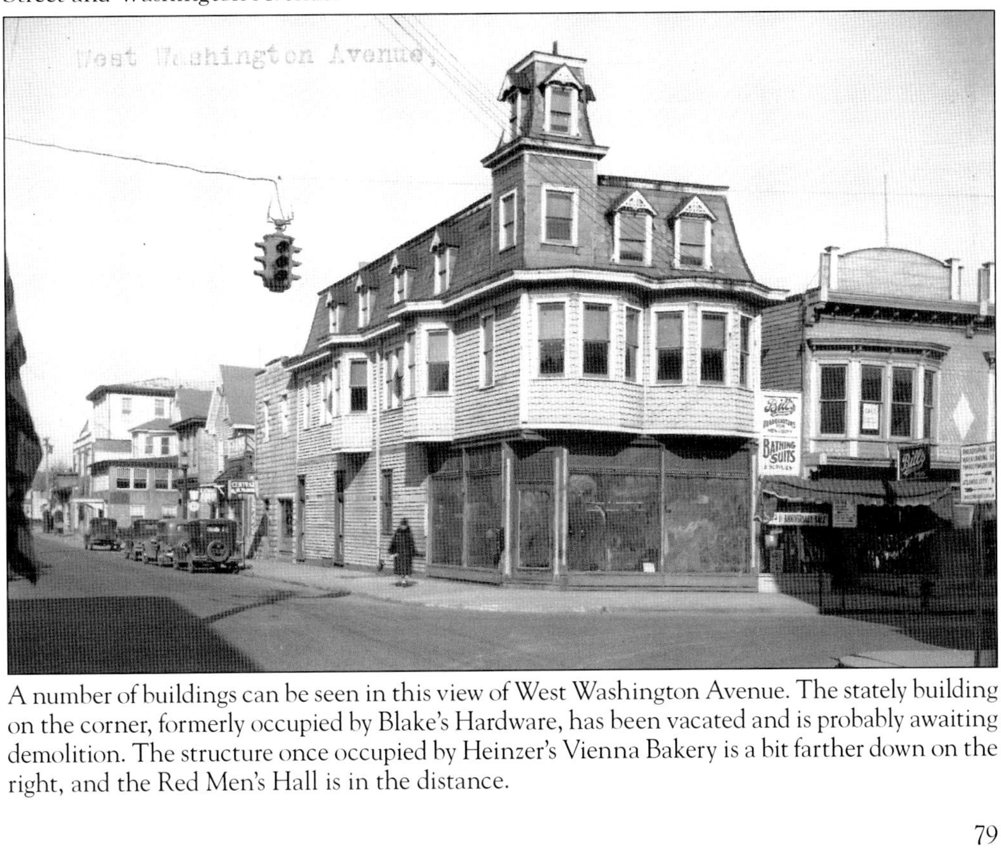

A number of buildings can be seen in this view of West Washington Avenue. The stately building on the corner, formerly occupied by Blake's Hardware, has been vacated and is probably awaiting demolition. The structure once occupied by Heinzer's Vienna Bakery is a bit farther down on the right, and the Red Men's Hall is in the distance.

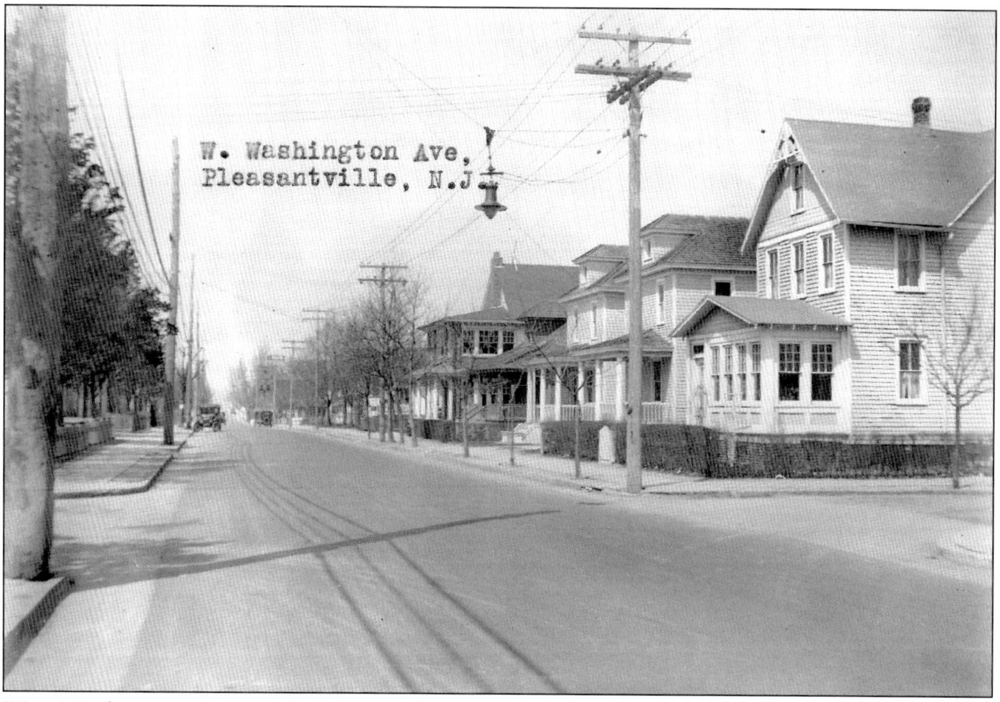

West Washington Avenue is seen here from the intersection with North Second Street. The Kirscht home is on the right.

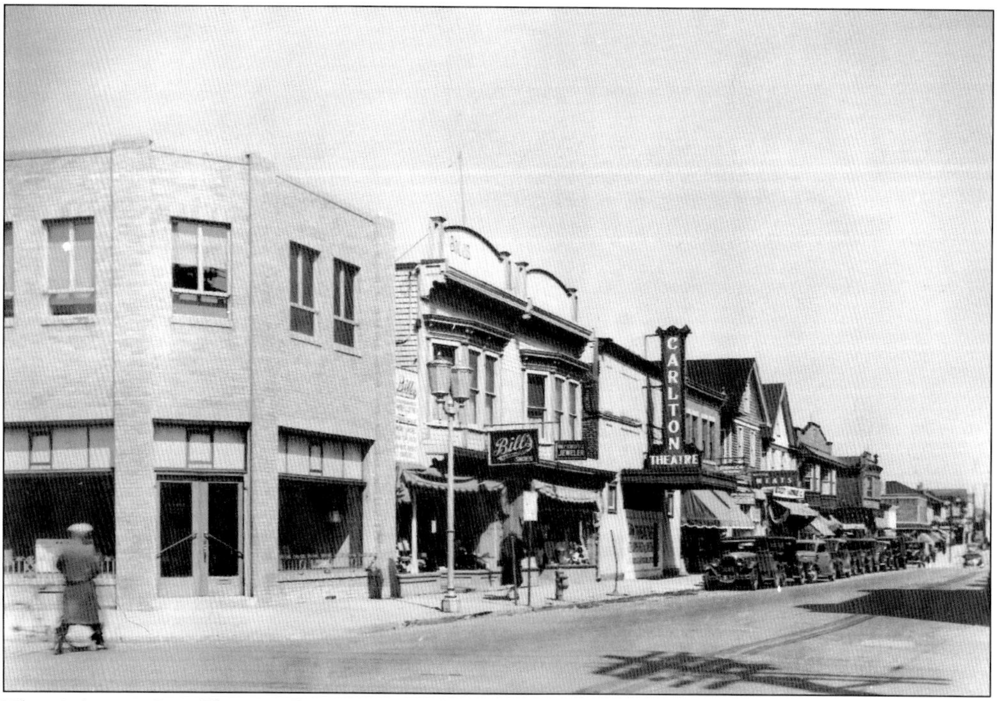

The Atlantic City Electric Company purchased the old Lore's Department Store property and had a brick building constructed on the site. The new structure was used for years by the electric company as a showroom and for sales. This building is also still standing.

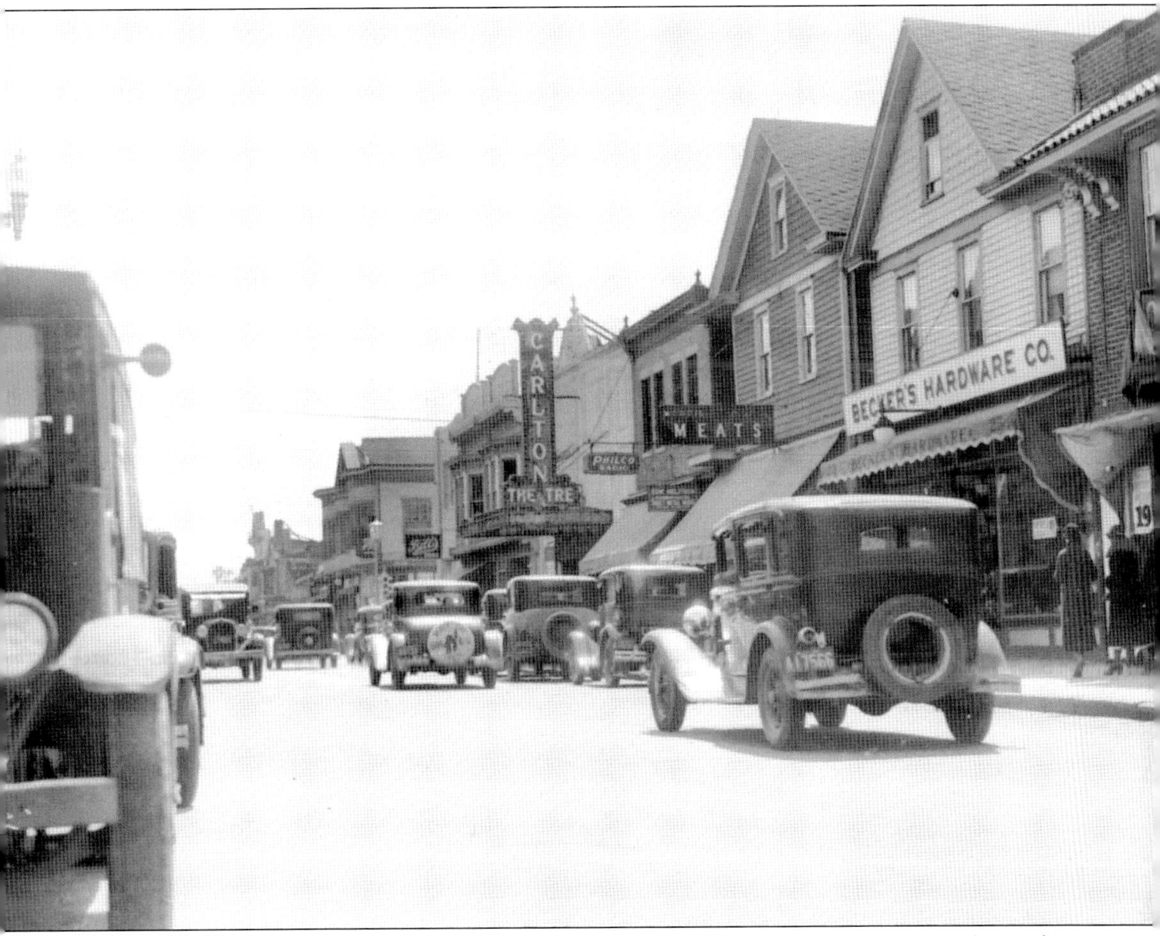

This is another shot of North Main Street, looking toward Washington Avenue in the mid-1920s. Lore's is gone, and the Atlantic City Electric Company's showroom is in its place. By this time, Pleasantville had become the shopping center of Atlantic County. Looking closely, the automobile in the middle of the street has a spare tire cover advertising the Black Cat Bar & Barbeque in Absecon.

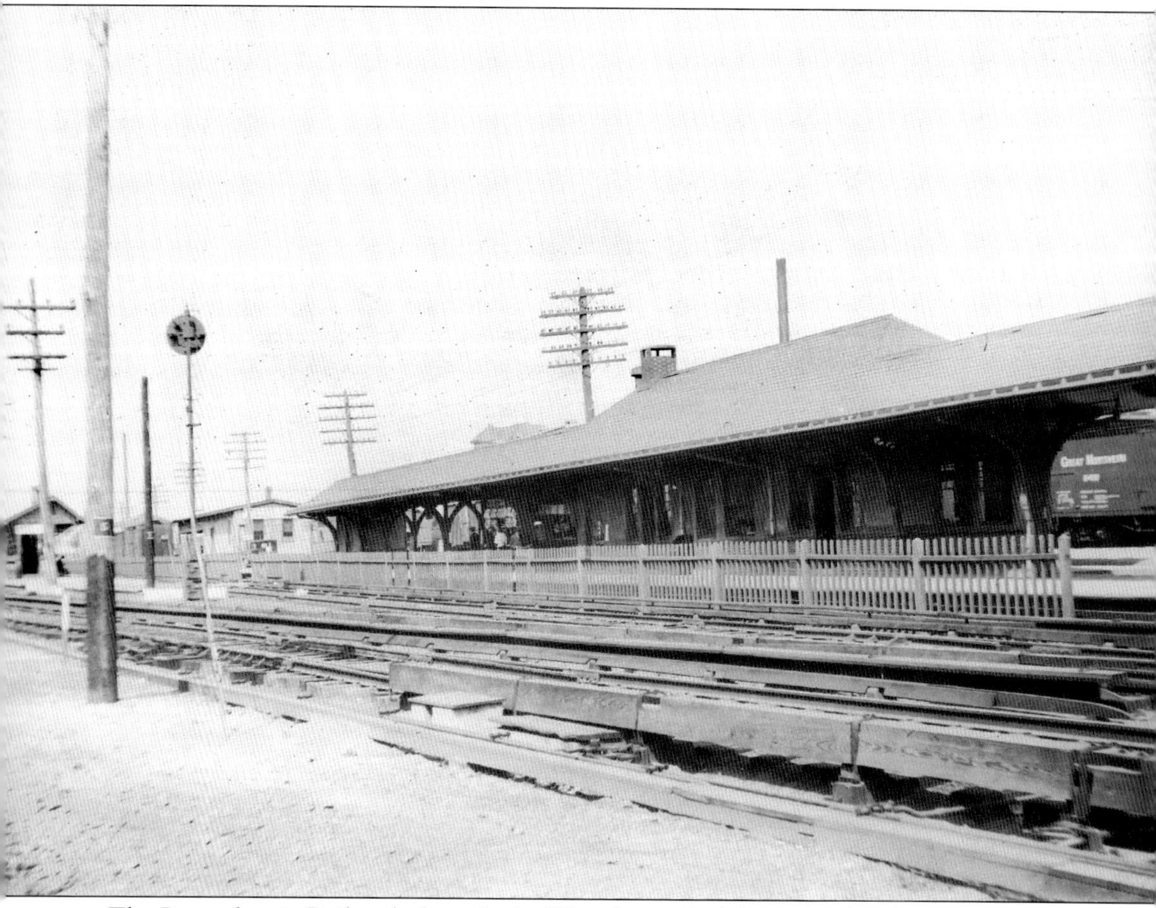

The Pennsylvania Railroad, through the West Jersey & Atlantic Railroad, was able to reach Atlantic City via a connection at Newfield in Gloucester County in the mid-1880s. During the summer of 1906, the railroad decided to electrify the line; by the following year, electric line service had begun to Atlantic City. Seen here is the railroad's Pleasantville station, located between West Jersey and Milan Avenues.

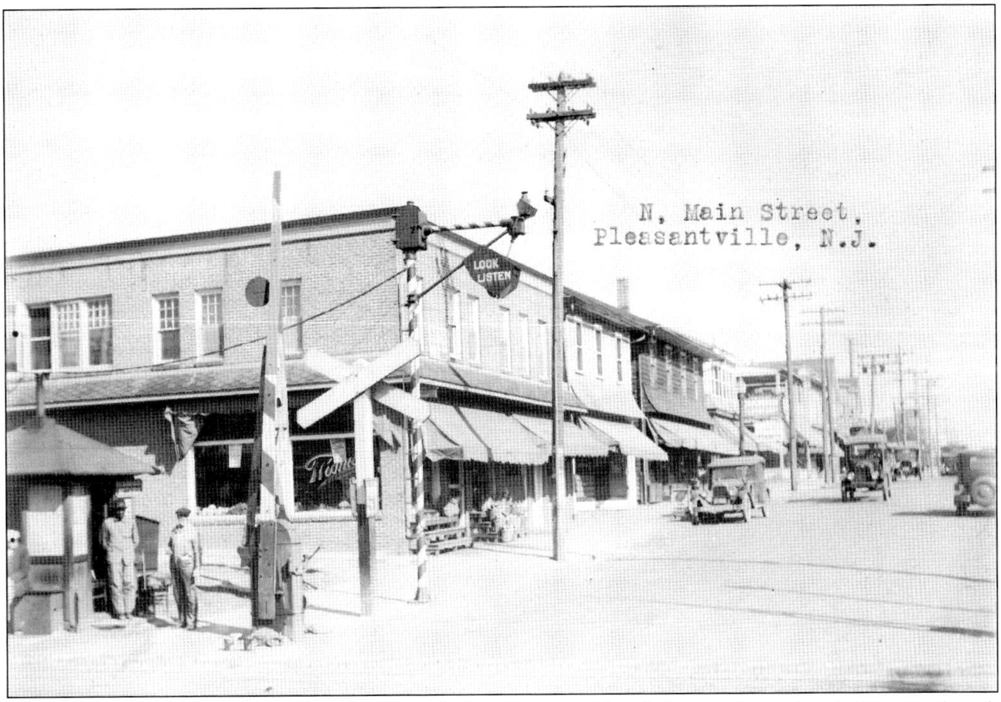

As with the Pennsylvania Railroad–controlled rail lines in South Jersey, the Atlantic City Railroad, commonly referred to as "the Reading" in many small towns in South Jersey, crossed North Main Street where Martin Luther King Jr. Avenue is today. The station was located adjacent to what is now the Casino Cleaners building.

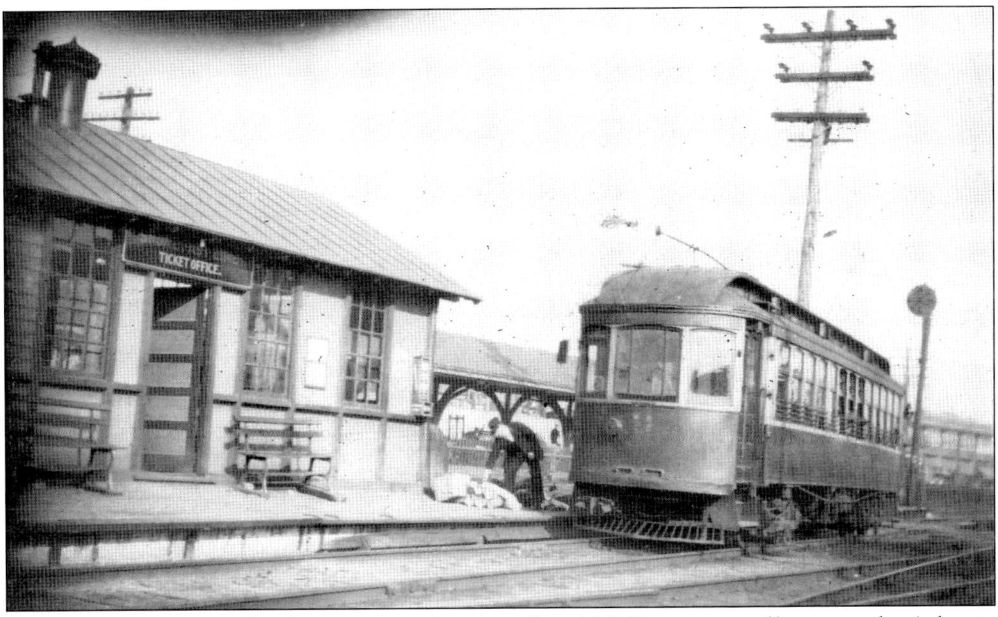

After the Atlantic & Suburban Traction Company line (A&S) went out of business, the Atlantic City & Shore Railroad, also known as the Shore Fast Line (SFL), became the only trolley service between the mainland communities and Atlantic City. Here, the conductor picks up mailbags at the SFL ticket office in Pleasantville.

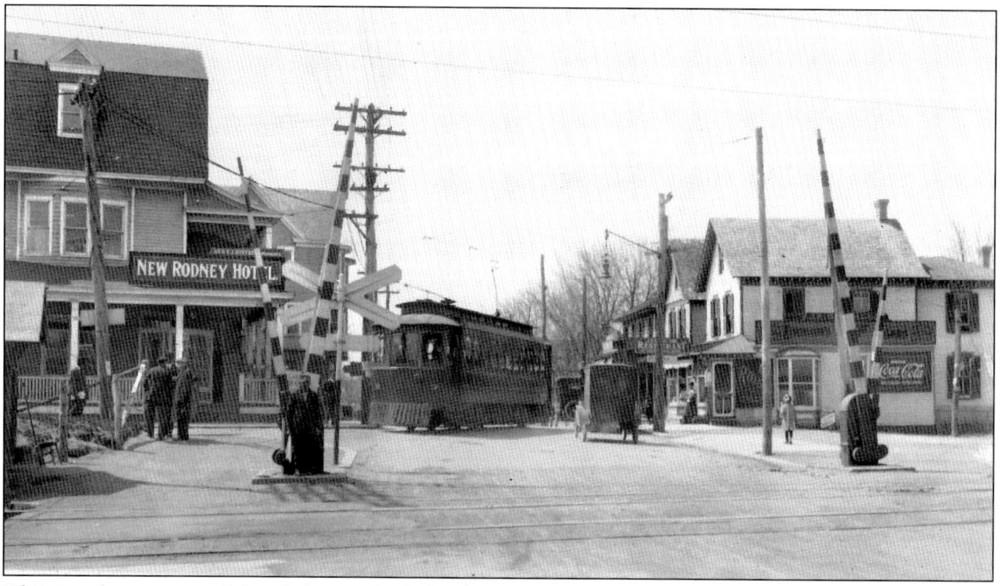

This is a later view of the Atlantic & Suburban Traction Company trolley from Absecon. The trolley is turning onto what became Milan Avenue. Part of the attraction of Pleasantville was its proximity to Atlantic City, as well as the mass transit options it had, with two trolley lines and two railroads.

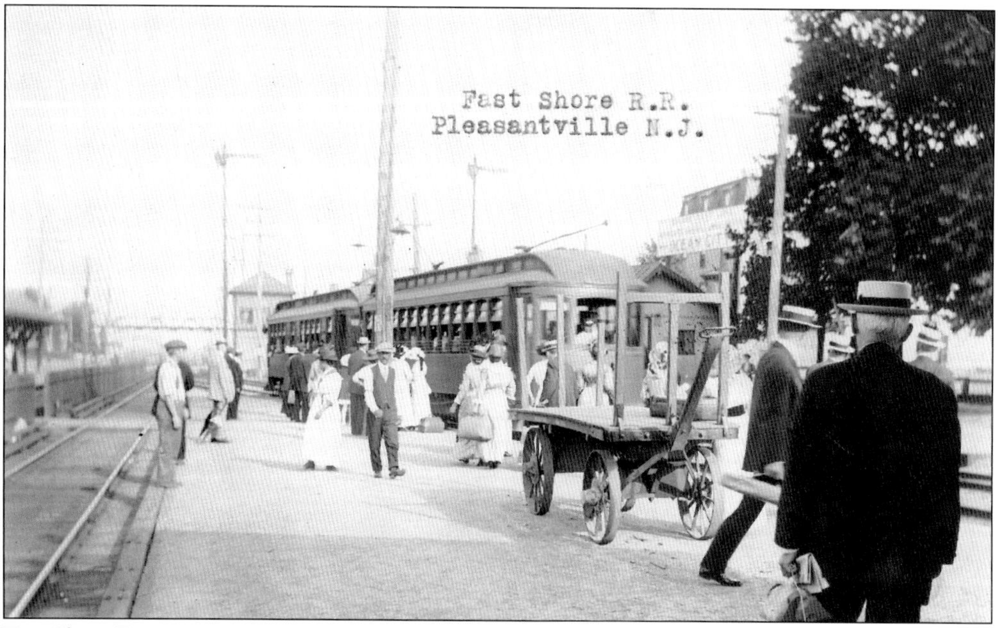

Two Shore Fast Line commuter cars wait for passengers to board at the line's Pleasantville station. The Atlantic & Suburban bridge over the West Jersey & Seashore Railroad right-of-way can be seen in the distance.

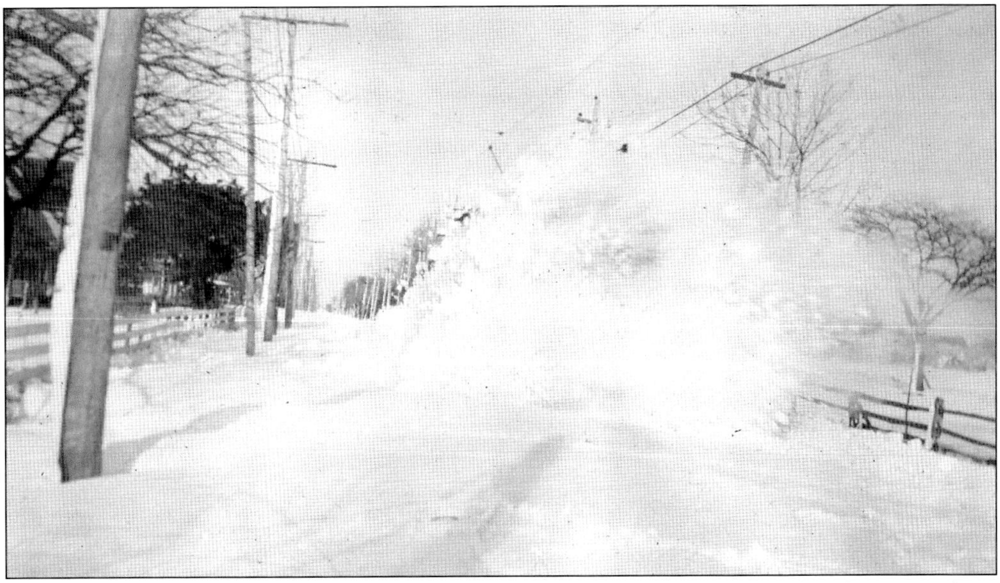

An Atlantic & Suburban trolley is behind a giant pile of snow in this photograph, taken somewhere along Main Street. After the A&S stopped operations, the Shore Fast Line, which had been incorporated in 1905, operated the remaining trolley service, including an extension to Ocean City, which was constructed during 1906 and 1907. SFL trolley service ended on January 18, 1948, and was replaced with buses.

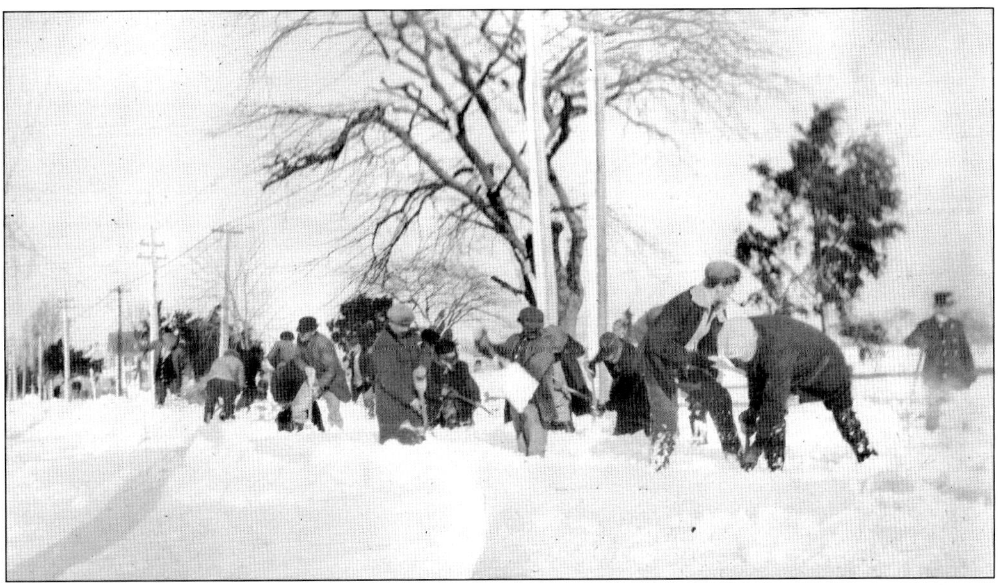

After the trolley hit the snow bank, it appears that the conductor enlisted a number of local men to help clear the tracks.

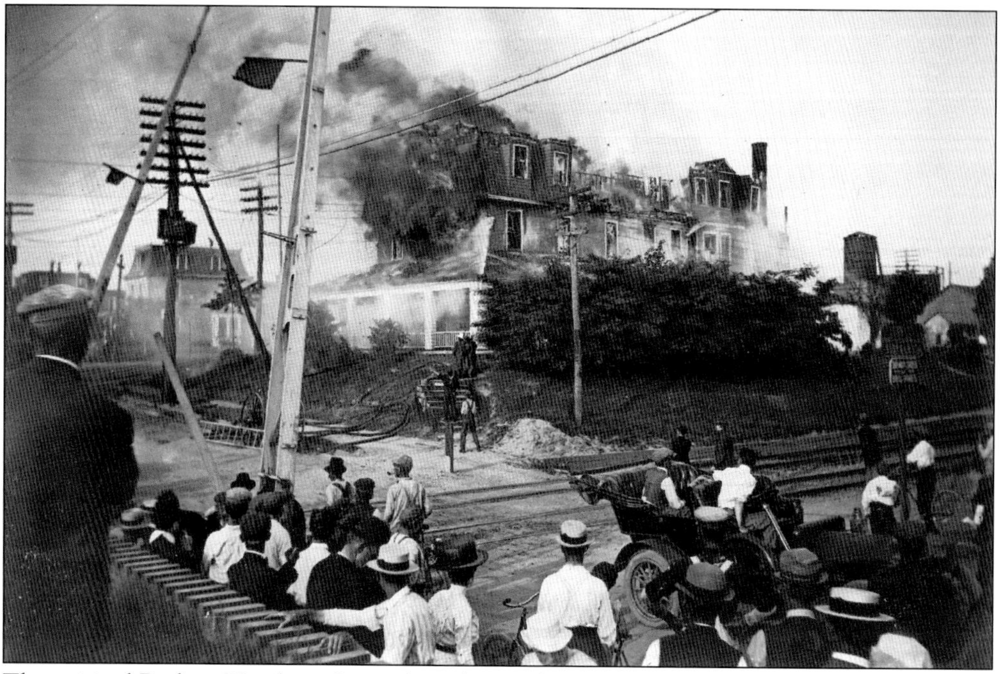

The original Rodney Hotel was located on the southeast corner of North Main Street and Old Turnpike, next to the Atlantic City Railroad. It later became the O'Donnell Hotel and was the scene of this disastrous fire in July 1910. The *Weekly Press of Pleasantville* reported that there was water pressure from the city hydrant for only several moments. The building was completely destroyed by the blaze.

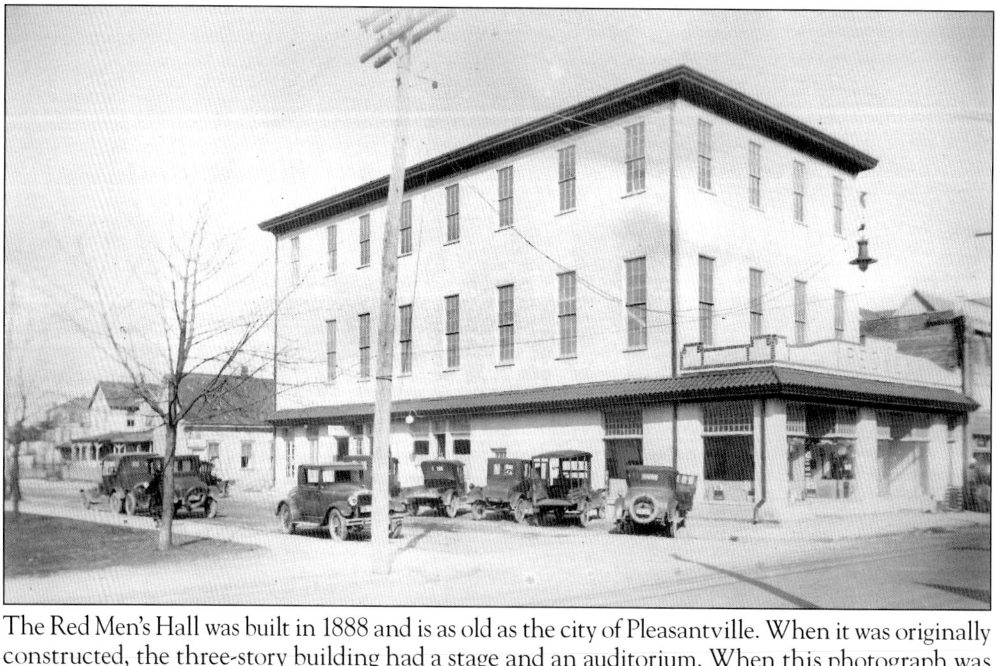

The Red Men's Hall was built in 1888 and is as old as the city of Pleasantville. When it was originally constructed, the three-story building had a stage and an auditorium. When this photograph was taken, the police department headquarters were on the ground floor on First Street. In the 1920s, the property was sold to the local lodge of the Independent Order of Odd Fellows.

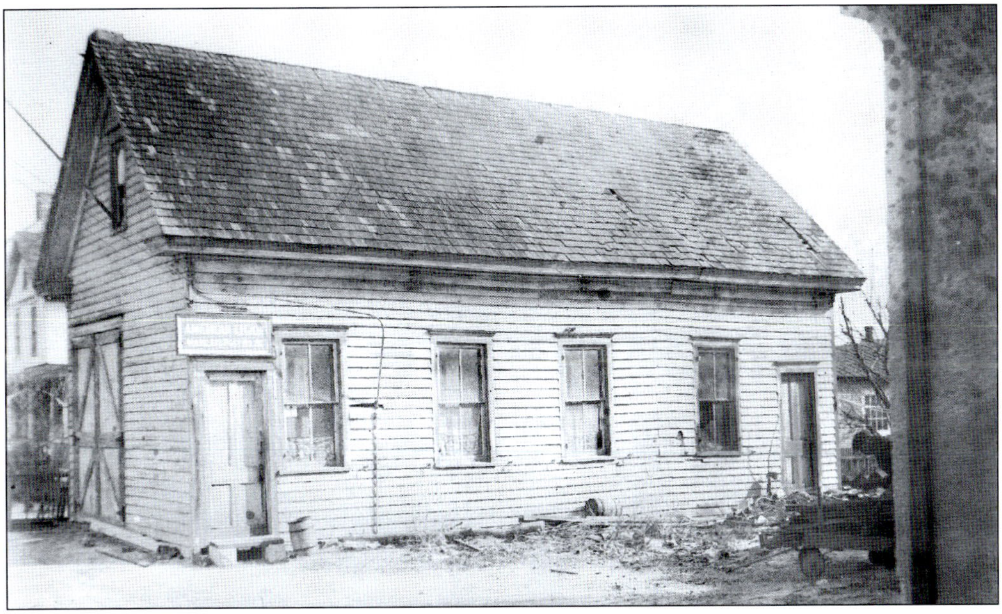

Pleasantville's original fire station was this building on First Street, situated behind the Red Men's Hall. Later, it became the first home of American Legion Mainland Post No. 81, which was founded on September 8, 1919. On January 16, 1922, the city council allowed the legion to use the old firehouse. The building is long gone now, and this site is currently a city parking lot.

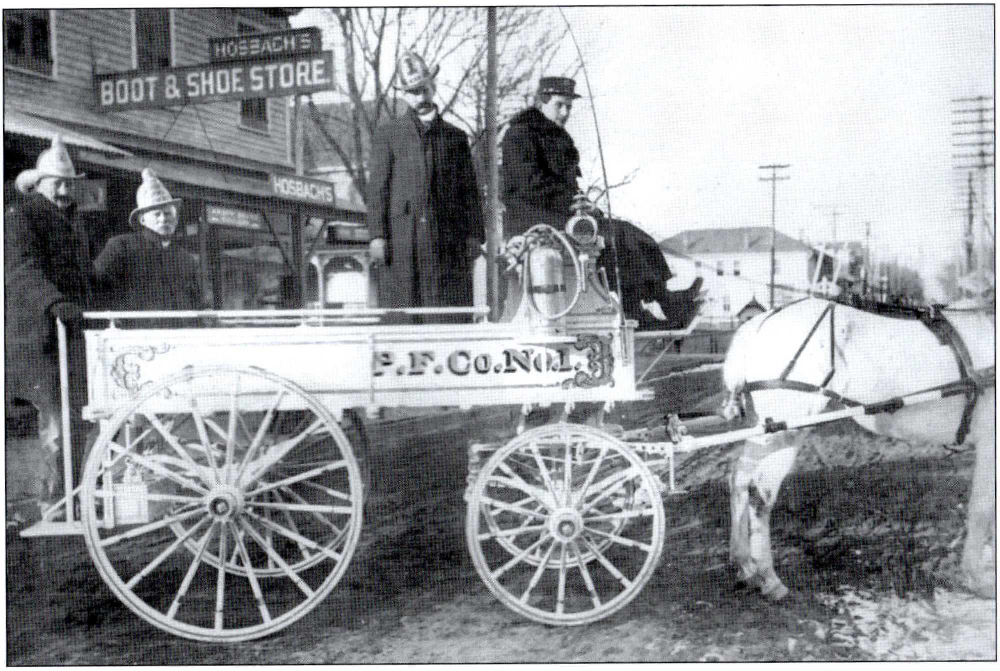

The carriage in this photograph was described as the first fire chief's wagon. The photograph was taken on North Main Street between Washington and Grant Avenues. The gentleman at the reins is Louis Zentmayer, who owned the Palace Livery and Boarding Stables on South Main Street. Assistant Fire Chief William Champion (left) and Fire Chief Frank Reinar stand on the back of the wagon, and Mark Fritsch is stands in the center.

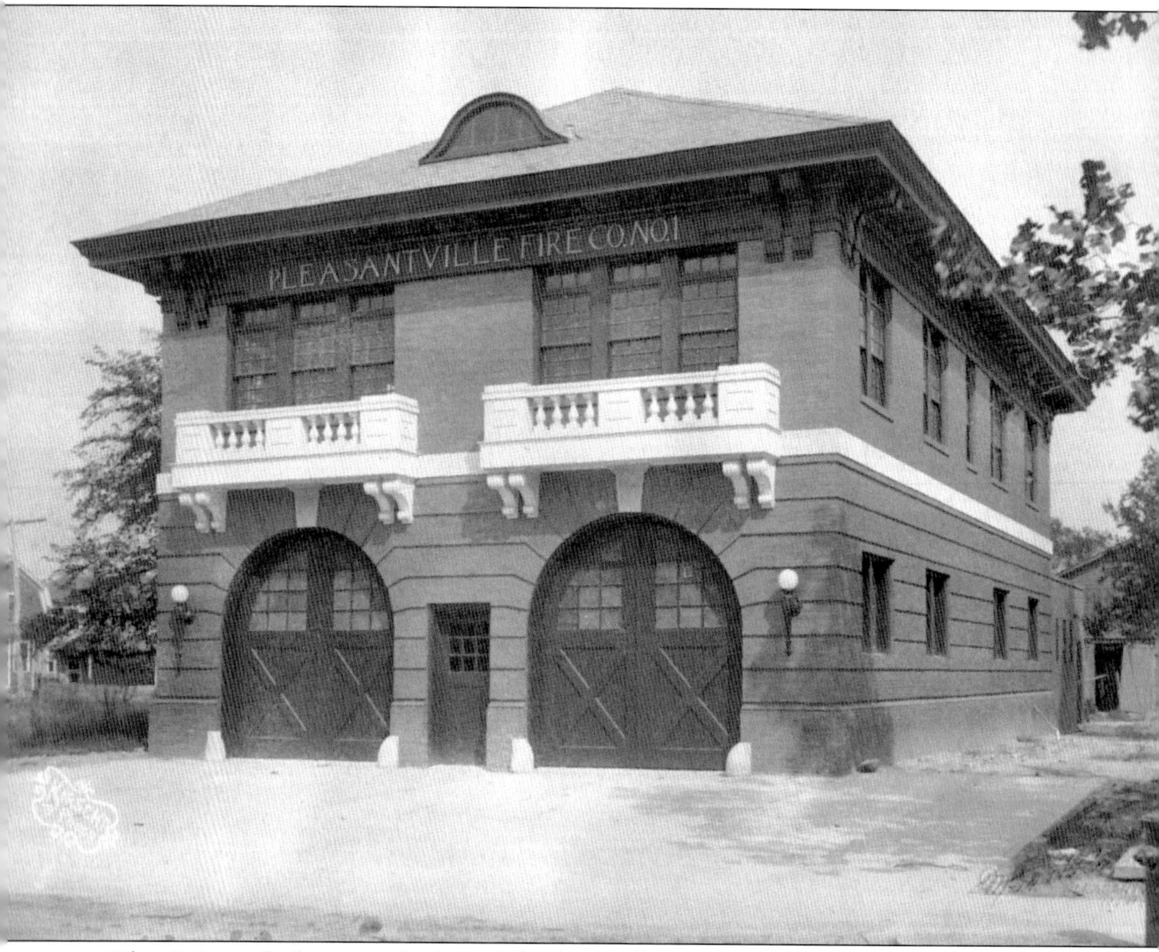

The city's new firehouse was built in 1912. The fire department was housed on the first floor, with the city jail in the rear. Municipal offices were on the second floor. Such buildings were common in small towns throughout South Jersey during the early 20th century.

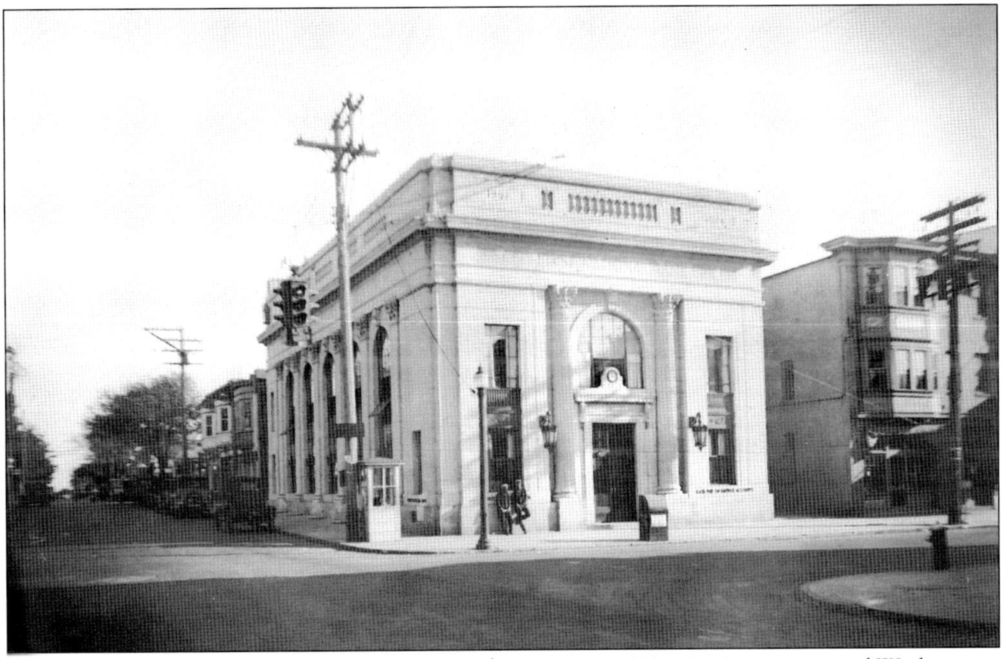

The First National Bank was located on the northeast corner of South Main Street and Washington Avenue. The building was constructed in 1902. It was torn down to make way for the New Jersey Department of Labor's One-Stop Career Center.

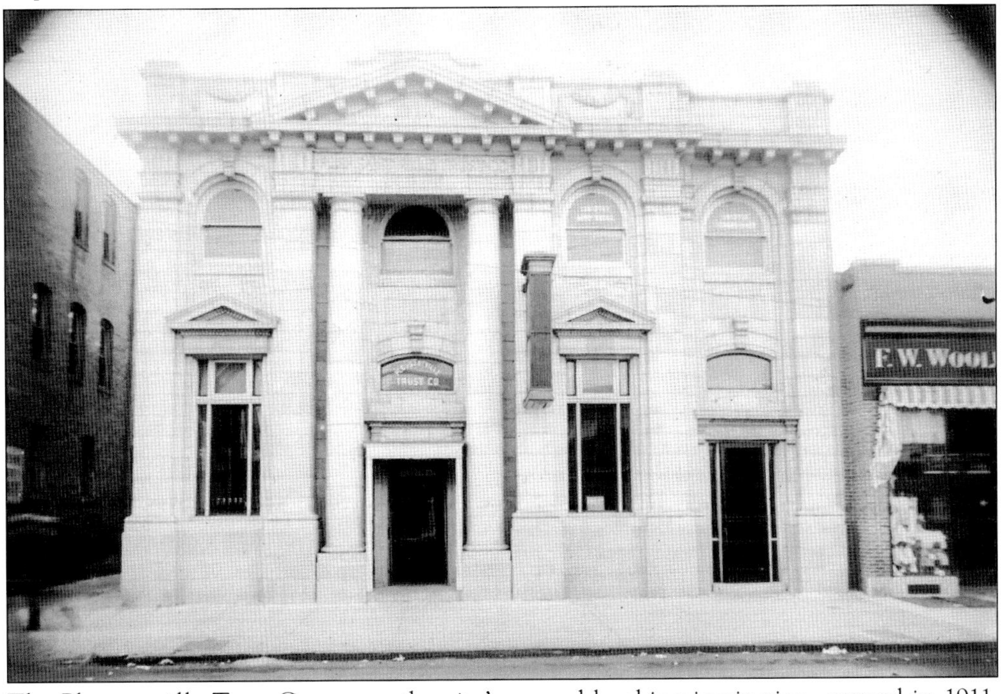

The Pleasantville Trust Company, the city's second banking institution, opened in 1911. This impressive building also housed a number of law offices and stood next to Woolworth's. Unfortunately, the bank could not survive the Depression and failed. Today, Sam's Bar and Grill occupies this site.

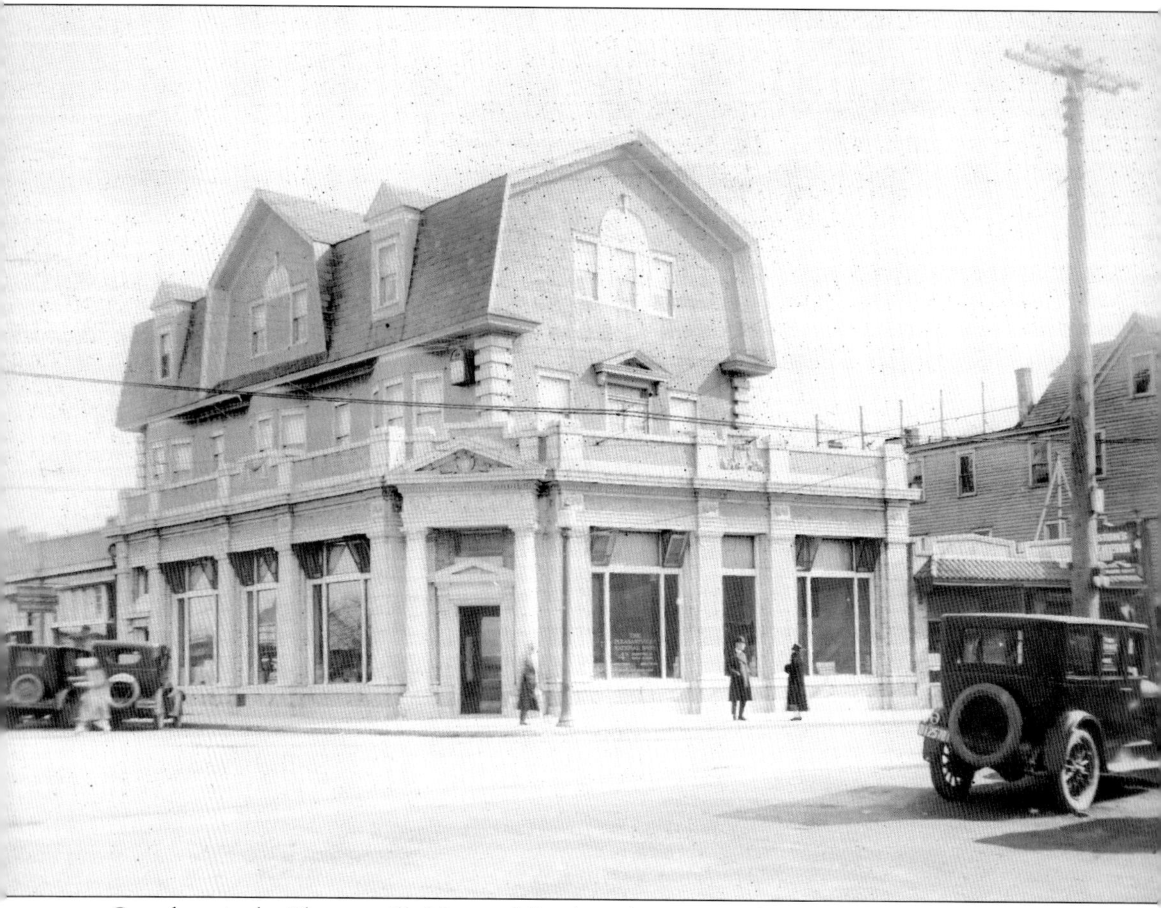

Seen here is the Pleasantville National Bank at the corner of Verona Boulevard (Black Horse Pike) and South Main Street. For years, this building has been the home of the Sherwin-Williams Paint Store. While the building has undergone a good deal of renovations, it still retains some of the feel of its original intent.

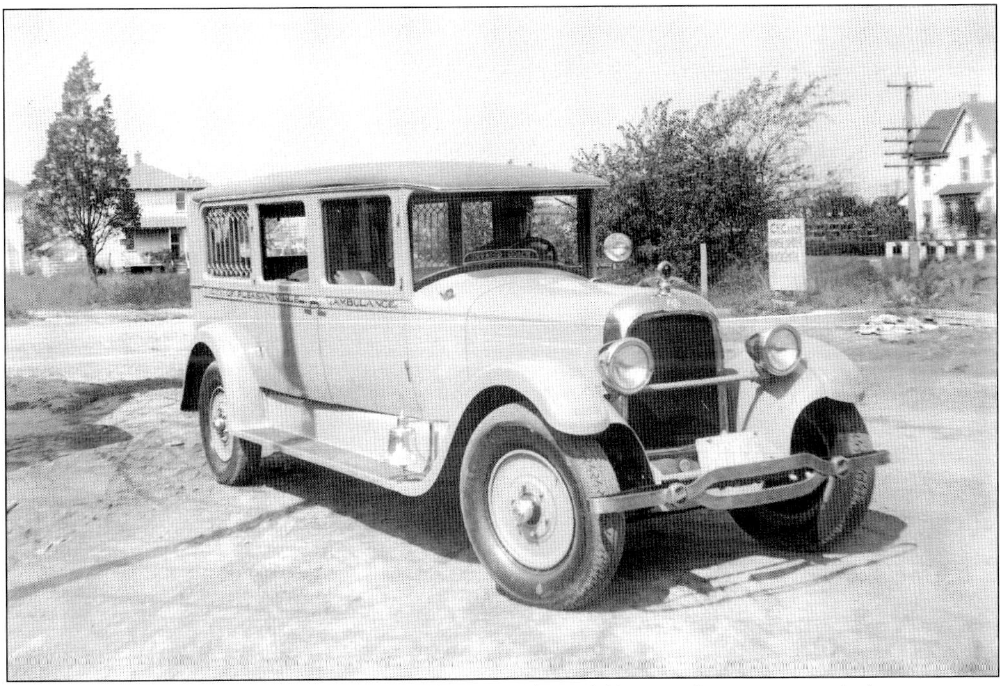

This vehicle was purchased by Pleasantville in April 1925. During those years, ambulance service was operated by the Pleasantville Police Department. The police department came into existence with the appointment of Clarence Krewson as chief on February 1, 1915. Before this, the city relied on marshals to enforce the law.

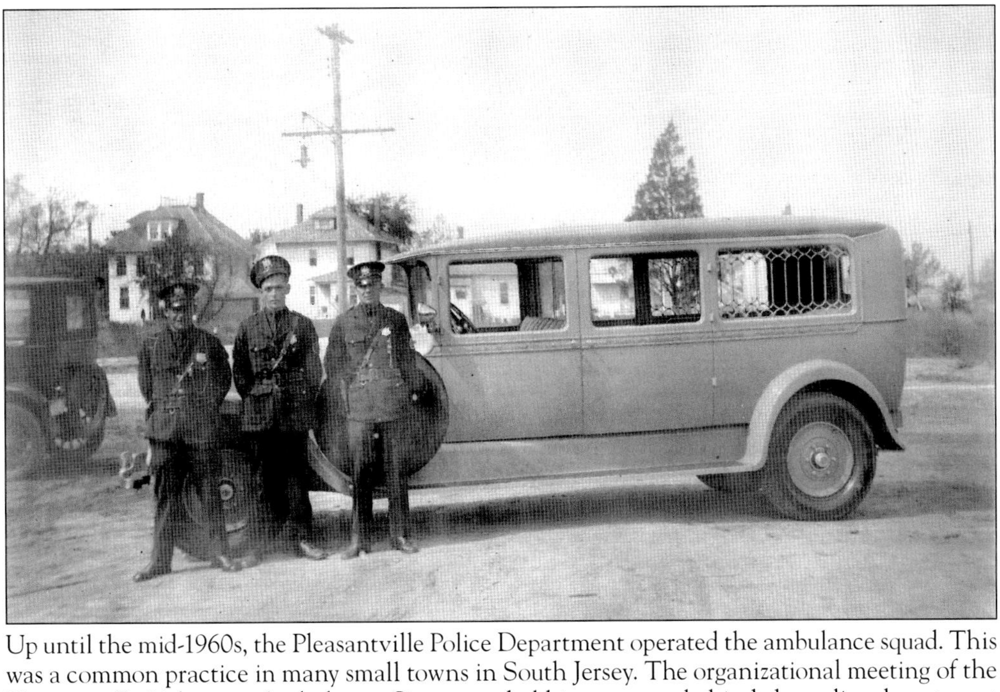

Up until the mid-1960s, the Pleasantville Police Department operated the ambulance squad. This was a common practice in many small towns in South Jersey. The organizational meeting of the Pleasantville Volunteer Ambulance Corps was held in a garage behind the police department on Saturday, September 19, 1964.

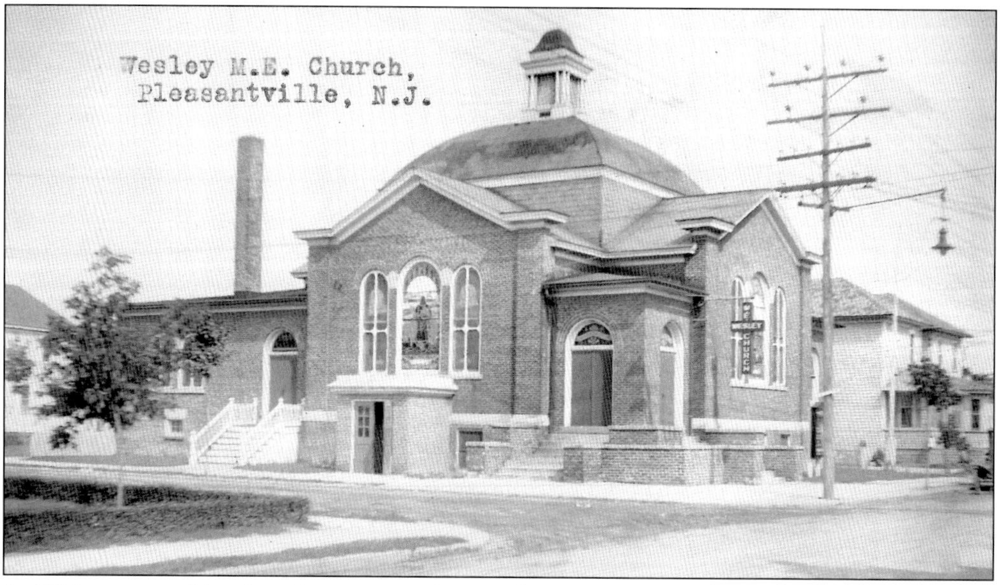

In 1903, a group of local residents met to discuss the construction of a Methodist church in the center of Pleasantville. Later that year, the Wesley Methodist Episcopal Church was organized. The corner of Pleasant and Linden Avenues was chosen as the site of the proposed church, which was dedicated in 1904. Max and Lola Kirscht were longtime members of this congregation, with Max as the organist.

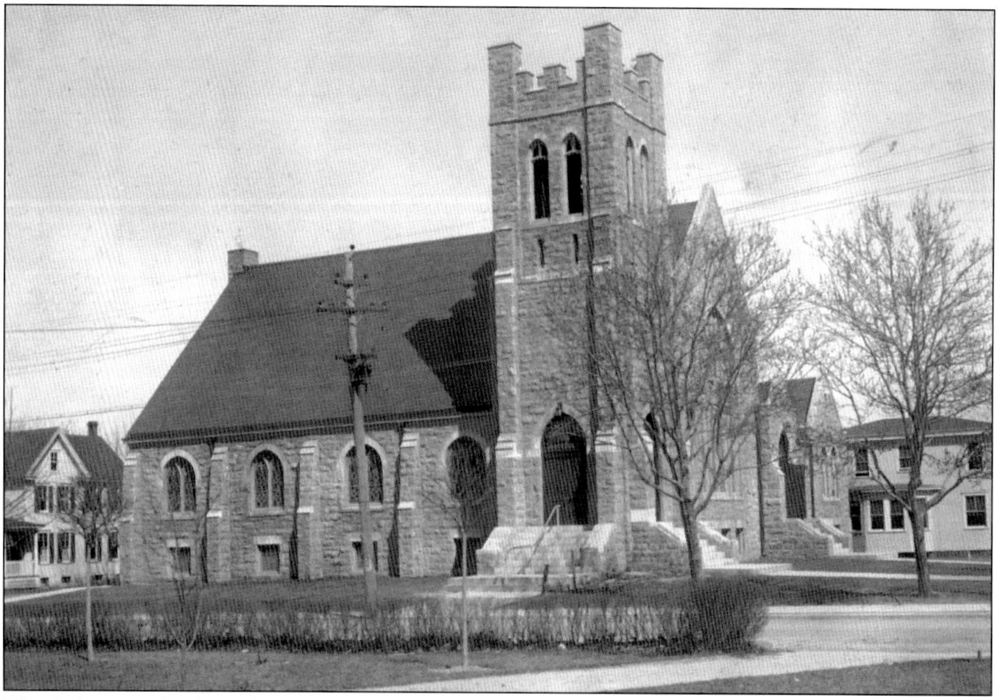

The Salem Methodist Church, located at South Main Street and West Park Avenue, is the oldest continually operated ministry in Pleasantville. The present church, seen here, was completed in late 1912 and dedicated in 1913. The church's cemetery is further down West Park Avenue, near the intersection of Doughty Road.

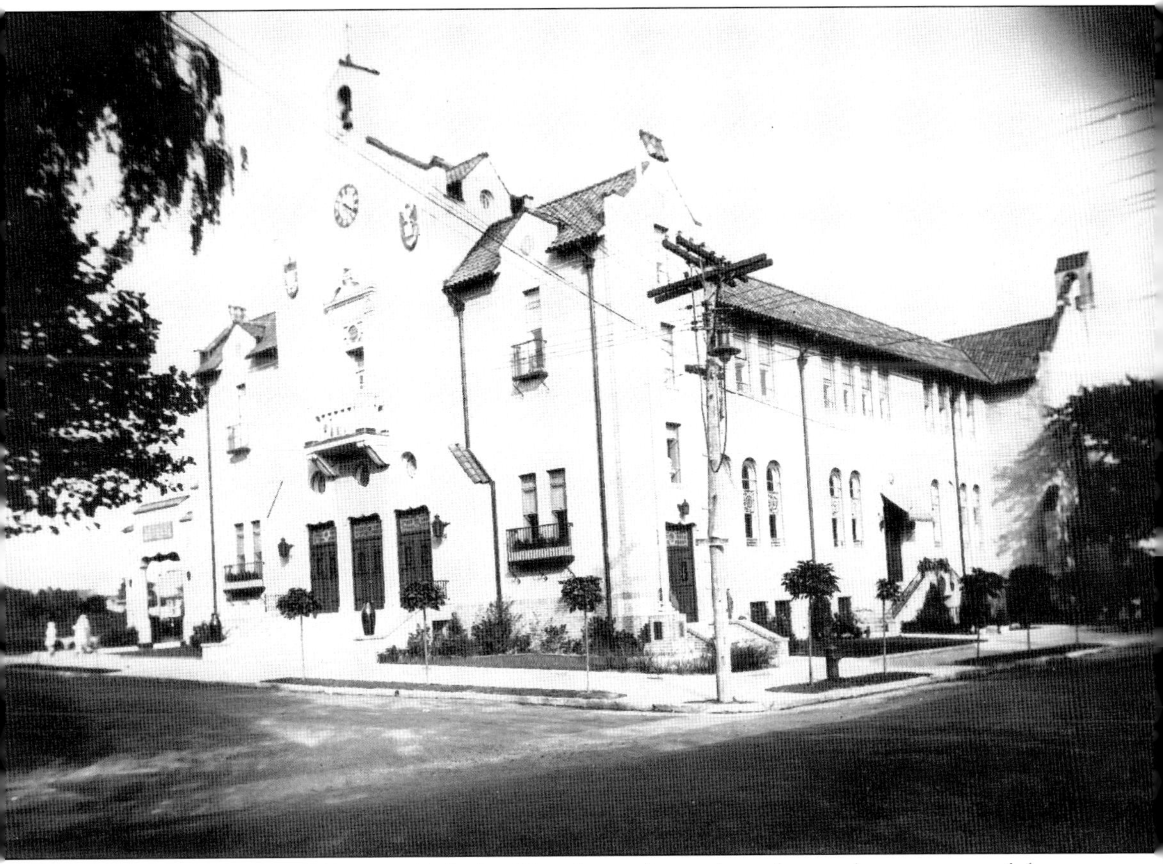

Built in 1898, St. Peter's Roman Catholic Church was located on the southeast corner of the Black Horse Pike and Chestnut Street. The Diocese of Camden closed the church in 2010 and merged the parish with St. Bernadette's in Northfield to create St. Gianna Beretta Molla Parish. Since 2011, this has been Our Lady Star of the East, a Maronite Catholic Church.

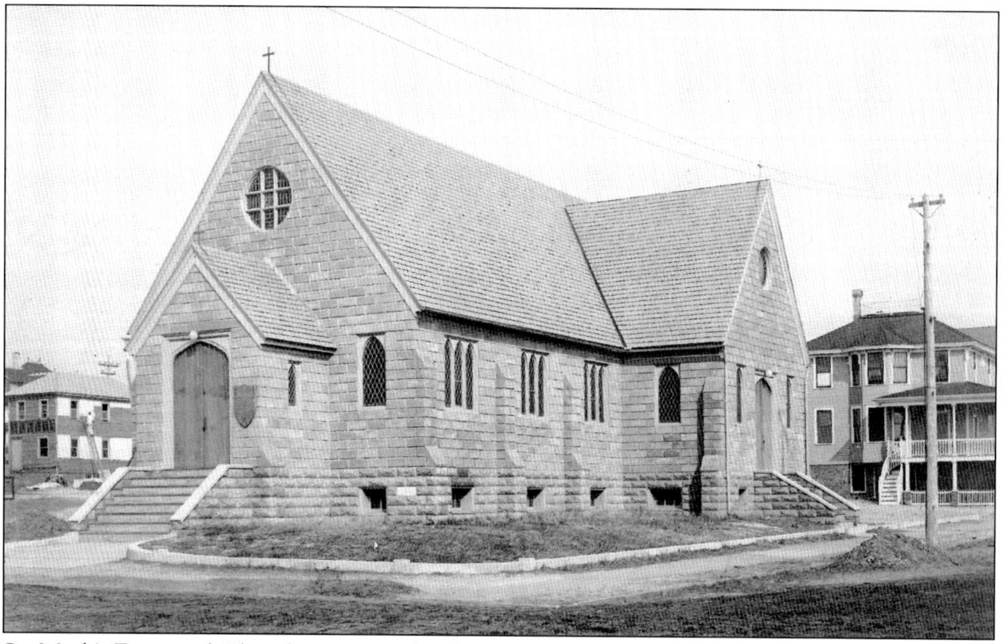

St. Mark's Episcopal Church was completed in 1907 and dedicated on November 1, 1907. The church was located at the northwest corner of Verona and Franklin Boulevards. This photograph, taken by Max Kirscht, was probably taken soon after the church was finished. Note that both thoroughfares have yet to be paved.

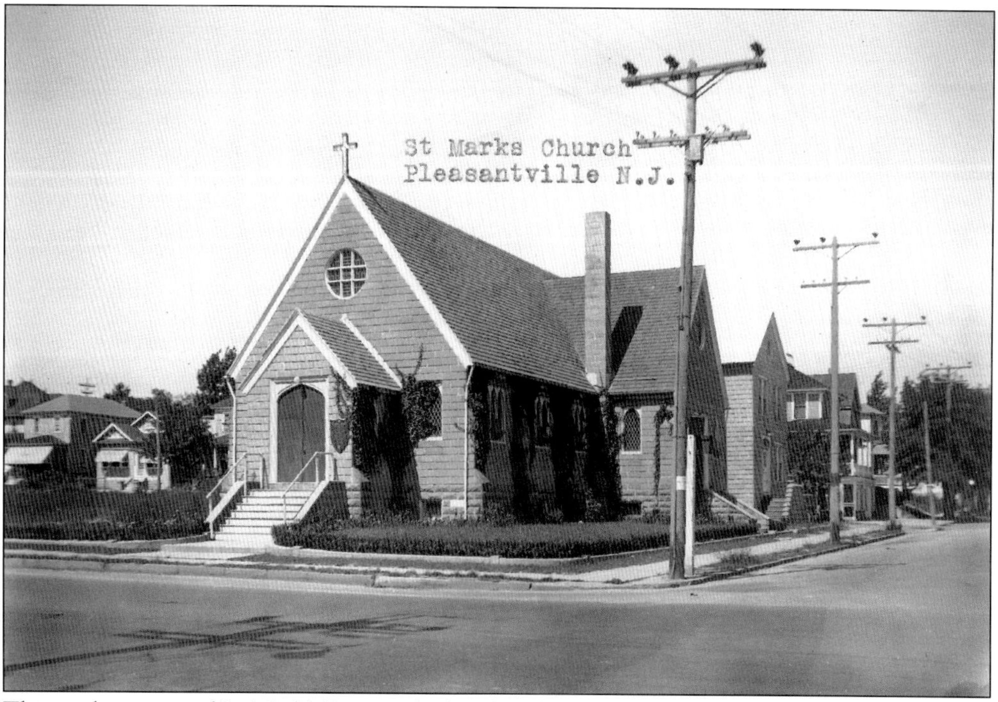

This is a later view of St. Mark's Episcopal Church, taken by Herman Kirscht sometime after 1923. The property was sold in 1982 and then used for some time as a union hall. Today, the building once again serves as a church.

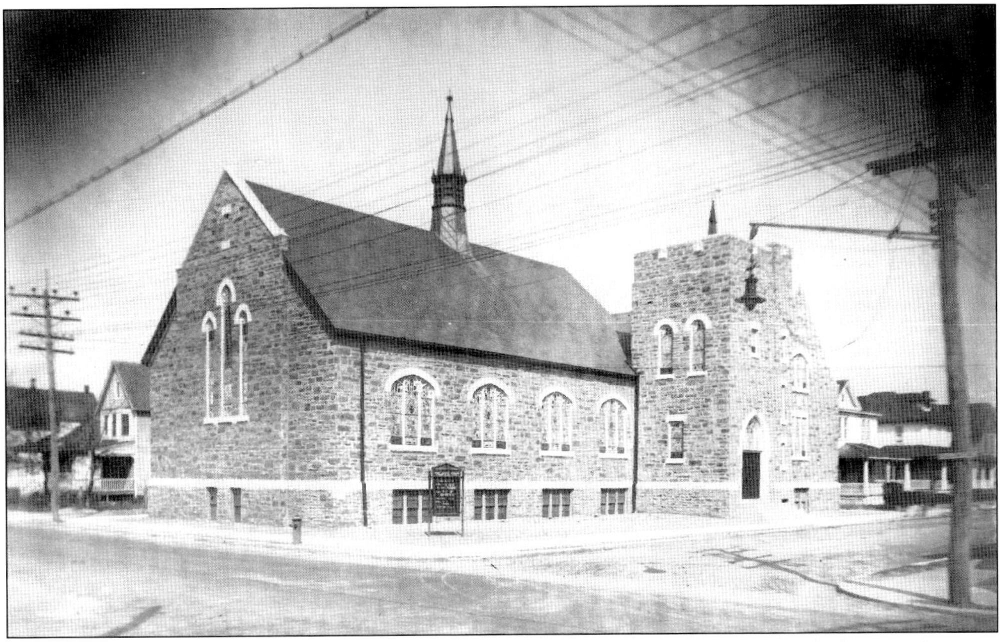

This is the Pleasantville Trinity Baptist Church, located at North First Street and Pleasant Avenue. This beautiful building was constructed in 1925. During the Depression, members mortgaged their homes to keep the church operating. Today, the property is the home of Crossroads Fellowship.

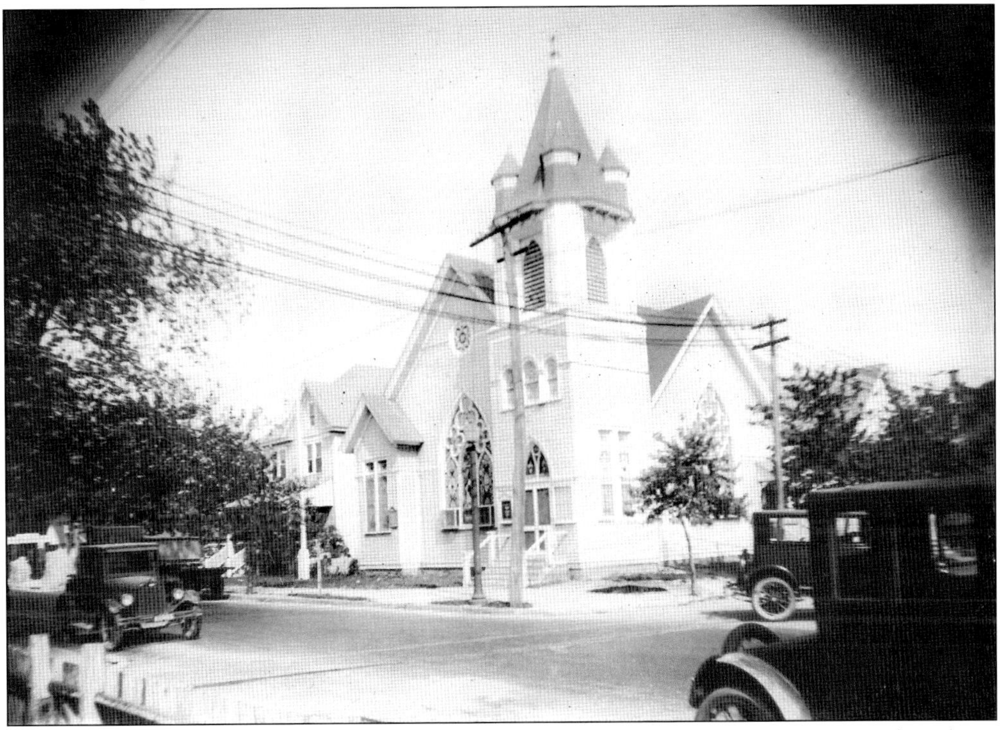

The Presbyterian Church at Pleasantville was located at East Washington Avenue and Madison Street. For years, this and several adjacent buildings were used by Weinstein Supply Company. The tracks of the Atlantic & Suburban Traction Company trolley line can be seen in the street.

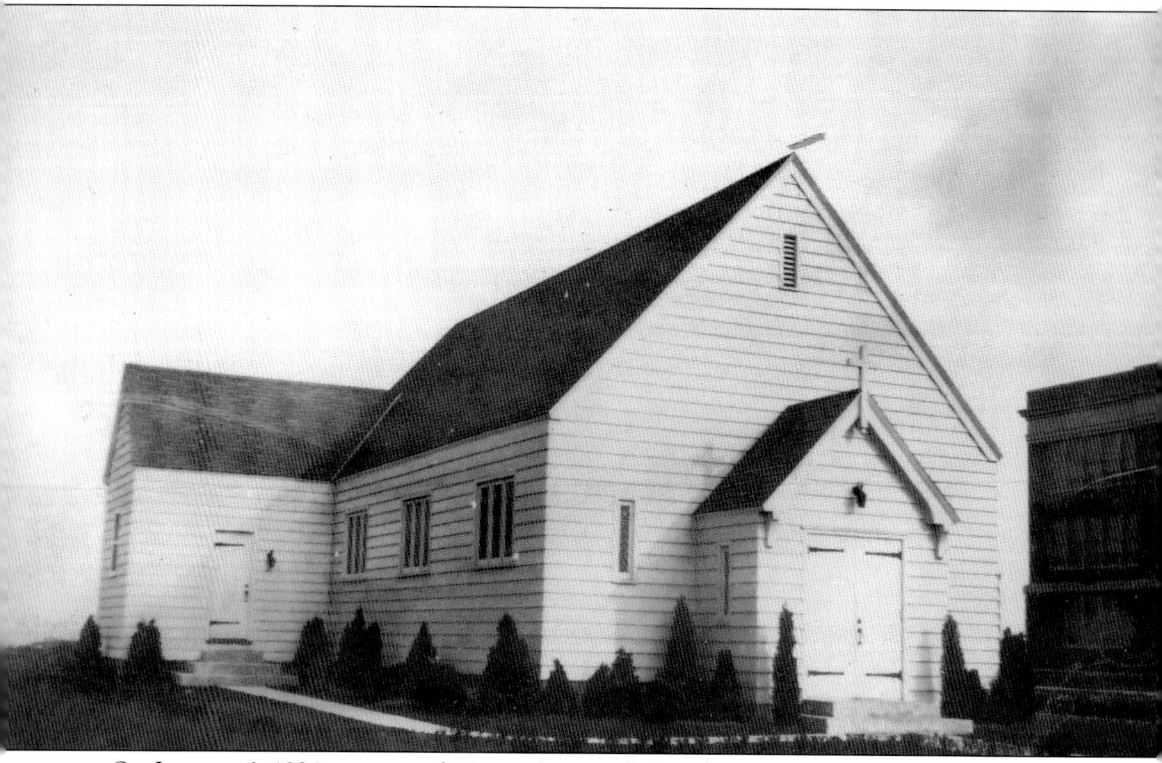

On January 6, 1924, a group of 12 people attended Lutheran services in Mechanics Hall in Pleasantville. A little more than a month later, Epiphany Evangelical Lutheran Church was organized. The church purchased lots in Ansley Park at the corner of Franklin Boulevard and Tunis Avenue, but it was not able to construct its own church until 1932. A larger church was constructed adjacent to the older building in 1961.

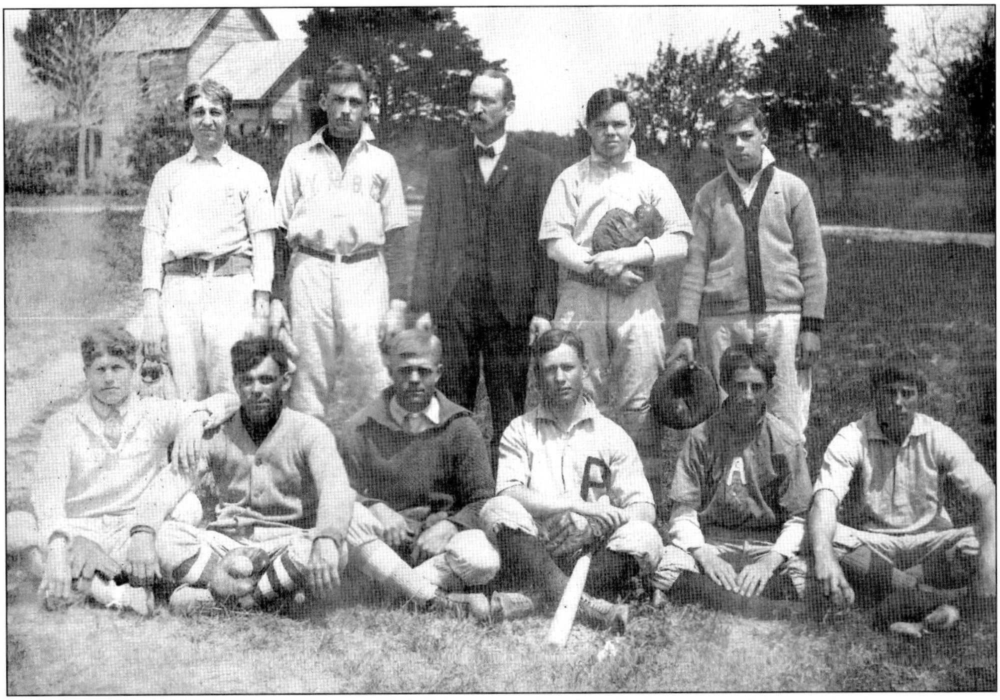

Around 1900, Pleasantville was a baseball town. One local player was Maxwell Manning, who pitched for Pleasantville High School before going on to play for the Johnson Stars, then managed by John "Pop" Lloyd. Later, Manning played in the Negro leagues and pitched for Satchel Paige's all-star team against Bob Feller's All Stars in 1946. He returned home and became a teacher.

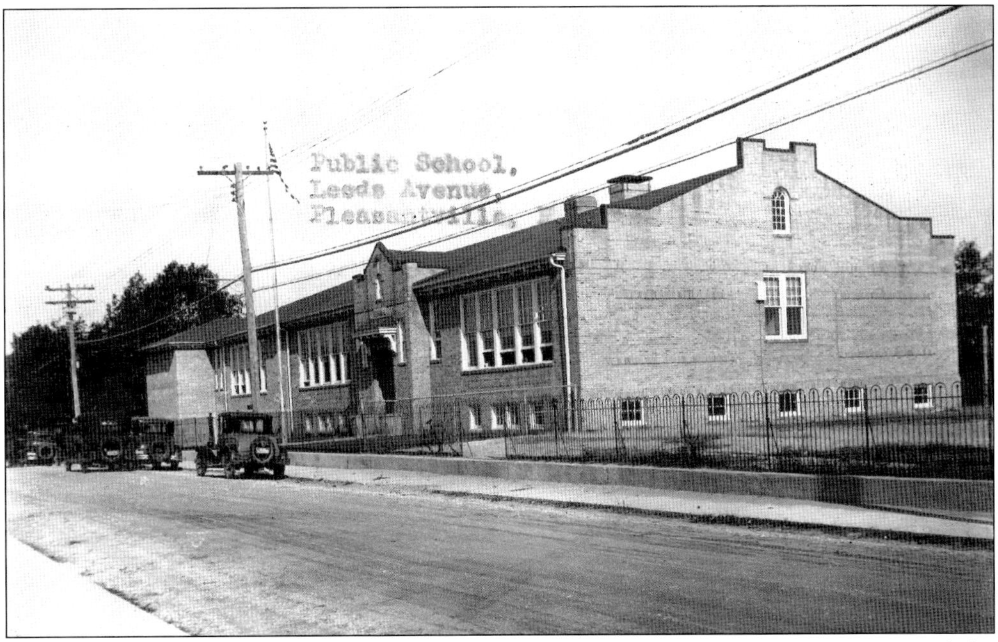

The Leeds Avenue School is Pleasantville's third school. It was constructed in 1910, and the addition at the far end of the building was put on in 1923. As the city grew, the school was added onto several more times before eventually being replaced with a new building in 1990.

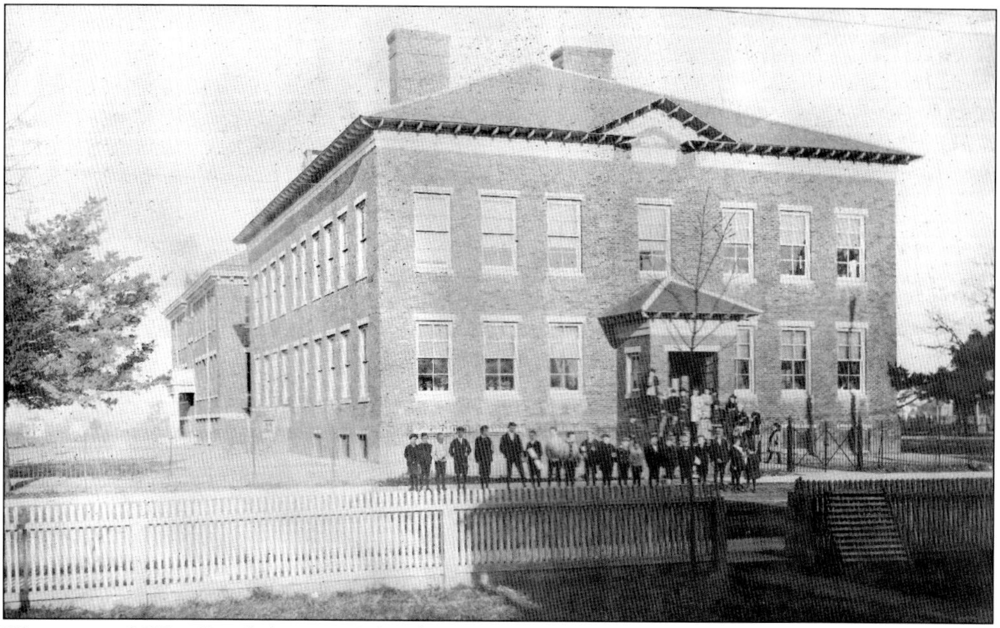

The original Woodland Avenue School was a wood-frame structure built in 1870. In 1900, a large brick building was added to the front of the school, and another was added in 1905. The addition was used to house high school students, who initially attended for only two years and then for three years. Students who wished to complete a fourth year were sent to Atlantic City High School.

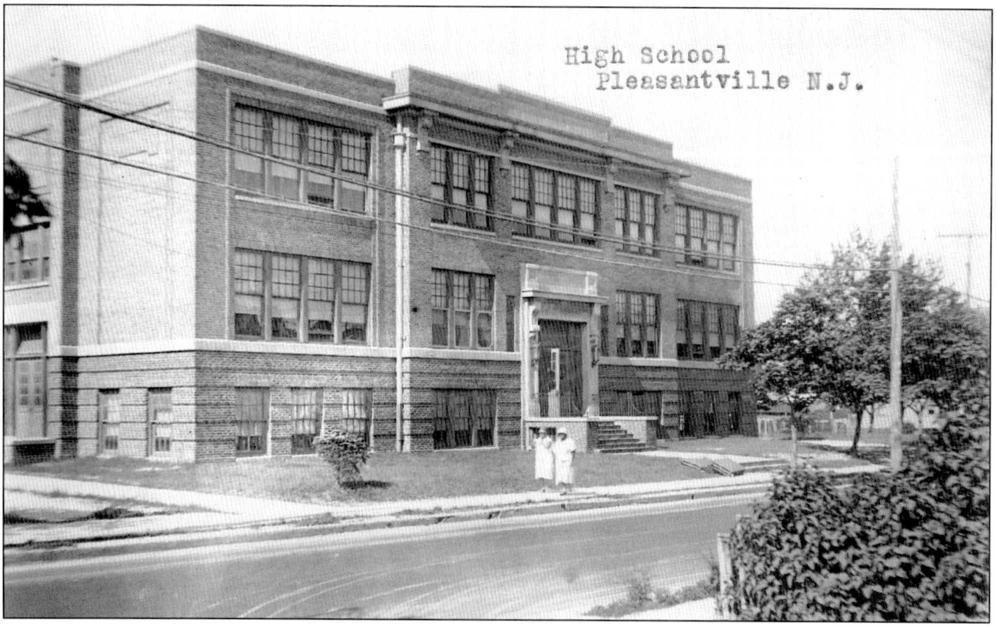

Needing desperately to accommodate the large number of students entering high school, particularly those from neighboring communities, the first Pleasantville High School was completed in 1915. This building was located on West Washington Avenue. After the new high school was built on Franklin Boulevard, this building became the junior high school. It later became an elementary school and has since been replaced with modern facilities.

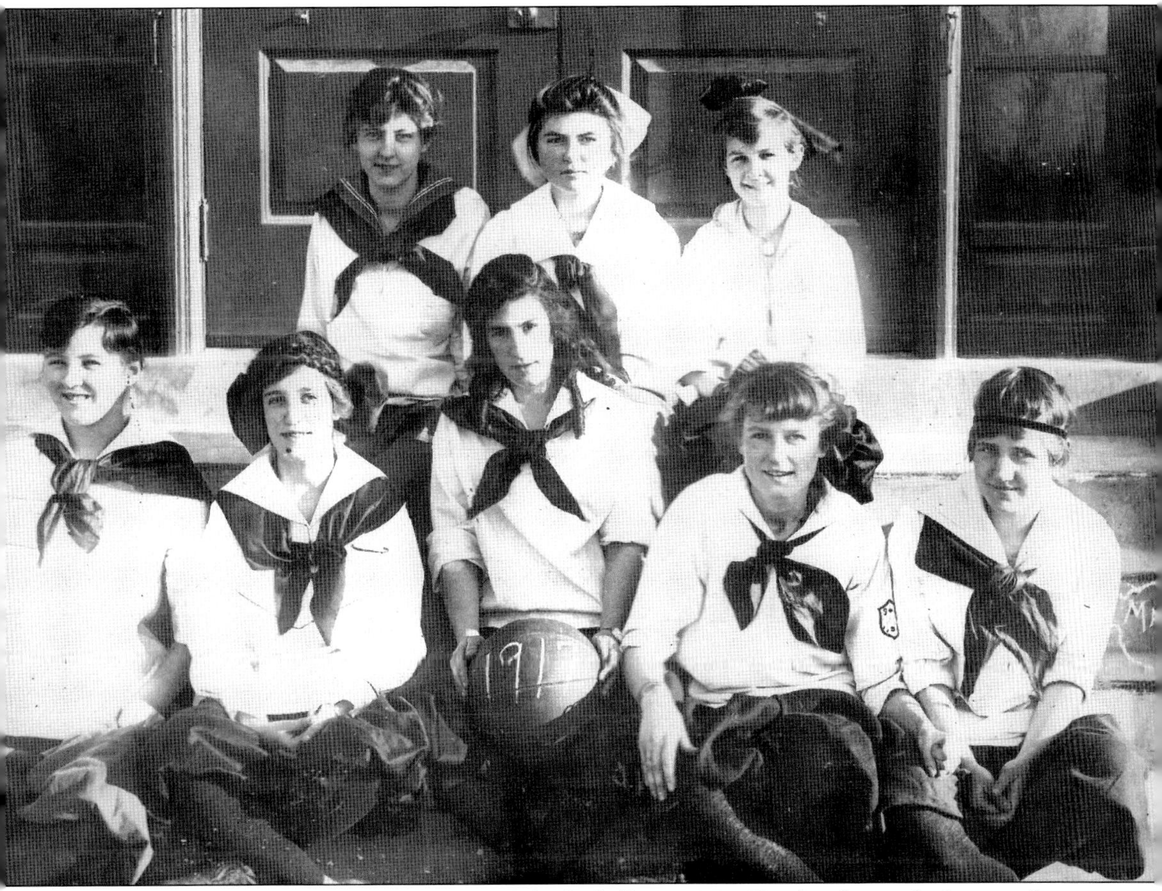

This is the 1917 Pleasantville High School girls' basketball team. Max Kirscht often took photographs of the high school athletic teams, which regularly appeared in the *Pleasantville Press*. Unfortunately, the names of these athletes were not recorded.

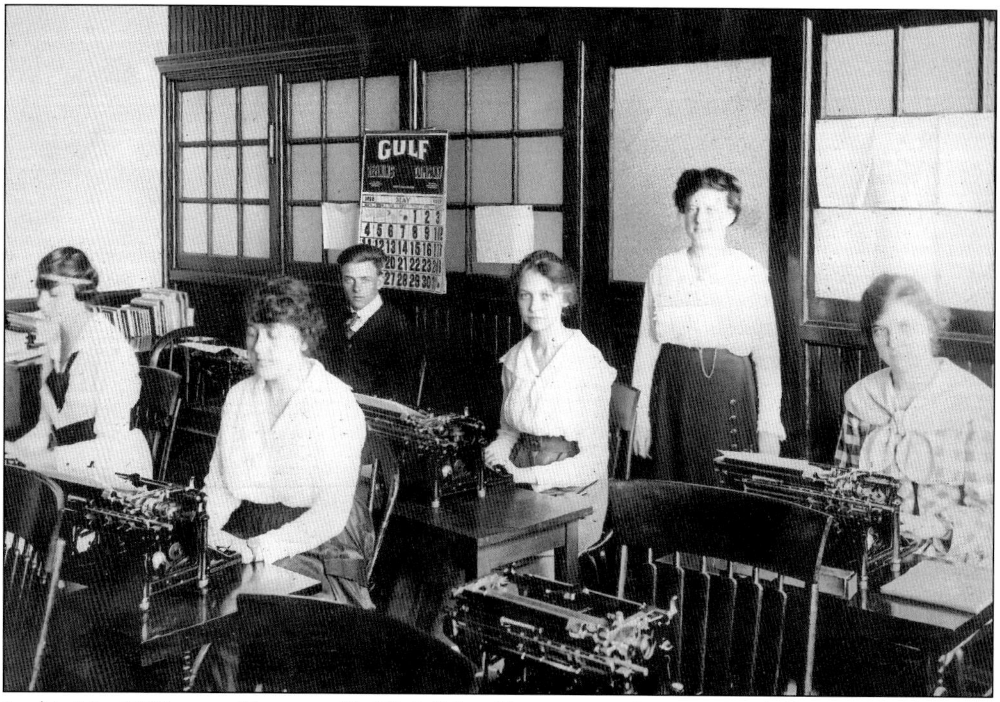

In this May 1919 scene, Pleasantville High School business students pause while Max Kirscht takes their picture. Throughout the 1910s, Kirscht took photographs at the high school, particularly of the sports teams.

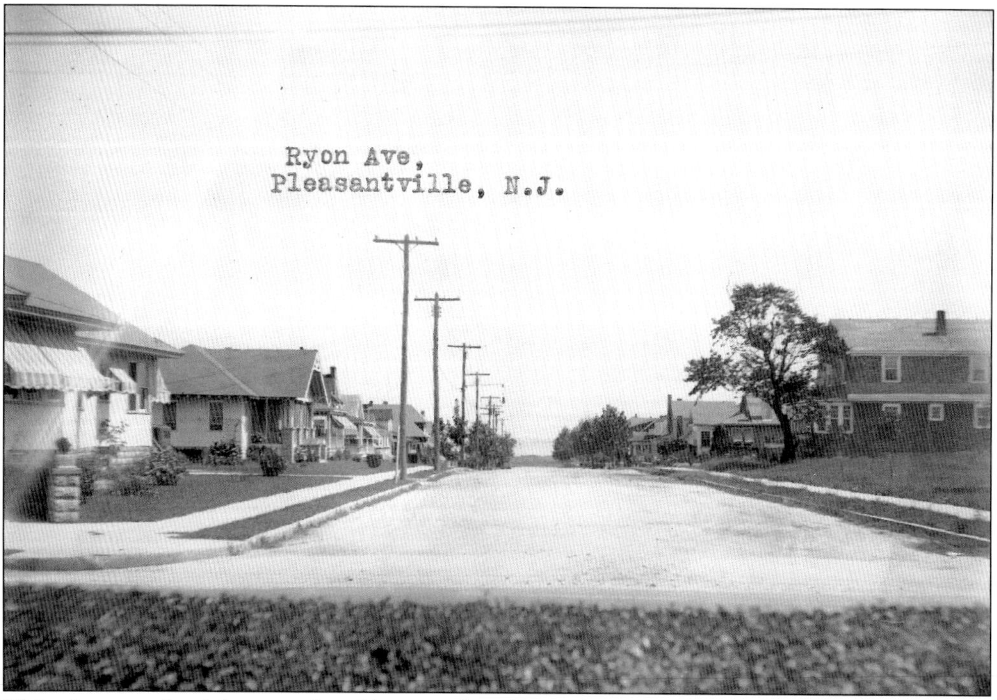

This photograph of the completed homes along Ryon Avenue was taken by Herman Kirscht. This view looks toward Lake's Bay from near South Main Street.

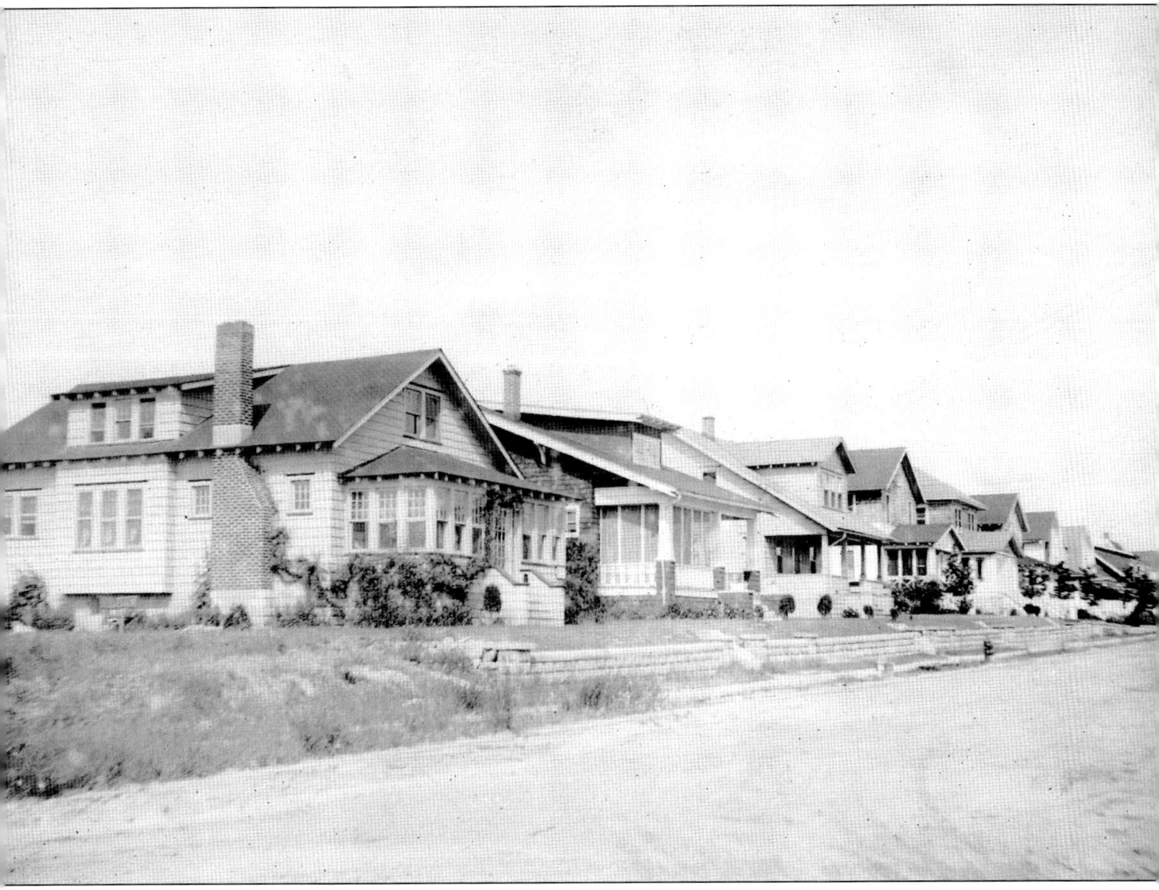

This is another view of the Ryon Avenue development taken by Herman Kirscht. In 1895, Pleasantville's population was 1,543 people. By 1900, there were 2,182 people living in the borough. Over the next 10 years, the municipality's population would more than double to 5,887 souls. Census records show that the new city's population would almost double by 1930, which was mostly due to such real estate endeavors.

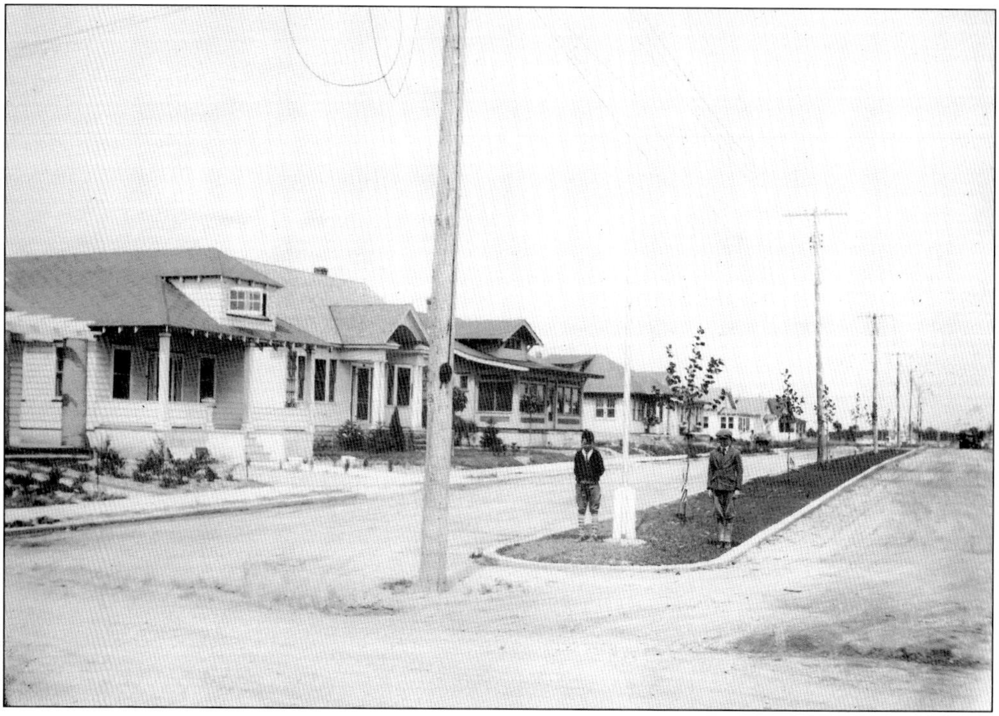

This is the southwest section of Wellington Avenue, taken by Herman Kirscht from the intersection of Linden Avenue. The shot is of the southwest side of the street. This was one of the first developments in this part of the then rapidly growing city.

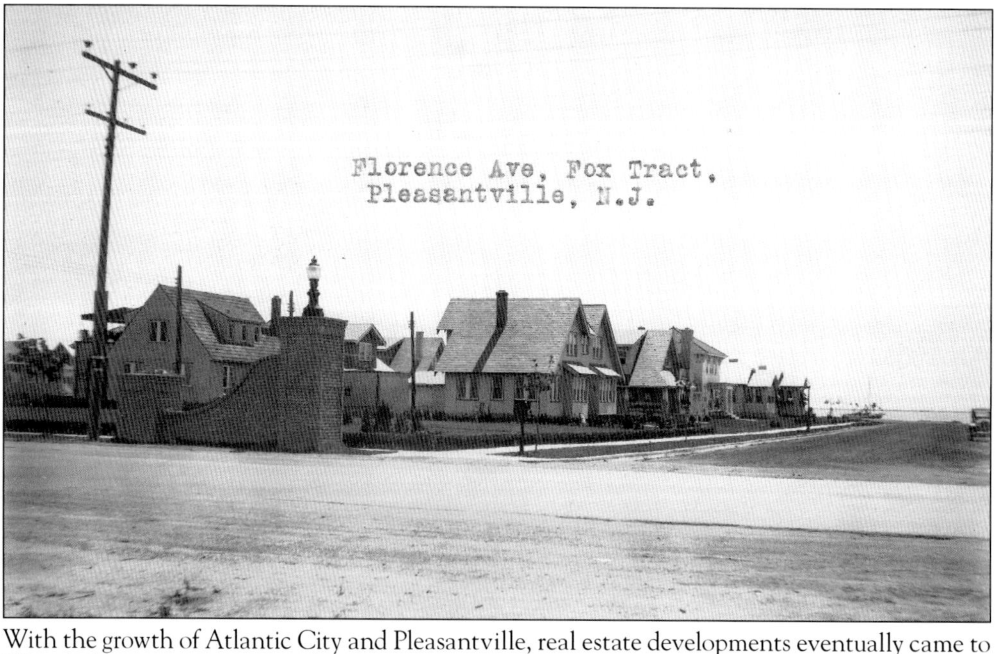

With the growth of Atlantic City and Pleasantville, real estate developments eventually came to West Atlantic City in Egg Harbor Township. It is believed that Herman Kirscht did photography work for developers and real estate agents in eastern Atlantic County. The author recalls that the curved wall at the entrance to this development remained standing into the 1980s.

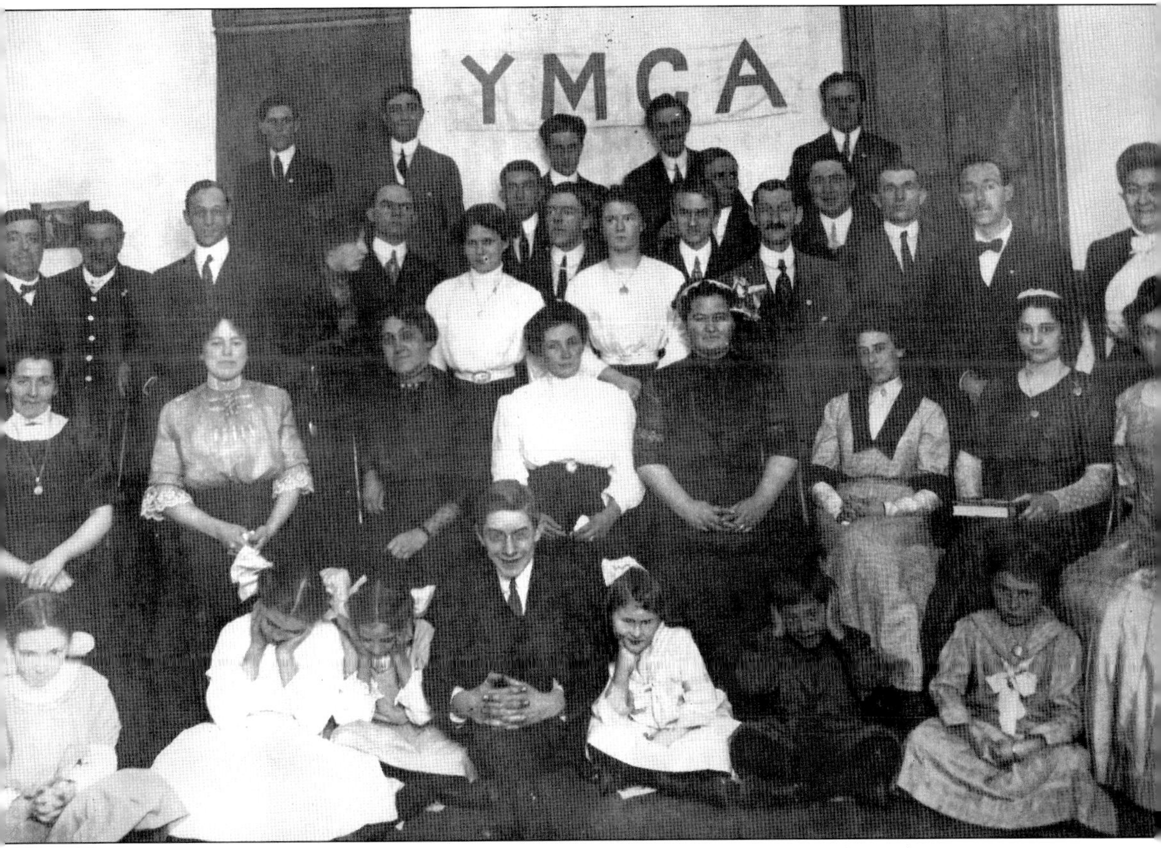

During the first quarter of the 1900s, Pleasantville had numerous fraternal and social organizations, including the Young Men's Christian Association (YMCA). Given the work and interests of the Kirscht family, it would only be natural that Max Kirscht would have taken a photograph of the association's members.

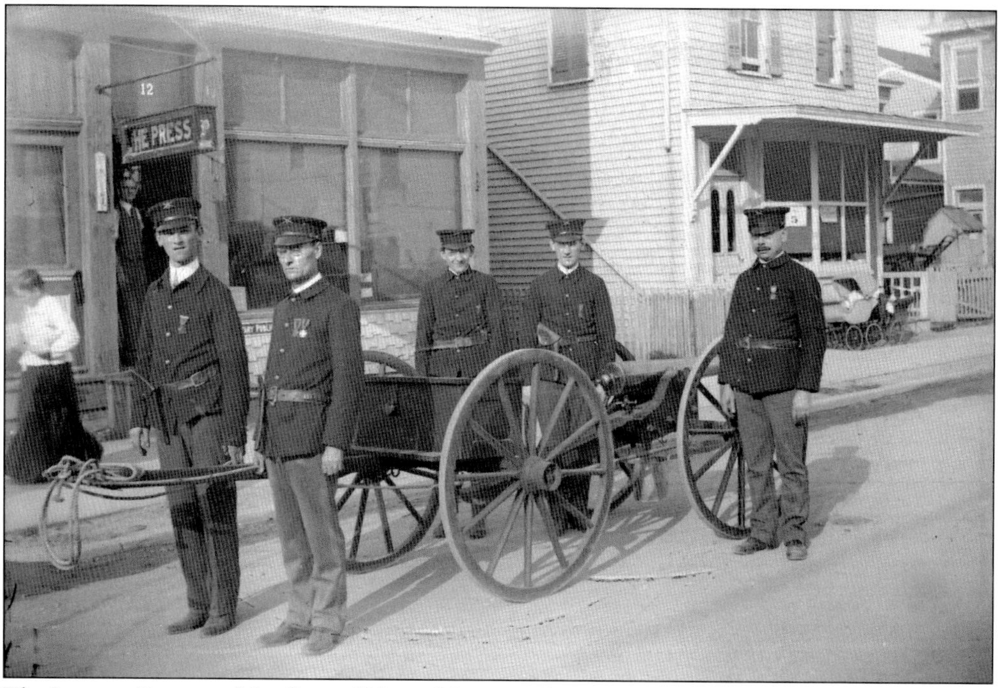

The Janeway Battery of the Sons of Union Veterans Camp 11 was involved in many local parades and events. Here, some of the members are stopped in front of the offices of the *Pleasantville Press*, which were located on East Washington Avenue. Walter Whitman, the publisher and editor, may well be standing in the doorway. This image was taken directly from a glass plate negative, one of only a few still surviving.

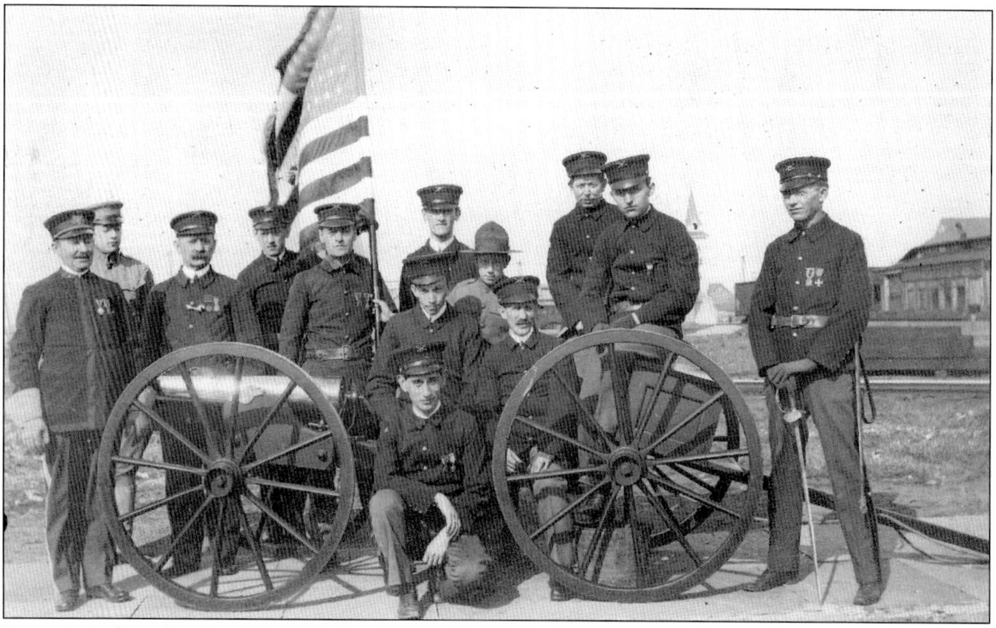

It appears that the entire compliment of the Janeway Battery is in this photograph. Max Kirscht was a member of this organization. Unfortunately, the location in the photograph is unknown, but it appears to have been taken in Atlantic City.

Four

Nearby Communities

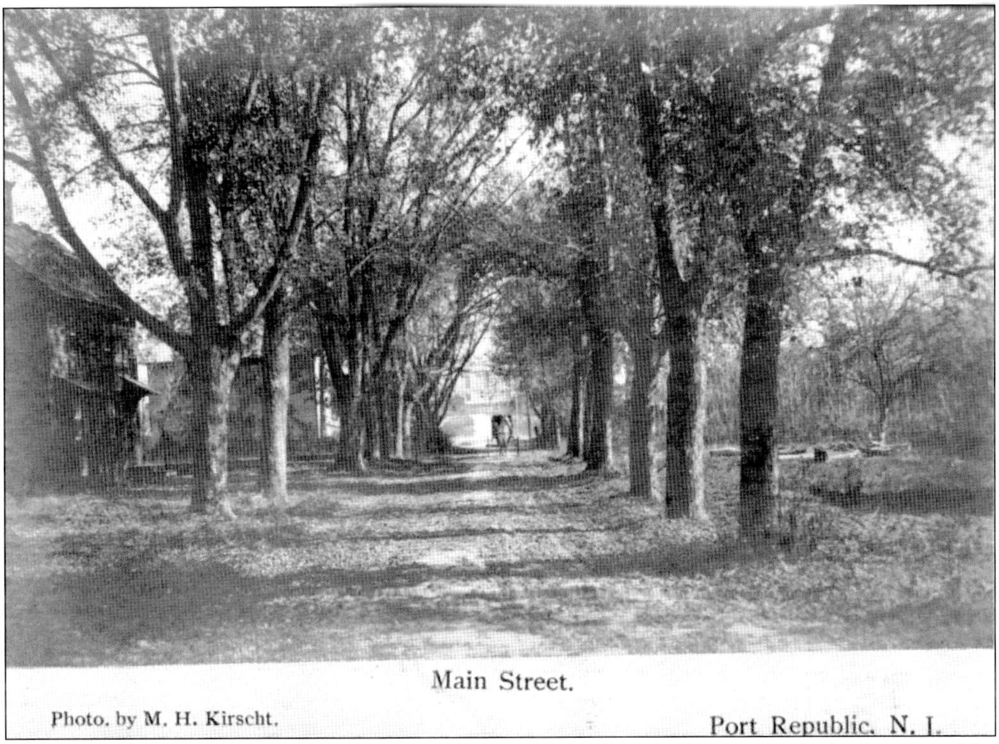

This view of Main Street was captured near its intersection with Mill Street, with the Port Republic Methodist Episcopal Church in the distance. The church is now called St. Paul's United Methodist Church. Port Republic, which includes the communities of Chestnut Neck, Clark's Mill, Gravelly Landing, Hewitt Town, Unionville, and Wrangleboro, still retains much of its small-town charm, with scenes like this having changed little over the last century.

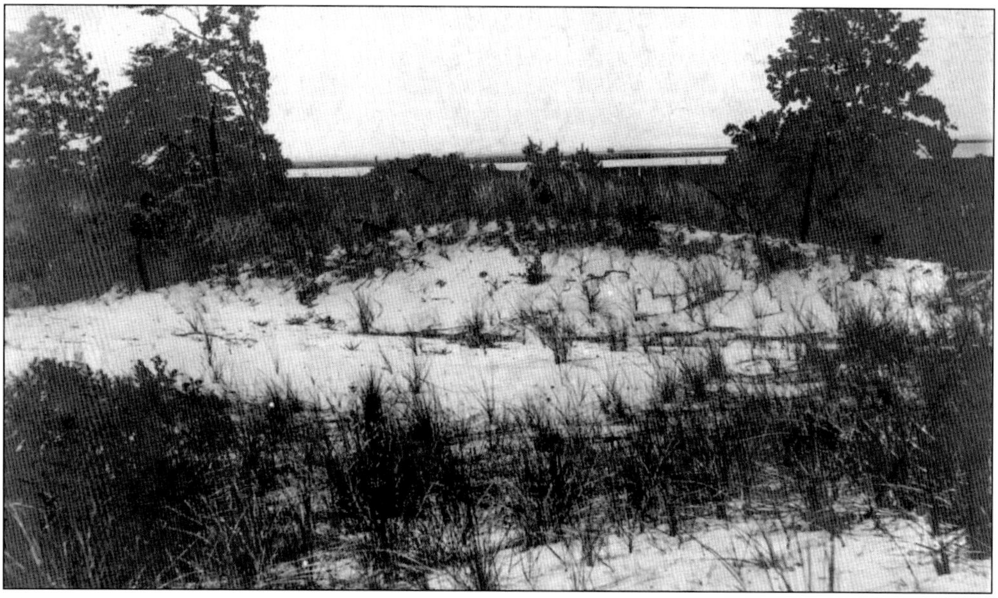

This photograph is from a postcard published by Max Kirscht, which claimed that this area on the Mullica River is where the monument commemorating the Battle of Chestnut Neck was originally to be placed. It is believed that this may be a view of Fort Fox Burrows or the immediate area, where the Americans constructed a fortification designed to protect Chestnut Neck and communities upriver from British attack. (Courtesy of Doris Bugdon.)

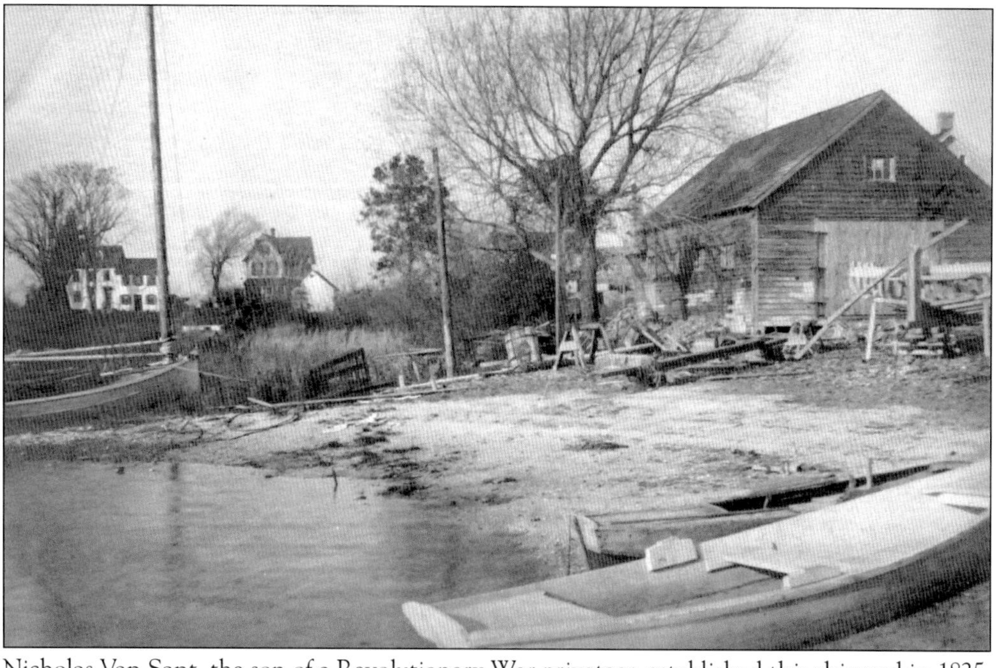

Nicholas Van Sant, the son of a Revolutionary War privateer, established this shipyard in 1825. The yard produced barges, catboats, houseboats, ketches, oyster schooners, sloops, and coastal schooners. By 1850, it was one of the principal shipbuilding communities in Atlantic County. The Port Republic City Council held their first city council meeting at the Van Sant House on May 15, 1905. (Courtesy of Doris Bugdon.)

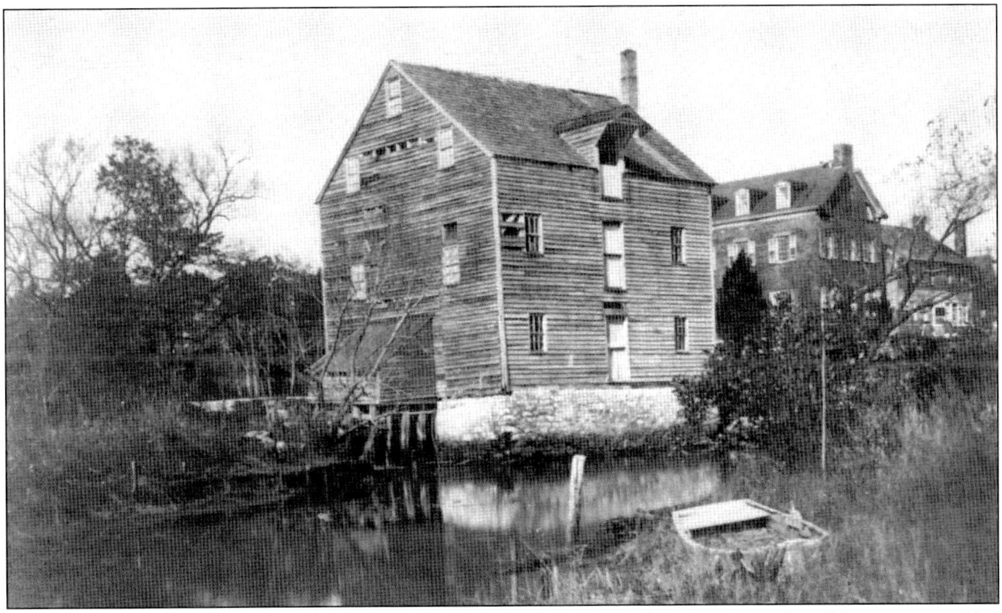

"An act for the erecting of a Dam, Mills and other Waterworks on Nacut Creek" was passed by provincial authorities on March 11, 1774. The act sanctioned the construction of a grain or grist mill above Indian Landing, located directly across Mill Street from the millpond. Note that the text on the original postcard is incorrect: the mill was chartered during the reign of King George III. (Courtesy of Doris Bugdon.)

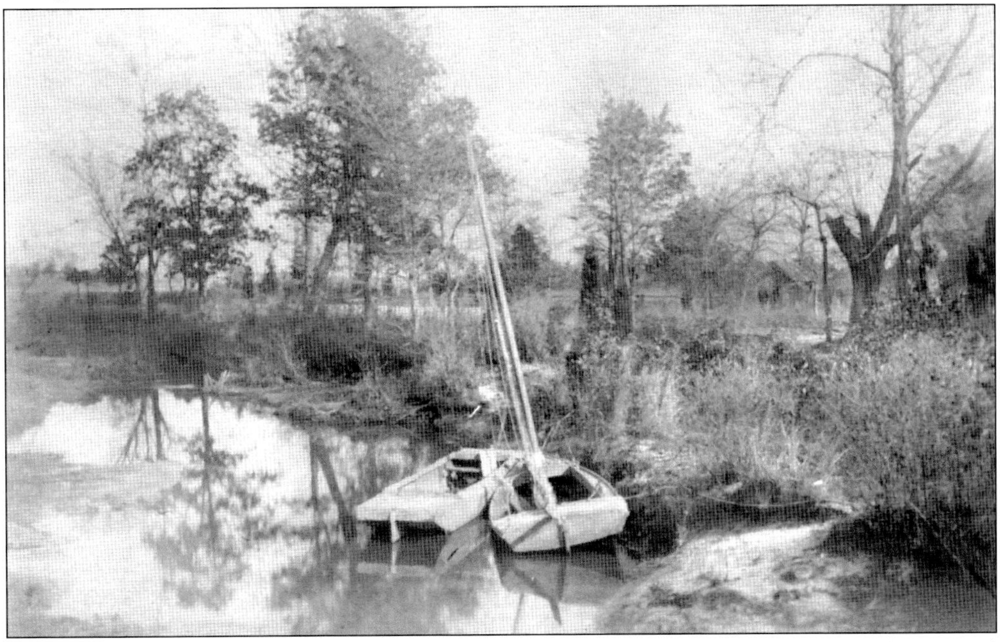

Since its completion more than two centuries ago, freshets have breached the millpond dam several times, requiring reconstruction. In his recollections, Rollin A. Cale wrote that the passing of Judge David Somers Blackman, who died on October 13, 1884, while trying to shore up the dam, was one of two "great catastrophes" to hit Port Republic; the other catastrophe was the rerouting of New York Road in 1922. (Courtesy of Doris Bugdon.)

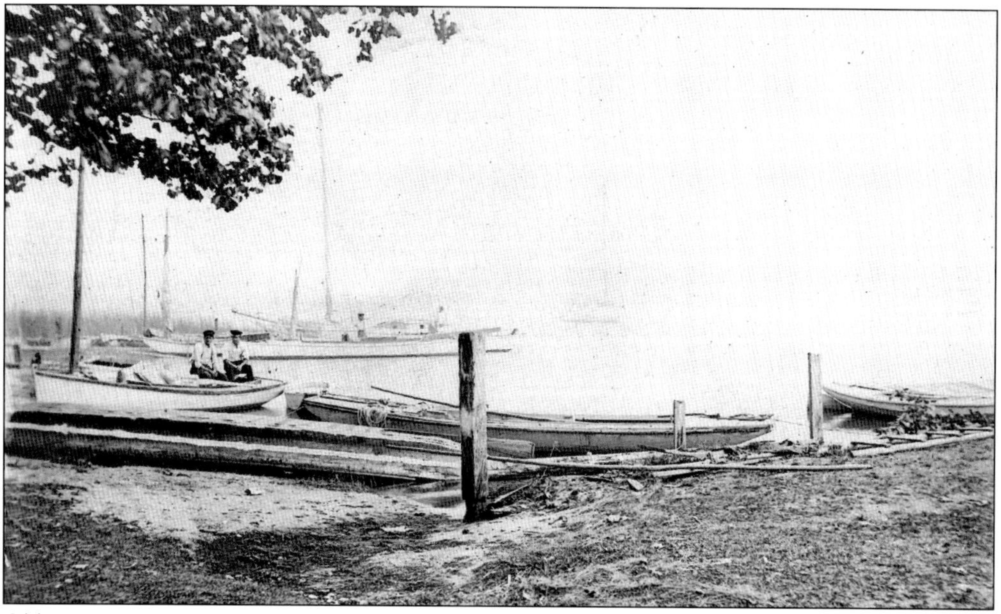

Old-timers report that in Port Republic in the early 1900s, most people worked either as a farmer or a waterman. In the early 1880s, almost 500 schooners and 750 small boats were engaged in the oyster industry, a vital business for many shore communities. This photograph by Max Kirscht was taken along Nacote Creek, near the Van Sant shipyard. (Courtesy of Doris Bugdon.)

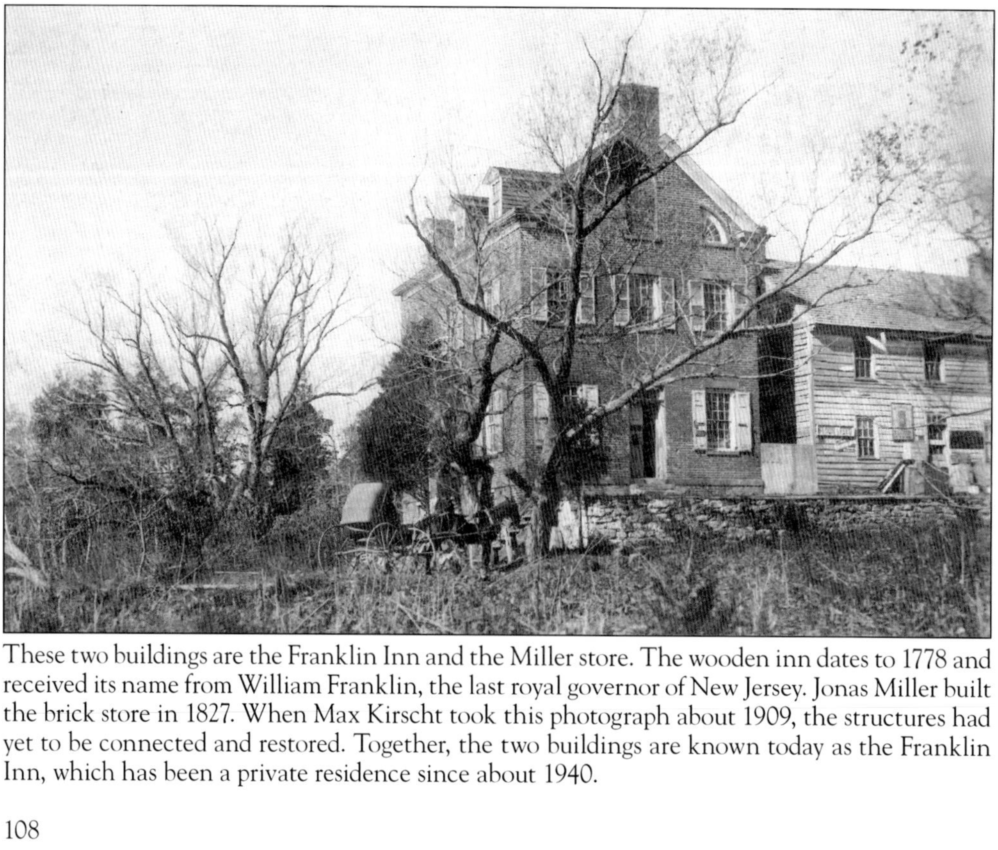

These two buildings are the Franklin Inn and the Miller store. The wooden inn dates to 1778 and received its name from William Franklin, the last royal governor of New Jersey. Jonas Miller built the brick store in 1827. When Max Kirscht took this photograph about 1909, the structures had yet to be connected and restored. Together, the two buildings are known today as the Franklin Inn, which has been a private residence since about 1940.

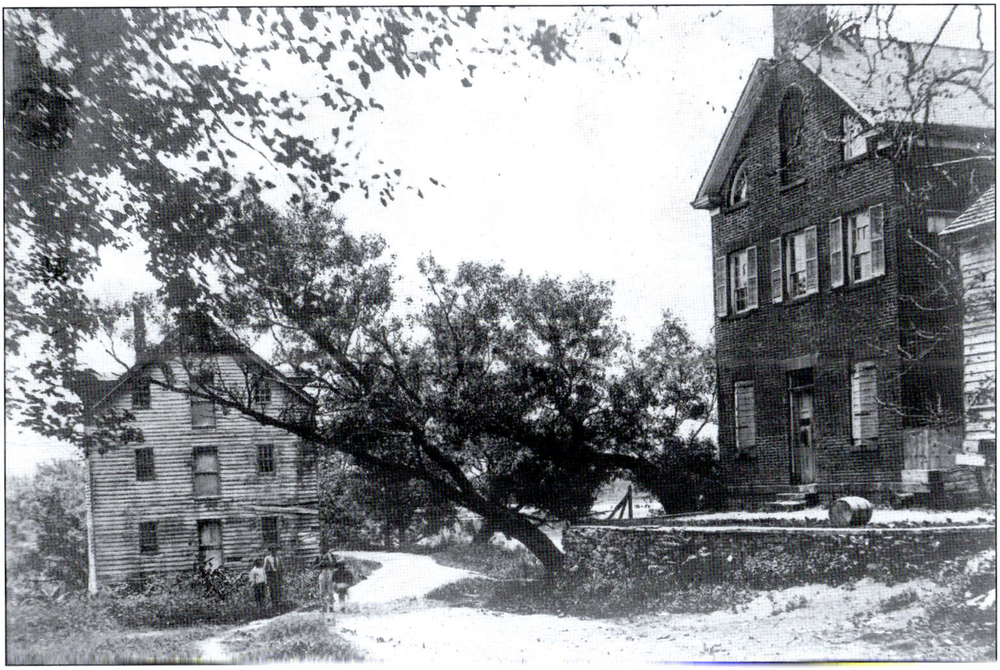

When Max Kirscht took this photograph in the early 1900s, Mill Street was much closer to the Franklin Inn and the Miller store than it is today. The gristmill and sawmill were also adjacent to the dam, with Mill Street meandering between the three properties. The location of the mill is marked today by the millstone on the western side of the street. (Courtesy of Doris Bugdon.)

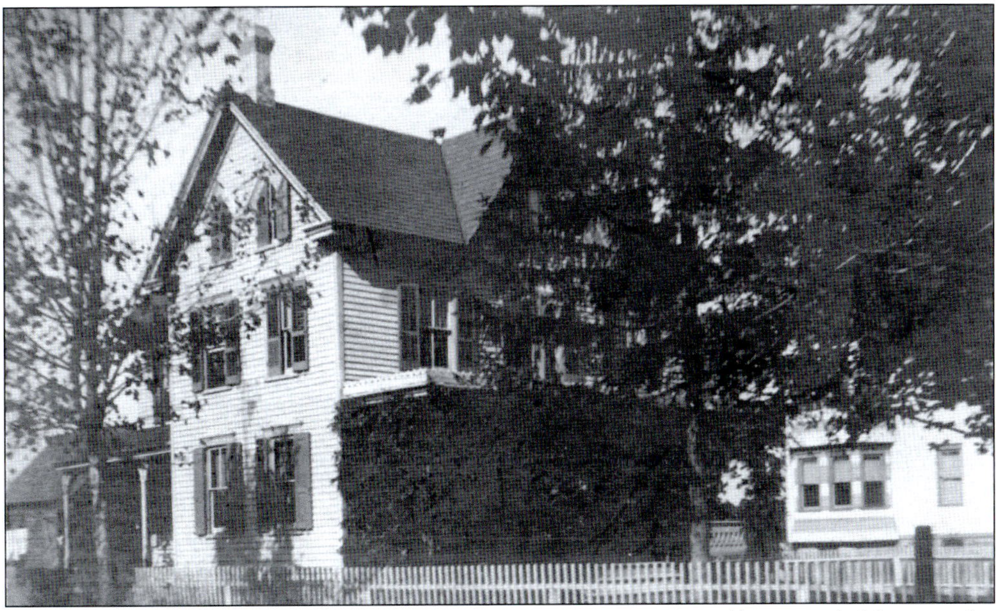

Roland Ashley's house still stands next to the Franklin Inn on Mill Street. Ashley was the postmaster and also operated the store in the inn. Ralph Ashley, an ancestor who settled in Port Republic in 1823, married Sarah Blackman, the daughter of Nehemiah and Sarah Smith Blackman. Sarah was the daughter of Micajah Smith, a privateer during the Revolution and a founder of Smith's Meeting House. (Courtesy of Doris Bugdon.)

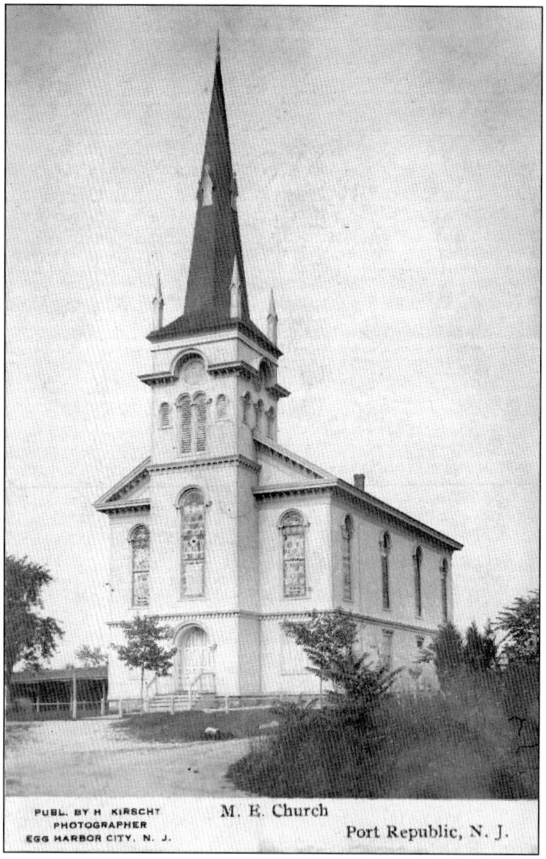

The first Methodist church was a small chapel built about 1800 near Blackman's Mills off Main Street. The congregants erected the Methodist Union Chapel across the street in 1832. As the result of a spiritual revival following the Civil War, construction of the present church began in 1871. Over the years, this building has been a favorite subject of photographers and is the most recognizable landmark in the city.

It is said that the original section of this building was constructed by Benjamin Endicott after the British invaded Chestnut Neck in late 1778, making it one of the oldest structures in Port Republic. Located on the northeast corner of Main Street and Blakes Lane, it served as the Methodist parsonage from 1868 to 1978. In the late 1970s, it was the headquarters of the Port Republic Historical Society. (Courtesy of Doris Bugdon.)

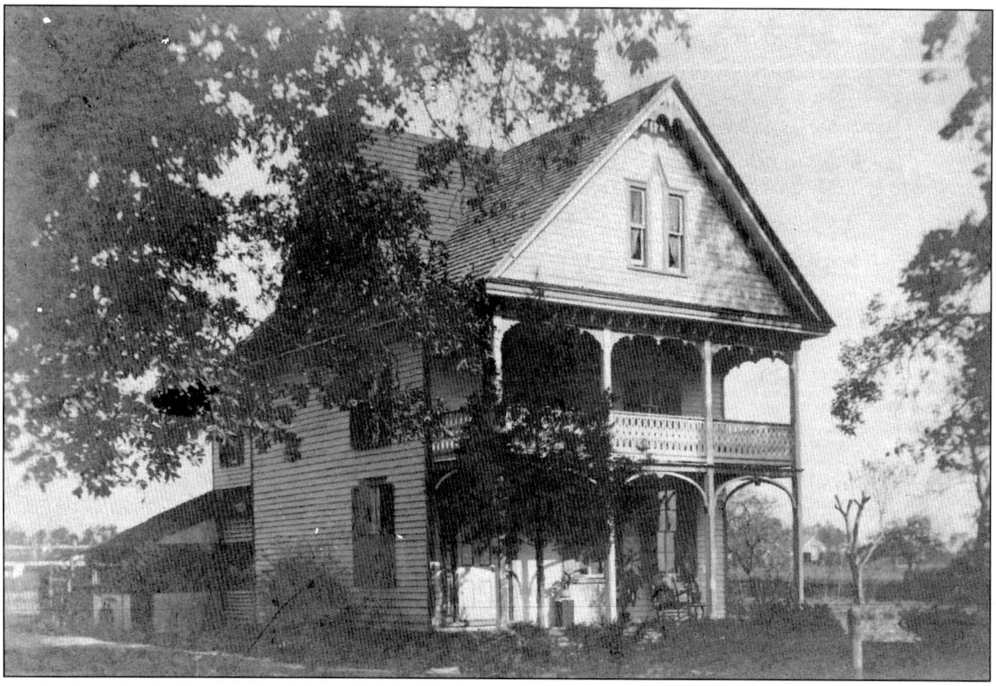

The Bartlett Meat Market, located on the southeast corner of Pomona Avenue and Mill Street, was an attractive structure when Max Kirscht took this photograph about 1910. Ralph Bartlett, the longtime owner of Bartlett Chevrolet in Absecon, was a member of this family. This building, now a private residence, retains much of its original appeal today. (Courtesy of Doris Bugdon.)

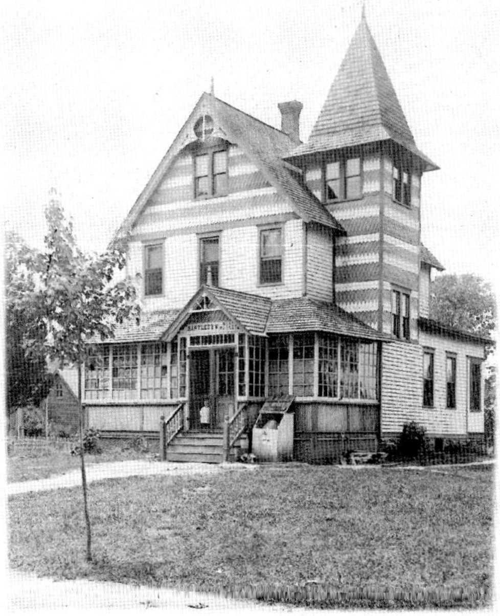

Bartlett's Meat and Grocery Store.
Photo. by Max H. Kirscht
Port Republic, N. J.

Photographed about 1910, these students are in front of the Clayhole School, located near the intersection of Chestnut Neck Road and Mill Street. Workmen removed the wood from this building and the other public school, known as the Gander Point School, which was on Riverside Drive, to construct a schoolhouse on Pomona Avenue, a more central location in the city. The present school was built not far from that site.

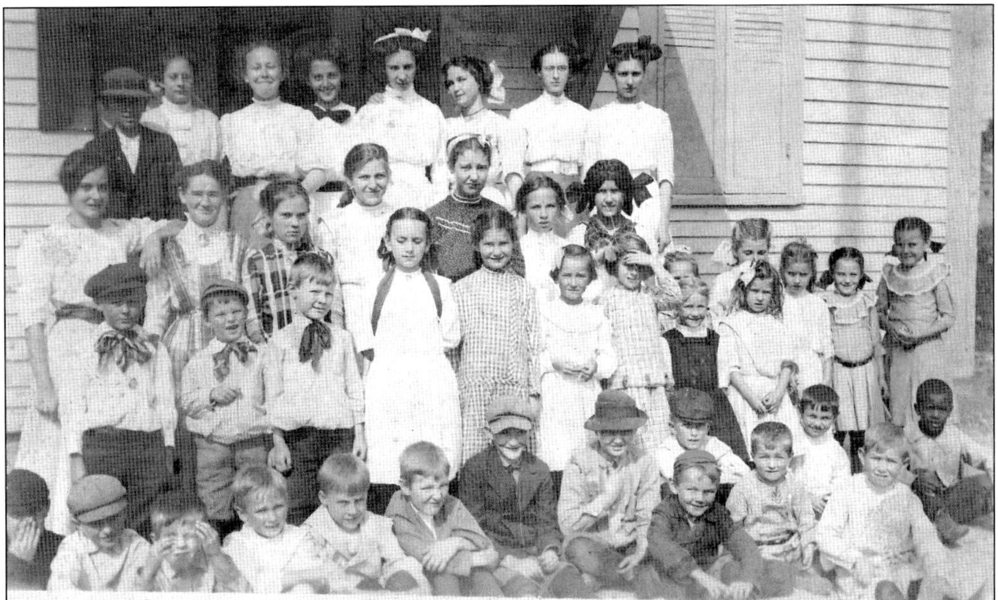

Photo. by Max H. Kirscht
Pleasantville, N. J.
SCHOLARS OF PUBLIC SCHOOL.—Port Republic, N. J.

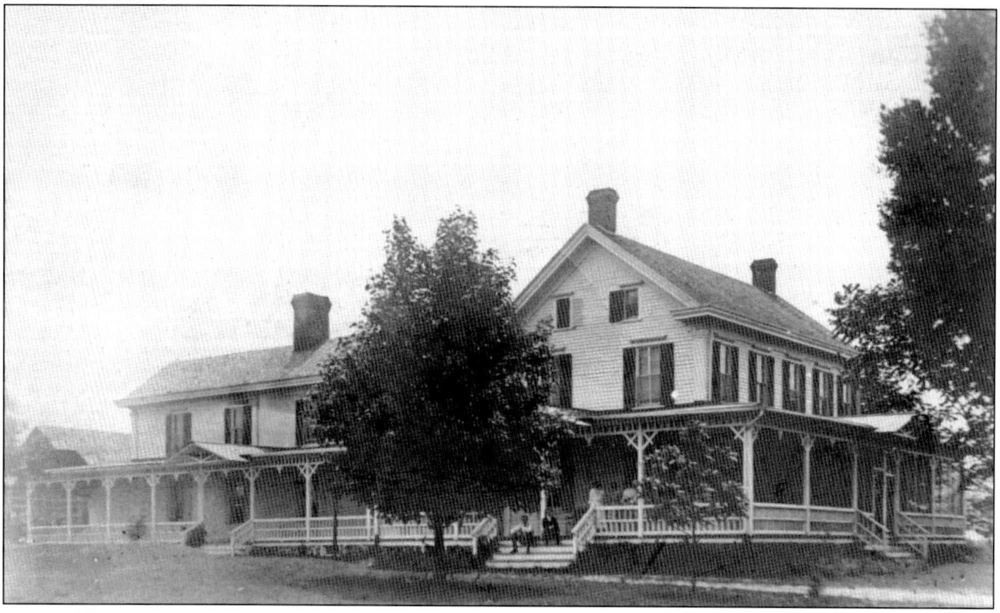

Owned by a member of the Clark family, this building became the home of Elmer D. French about 1900. It was located in the triangle between Pitney and Old New York Roads. French ran the stage from Pomona to Brigantine via Port Republic. It became Willow Grove Cottage, a hotel and store operated by a Mrs. Brand. Later, it was destroyed by a fire. (Courtesy of Doris Bugdon.)

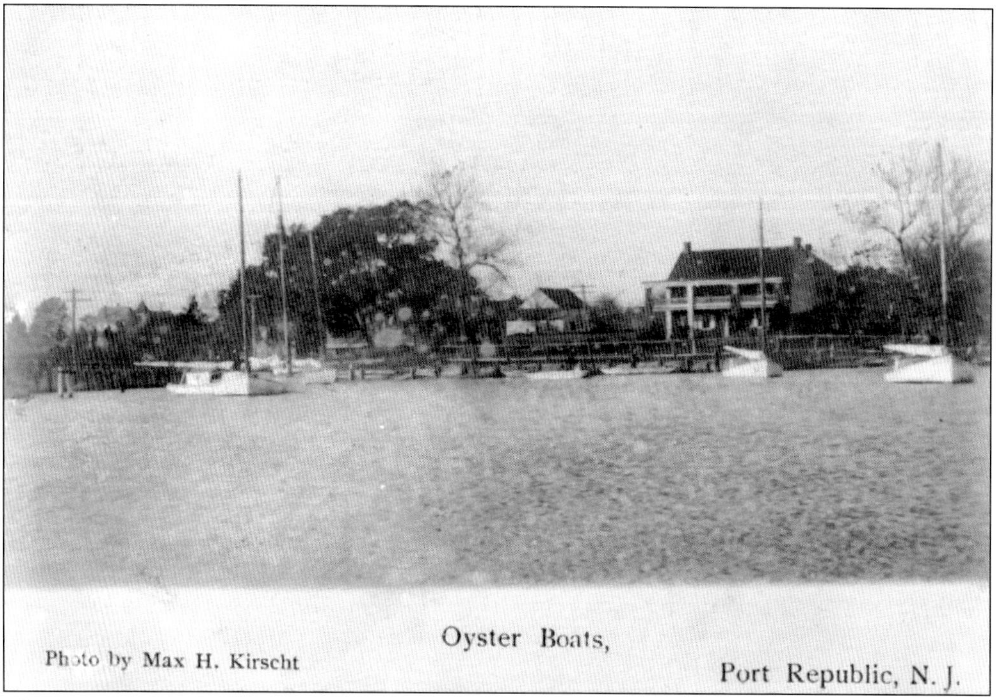

The building to the right in this photograph, known as the Endicott House, was constructed by Jonas Miller in 1792. It is said that Alice Clark, Port Republic's first public school teacher, taught in the parlor of this home. It is still located on Old New York Road near Nacote Creek Bridge, which is just out of view to the left. It was owned for many years by Louis Adams.

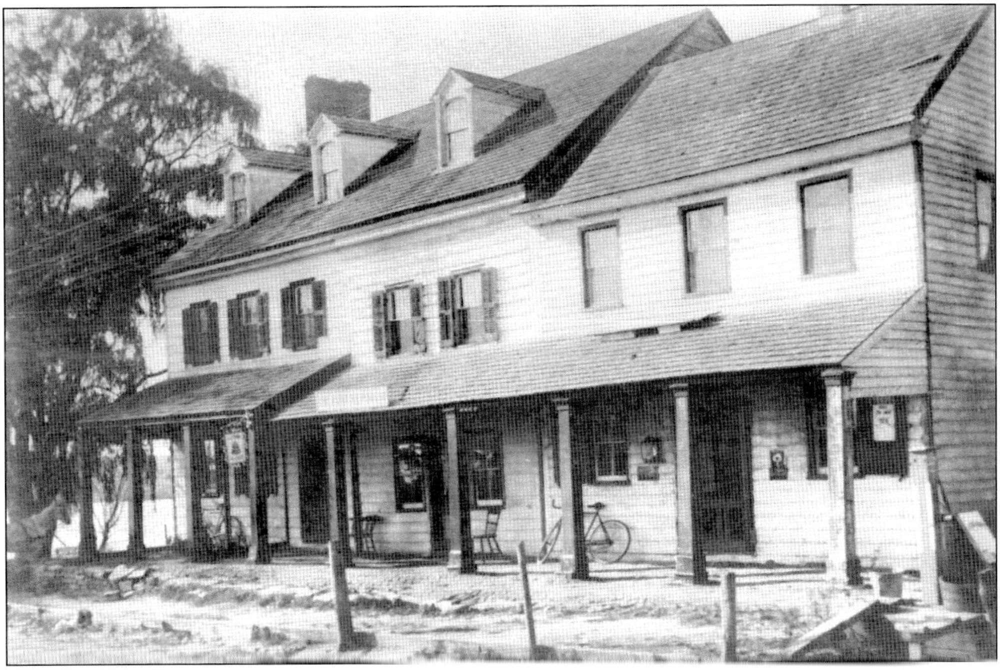

The Port Republic Inn was located on Old New York Road, south of the intersection of St. John's Lane and opposite the Endicott House. The portion of the building on the far left was constructed prior to 1800. Later, it was owned by Fred and Ethel Noyes, who stored antiques in it. The site was proposed as the original location for the Noyes Museum. It was later demolished. (Courtesy of Doris Bugdon.)

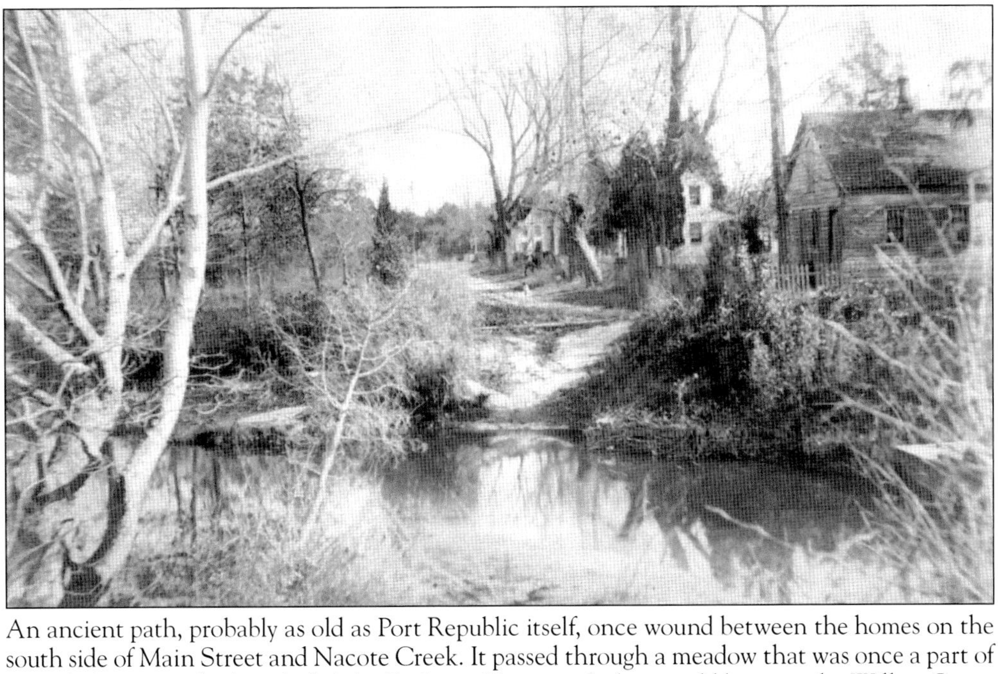

An ancient path, probably as old as Port Republic itself, once wound between the homes on the south side of Main Street and Nacote Creek. It passed through a meadow that was once a part of the Clark estate, which included the Endicott House and what would become the Willow Grove Cottage and then the Port Republic Inn. (Courtesy of Doris Bugdon.)

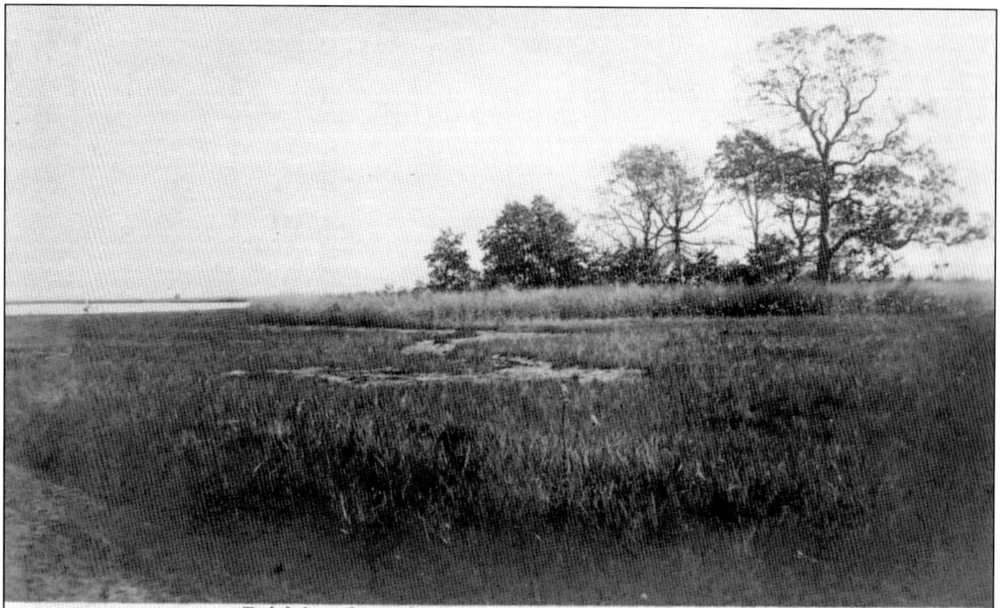

British—American Battlefield, Oct. 15, 1778.

Photo. by M. H. Kirscht. Chestnut Neck, N. J.

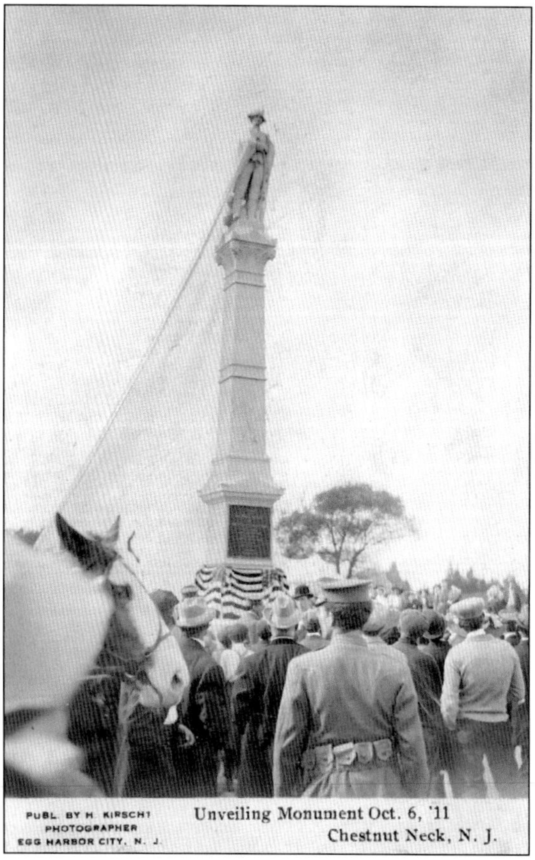

PUBL. BY H. KIRSCHT PHOTOGRAPHER EGG HARBOR CITY, N. J. Unveiling Monument Oct. 6, '11 Chestnut Neck, N. J.

Angered by the loss of ships and the interruption of trade, the British military ordered the destruction of the privateering center at Chestnut Neck in September 1778. During the 23-day campaign, the British decided to attack Count Casmir Pulaski's legion in Little Egg Harbor Township. During the early-morning hours of October 15, 1778, the British massacred upwards of 50 legionnaires. (Courtesy of Doris Bugdon.)

On October 6, 1911, the General Lafayette Chapter of the Daughters of the American Revolution dedicated this monument to mark the site of the Battle of Chestnut Neck. The monument pays homage to those men who defended Chestnut Neck on October 6, 1778. Sadly, the small community was burned to the ground by British forces. This postcard shows the moment that officials unveiled the memorial. A rededication ceremony was held on October 8, 2011.

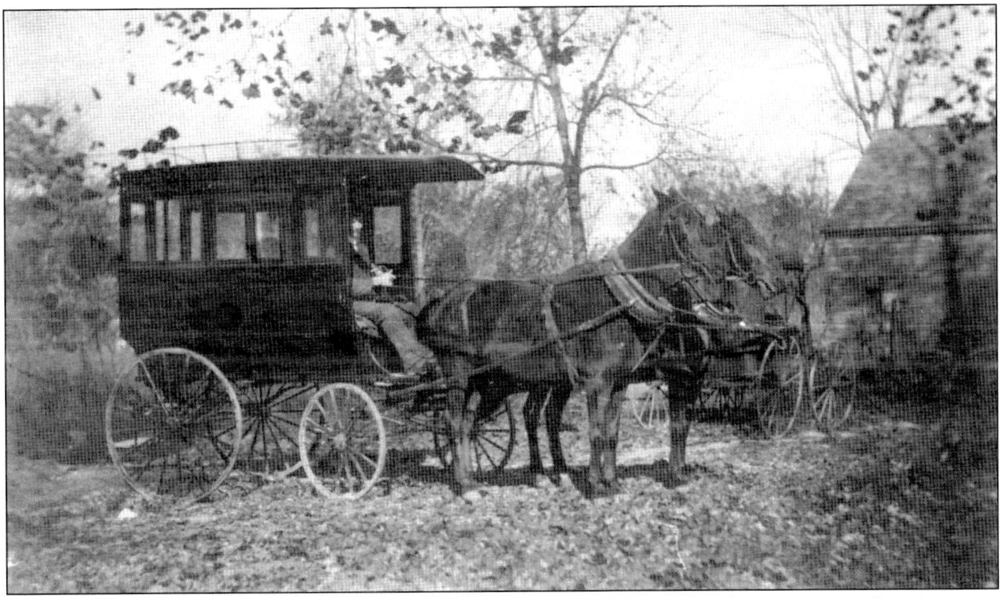

Wesley Brown was one of several men who operated the stage between the Pomona railroad station and Port Republic. In the early 1900s, stage drivers provided a necessary service in many small towns, transporting passengers, mail, and freight. It was the bus—not the train—that brought the end of stagecoach service in the country. (Courtesy of Doris Bugdon.)

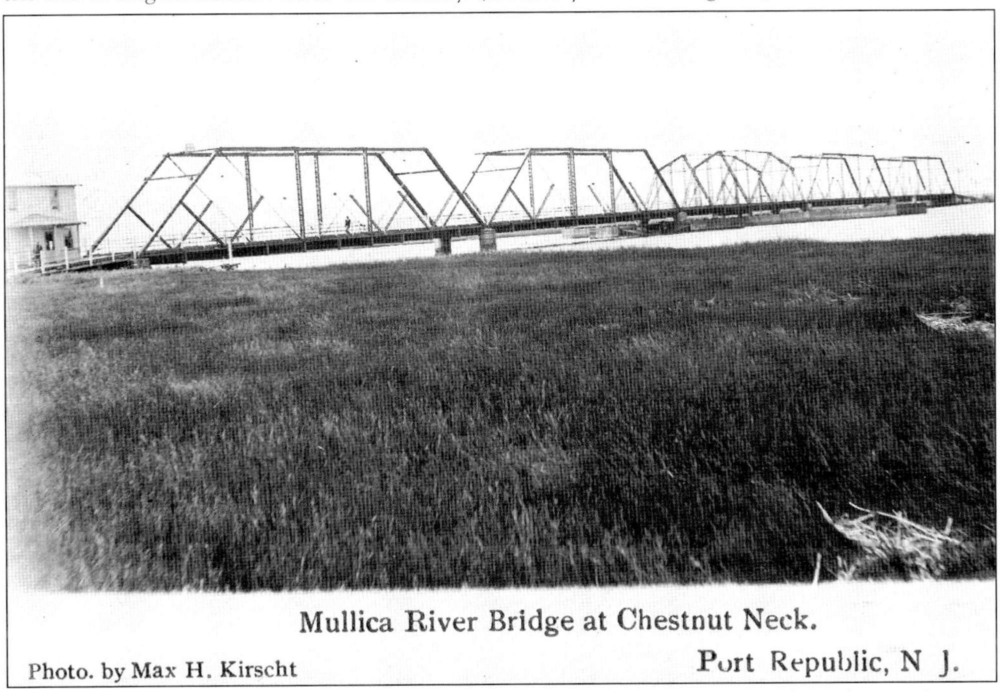

This iron bridge once spanned the Mullica River between Chestnut Neck and New Gretna. Standing on the span is Horatio D. Cramer, the bridge tender. His son Stanley "Tater" Cramer stands in front of the old tollhouse, where he rented rowboats and garveys. Tater was the longtime owner of the Chestnut Neck boatyard. The span was replaced by the Garden State Parkway Bridge. (Courtesy of Doris Bugdon.)

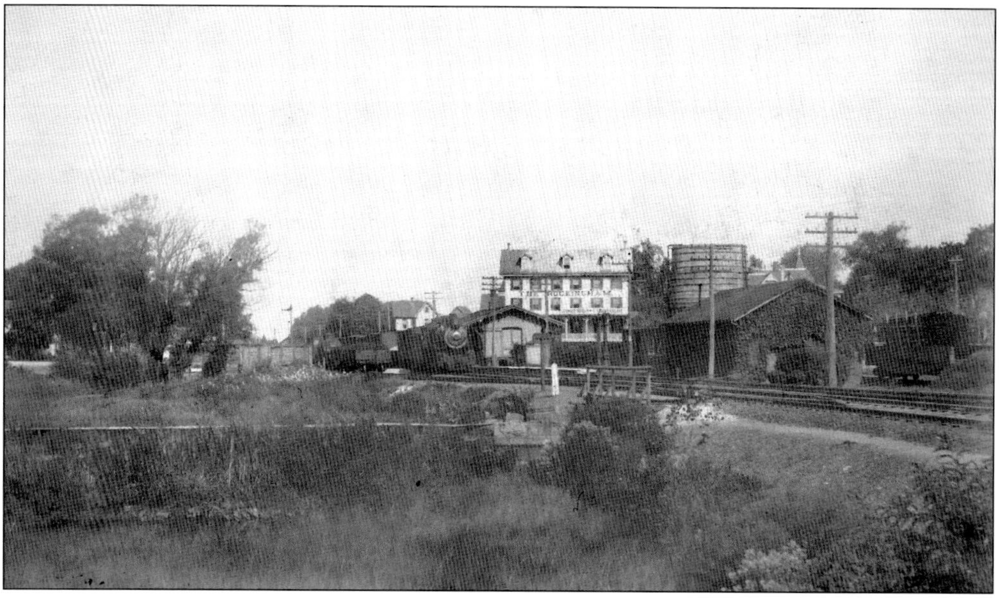

Decades before the Pennsylvania-Reading Seashore Lines constructed the viaduct that spanned Station Avenue, Absecon Creek, and Shore Road in 1940, this was the view of the West Jersey & Seashore Railroad station at Absecon. Much of the railroad's passenger and freight operations in the city can be seen in this view, taken from near Shore Road. The Rockingham Hotel, still in its original location and operated by Martin Keane at the time, is in the background.

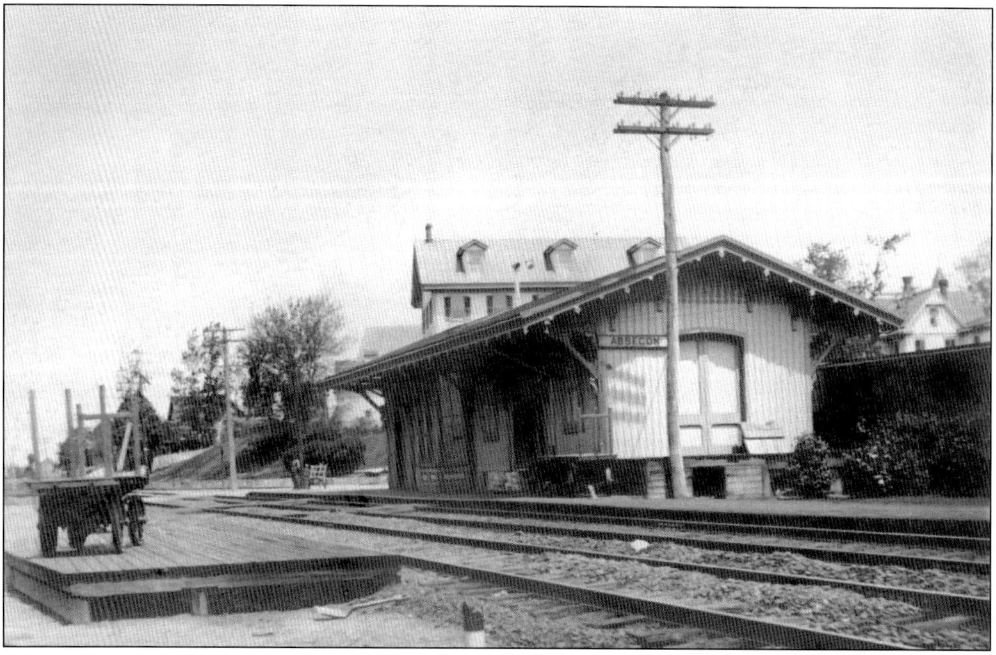

After more than a year of wrangling in the boardroom and the courtroom, the Pennsylvania Railroad (PRR) gained control of the Camden & Atlantic Railroad on February 22, 1883. In 1896, the PRR consolidated many of the rail lines it owned and controlled in South Jersey under the title of the West Jersey & Seashore Railroad. In many small towns, the line was simply known as "the Pennsylvania."

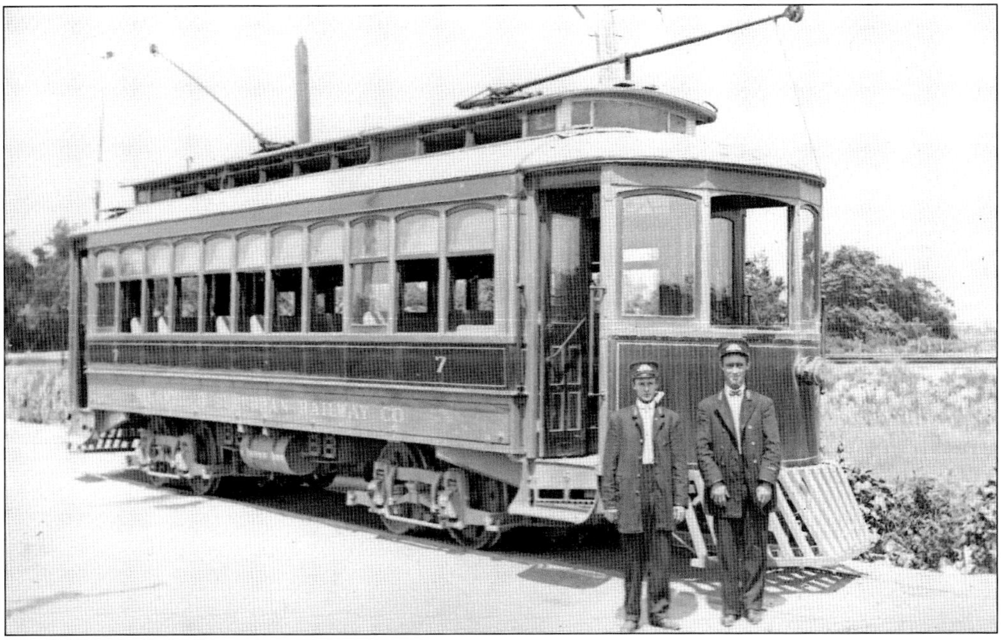

In addition to regular railroad service, Absecon also enjoyed trolley service. Founded in 1903, the Atlantic & Suburban Traction Company line ran up Shore Road, terminating just before the West Jersey & Seashore tracks, where this photograph was taken in the early 1920s. Original plans called for the line to be extended up New Jersey Avenue, but that goal was never realized. Service on the line ended on April 30, 1929.

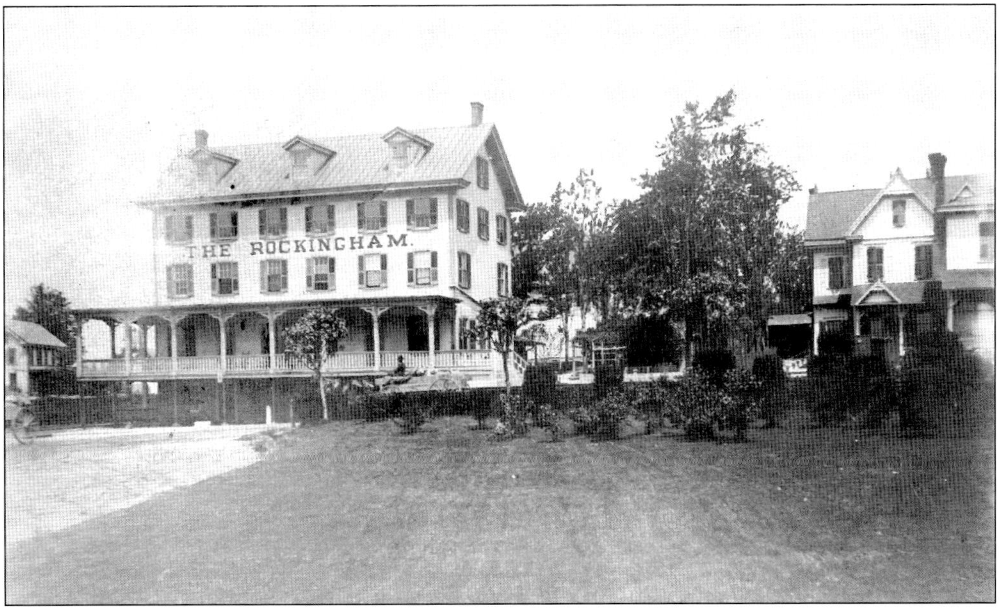

Both Herman and Max Kirscht produced a number of postcards featuring images of Absecon. Many of those cards have become well-known images, including this view of the Rockingham Hotel. Located on Station Avenue, directly across from the city's train station, the hotel had a long and varied history, including being turned to face the White Horse Pike in 1925. It was damaged by a fire on November 4, 1983, and demolished the following month.

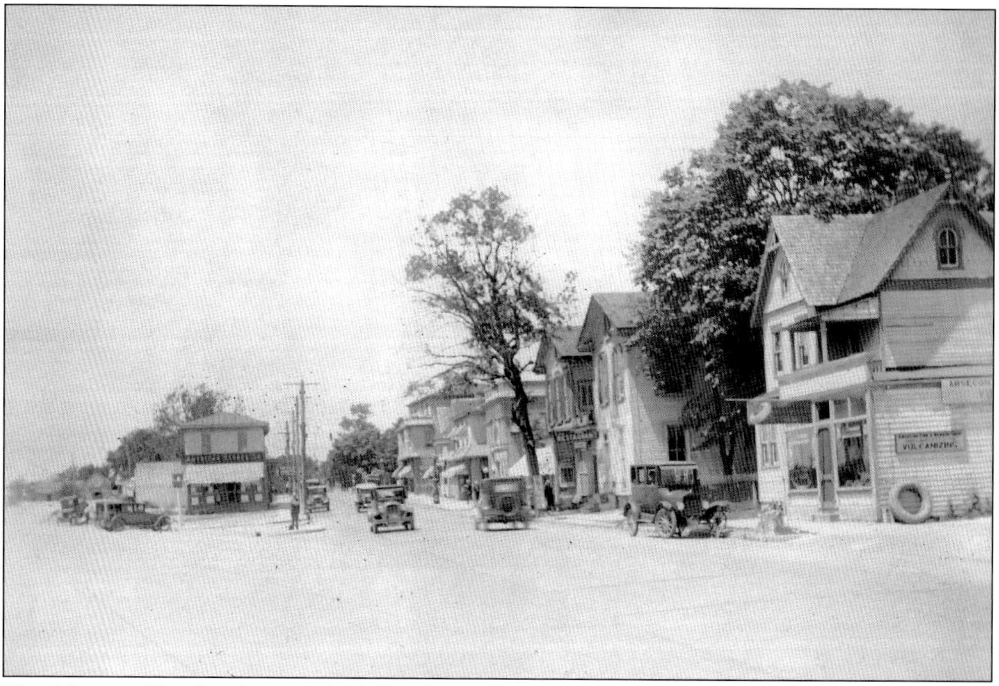

This Herman Kirscht photograph shows the intersection of the White Horse Pike and New Jersey Avenue around 1928. An improved Absecon Boulevard, dedicated on August 15, 1925, provided the motoring public with a viable alternate route to Atlantic City. By this time, Absecon had become a bedroom community to the ever-popular Atlantic City, and it finally had both rail and motor routes to the "World's Playground."

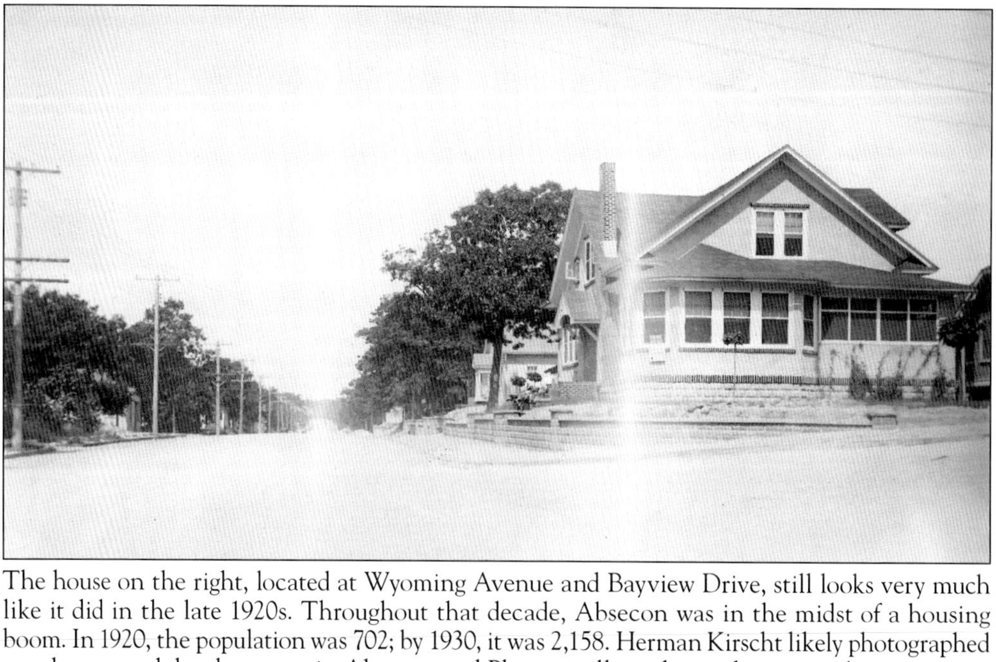

The house on the right, located at Wyoming Avenue and Bayview Drive, still looks very much like it did in the late 1920s. Throughout that decade, Absecon was in the midst of a housing boom. In 1920, the population was 702; by 1930, it was 2,158. Herman Kirscht likely photographed new homes and developments in Absecon and Pleasantville and sent them to real estate agents throughout the country.

Tradition states that the first Methodist meetinghouse in Absecon was on Shore Road, a short distance north of the present church. Feeling the need for a new building, they incorporated the Methodist Episcopal Church at Absecon on March 3, 1823. This was done in order to build a house to "worship Almighty God," "procure a suitable burying ground for the dead," and "for the more effectually accomplishing and better regulating of the same."

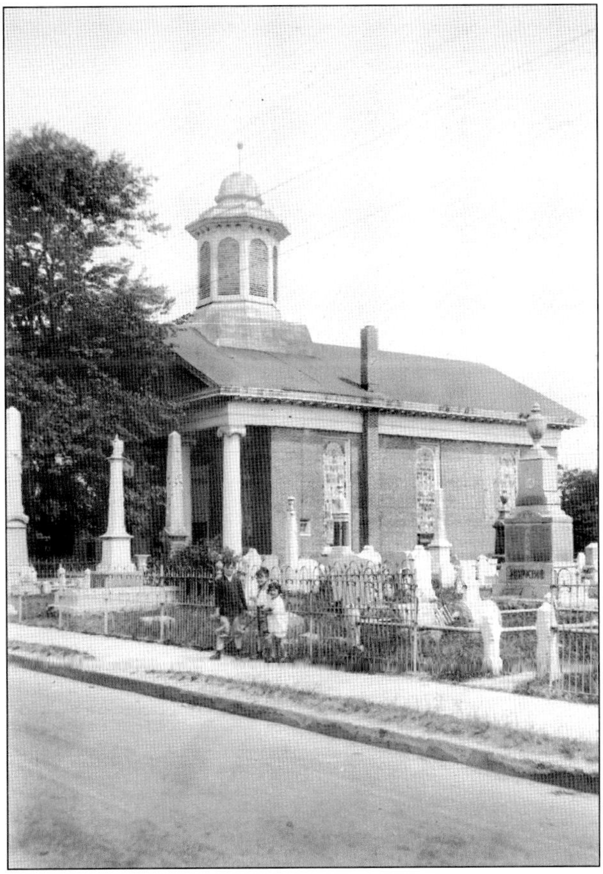

The brick Methodist Episcopal Church at Absecon was finished in 1829. In 1856, the church was completely rebuilt and enlarged. While no record of the changes exist, it is believed that the porch with the Ionic columns and the large belfry, which give the building its unique look, were added that year. A new gallery, pulpit, and vestibule, as well as new seating, were also included at this time.

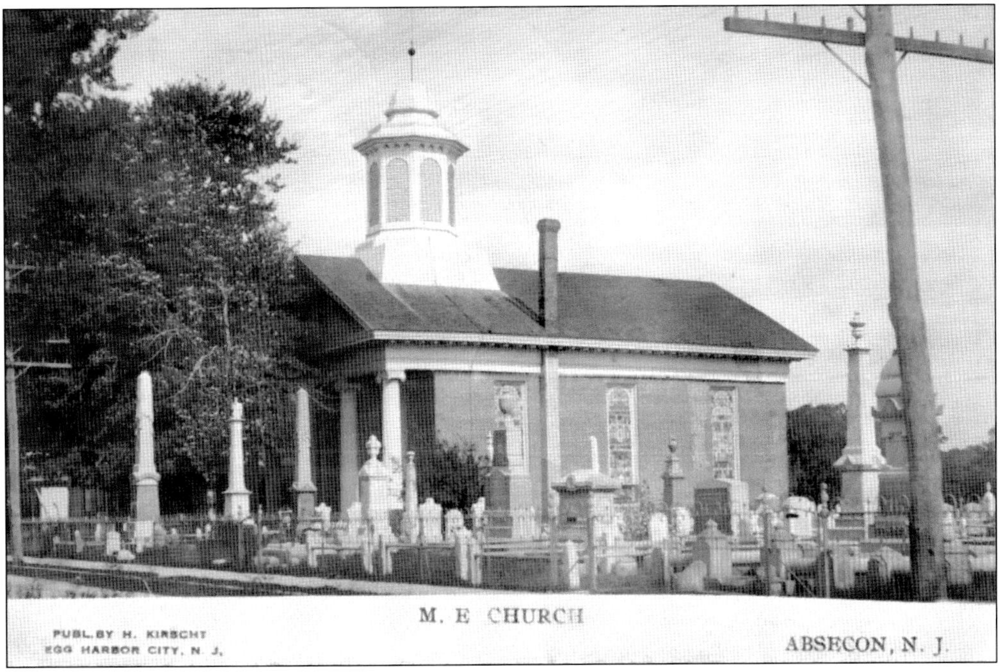

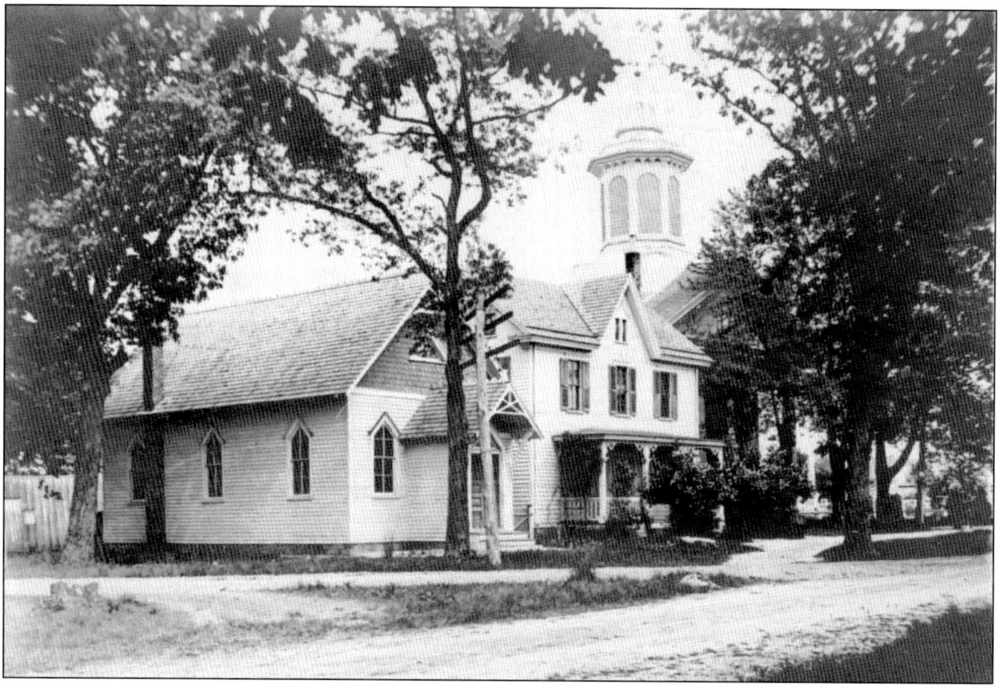

In 1869, the church decided to build a parsonage, seen in the center of this image. It was completed in 1870 and furnished the following year. In 1902, Reuben Babcock presented the congregation with the chapel on the far right. After his death in 1908, his widow enlarged and upgraded the building. While the chapel still exists, the parsonage no longer stands.

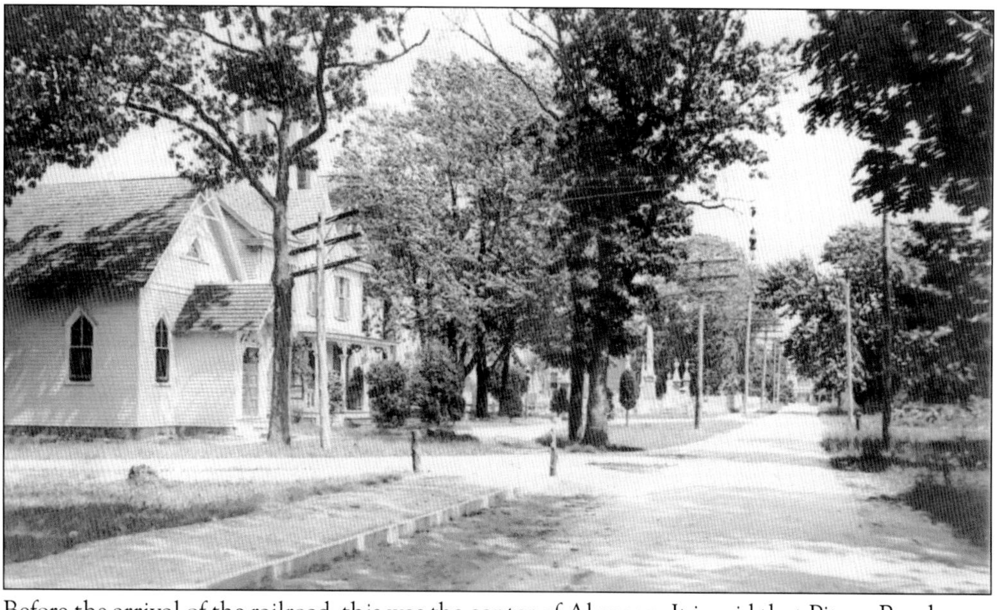

Before the arrival of the railroad, this was the center of Absecon. It is said that Pitney Road, seen on the left, was constructed so that Dr. Jonathan Pitney could travel to Port Republic to attend to his patients. This route allowed the doctor to bypass the longer and less direct New York Road. Compared to the previous image, the intersection has undergone some improvement.

Through the hard work and persistence of Rev. Allen H. Brown and local residents, the Presbyterian Church at Absecon was formally organized on February 13, 1859. Property between Church Street and New Jersey Avenue was purchased. Later, a school was constructed, and a cemetery was cleared. Meanwhile, the tiny congregation worshiped in rented halls and in their own school until the new church was completed. This beautiful edifice was dedicated on June 20, 1867.

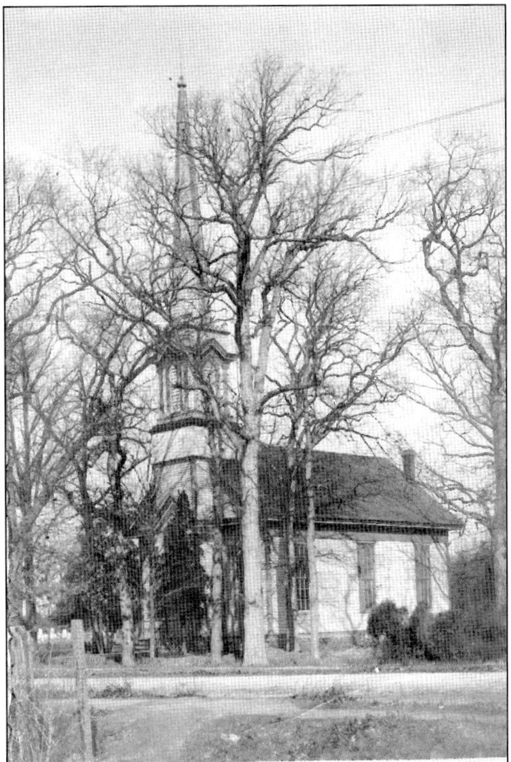

Presbyterian Church.

Photo. by Max H. Kirscht, Pleasantville, N.J.

Absecon, N. J.

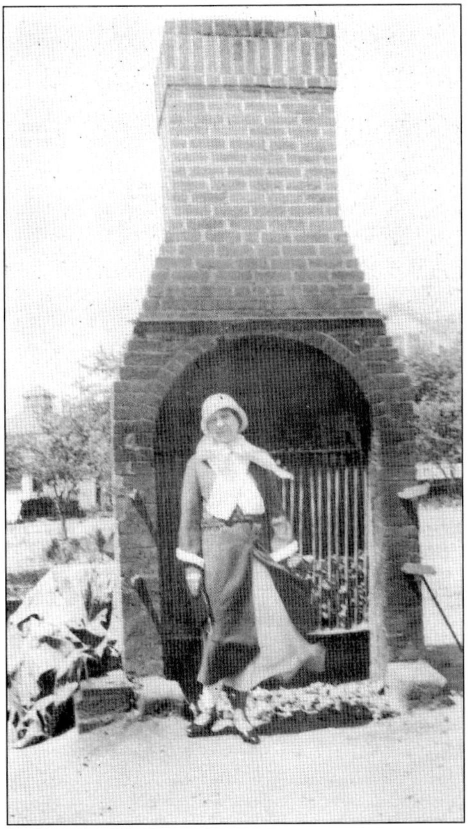

This and another photograph are the only known images of the barbeque pit at the Black Cat Inn. For decades, Al Royer and his son offered their famous "Bar-B-Q Sandwiches." In 1951, they only cost 50¢, or 60¢ with French fries. Clara Kirscht poses in front of the pit in January 1932 while visiting friends in the city with her father.

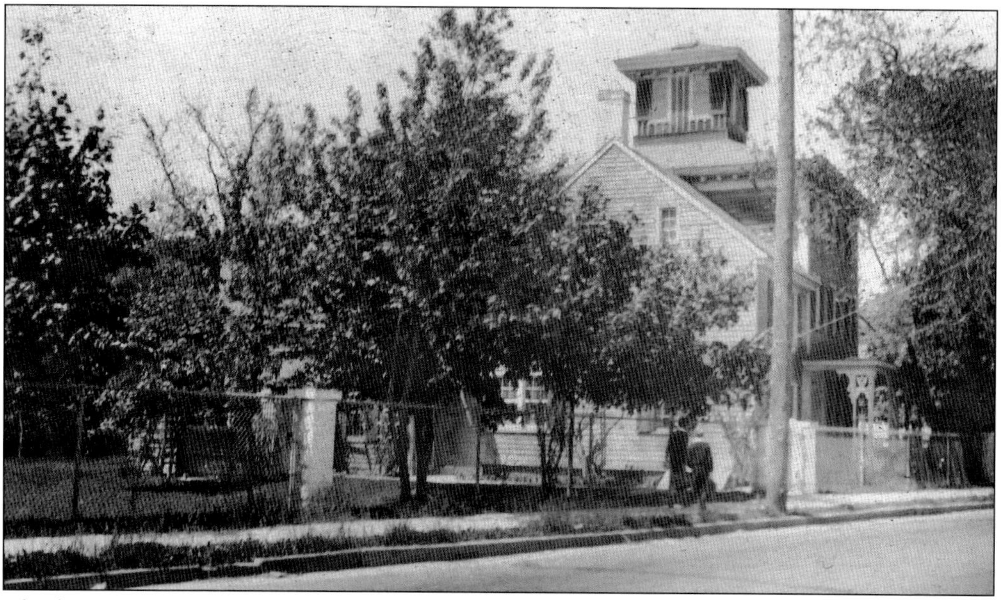

Charlotte Pitney, the daughter-in-law of Dr. Jonathan Pitney, wrote, "One morning in May 1820, Dr. Jonathan Pitney rode into Absecon on horseback with only his saddle bags. The first person he saw and shook hands with was my grandfather, General Enoch Doughty, and from that day in May, all their long lives they were fast friends in everything that transpired." The Pitney House, seen here, still stands at the corner of Shore Road and Church Street.

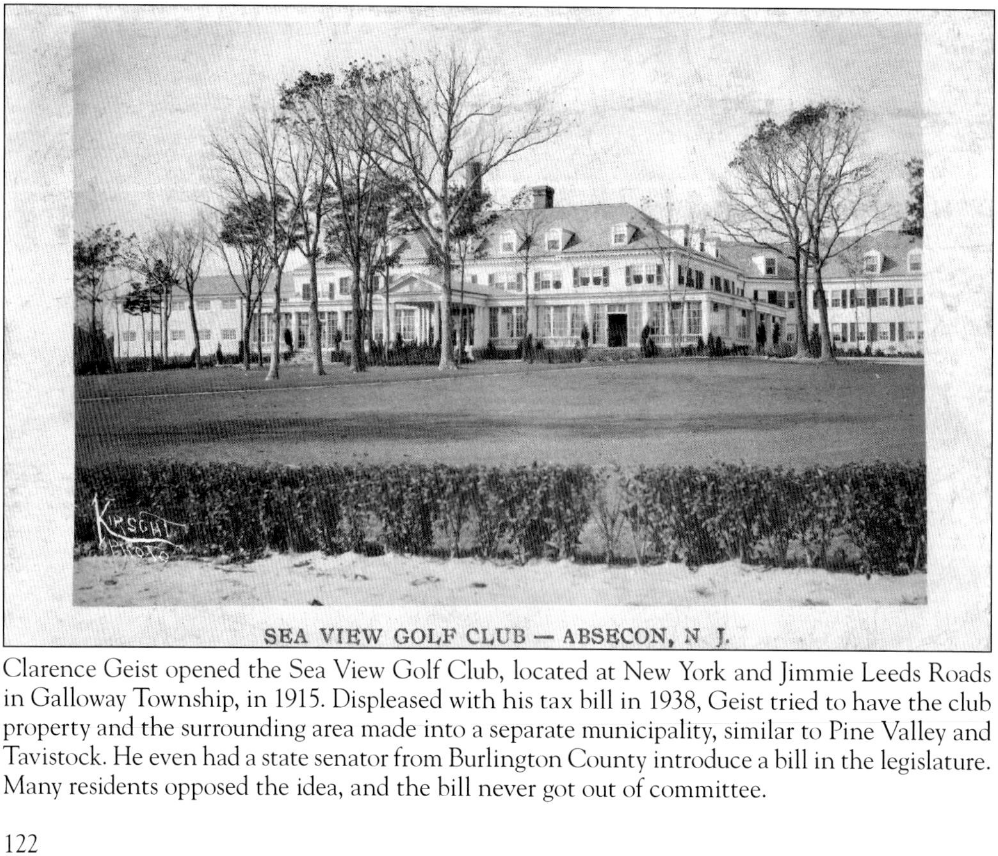

SEA VIEW GOLF CLUB — ABSECON, N. J.

Clarence Geist opened the Sea View Golf Club, located at New York and Jimmie Leeds Roads in Galloway Township, in 1915. Displeased with his tax bill in 1938, Geist tried to have the club property and the surrounding area made into a separate municipality, similar to Pine Valley and Tavistock. He even had a state senator from Burlington County introduce a bill in the legislature. Many residents opposed the idea, and the bill never got out of committee.

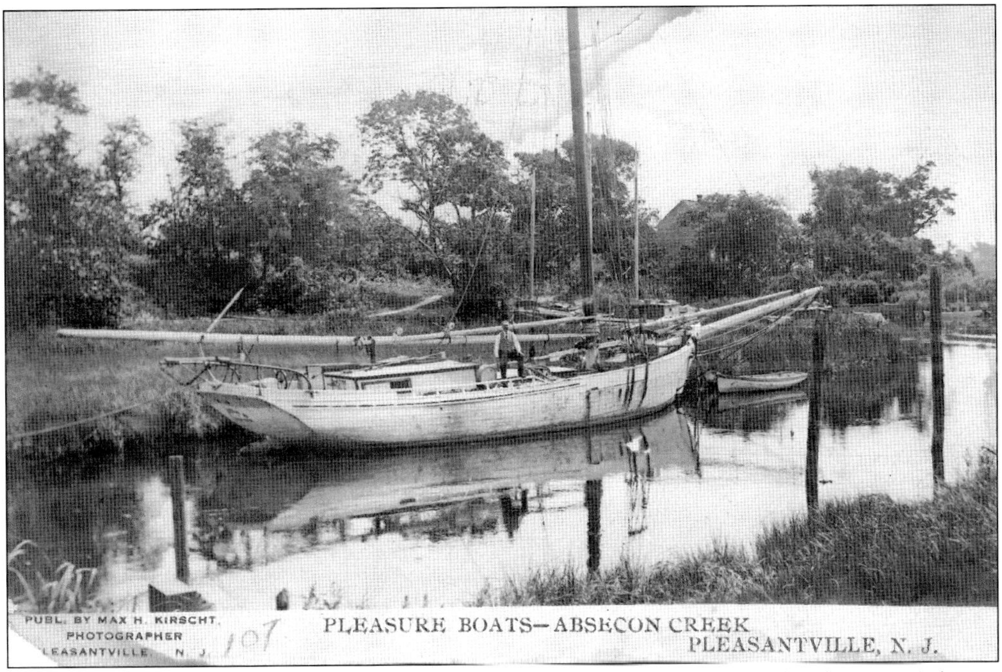

As early as 1776, Absecon served as one of the shipbuilding centers in what became Atlantic County, and many residents made a living from the sea. It was a small, insular community when the Camden & Atlantic Railroad had its inaugural run on July 1, 1854. While shipbuilding continued on as an industry for several decades, it was the railroad, more than any other force, that shaped the development of the community.

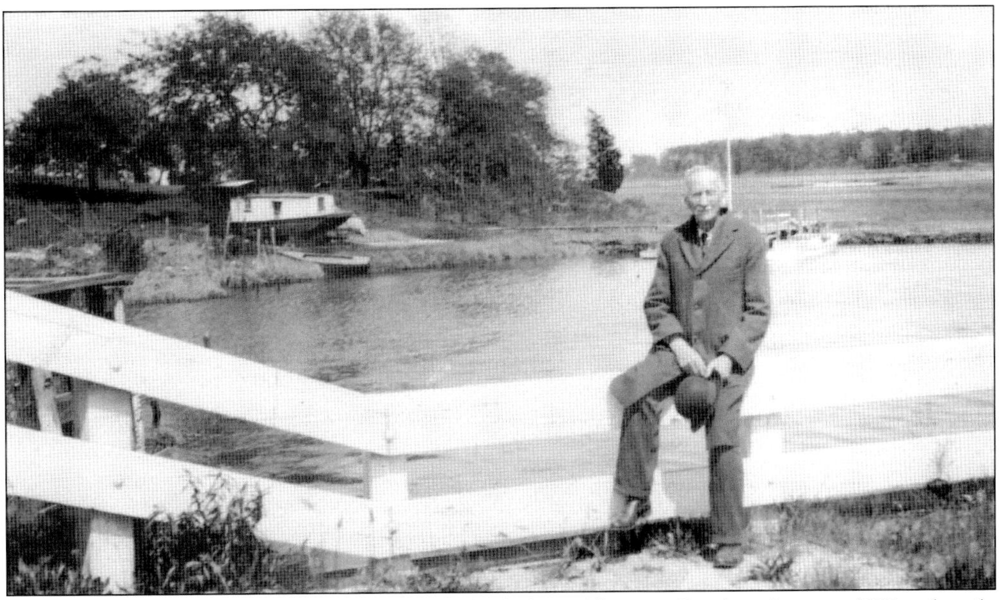

Herman Kirscht is seen here sitting on a guardrail along Absecon Creek in January 1932, a decade after his son had taken the photograph at the top of this page for one of his postcards near this very spot. This image was captured by Clara Kirscht and is proof that the apple did not fall far from the tree when it came to framing a moment.

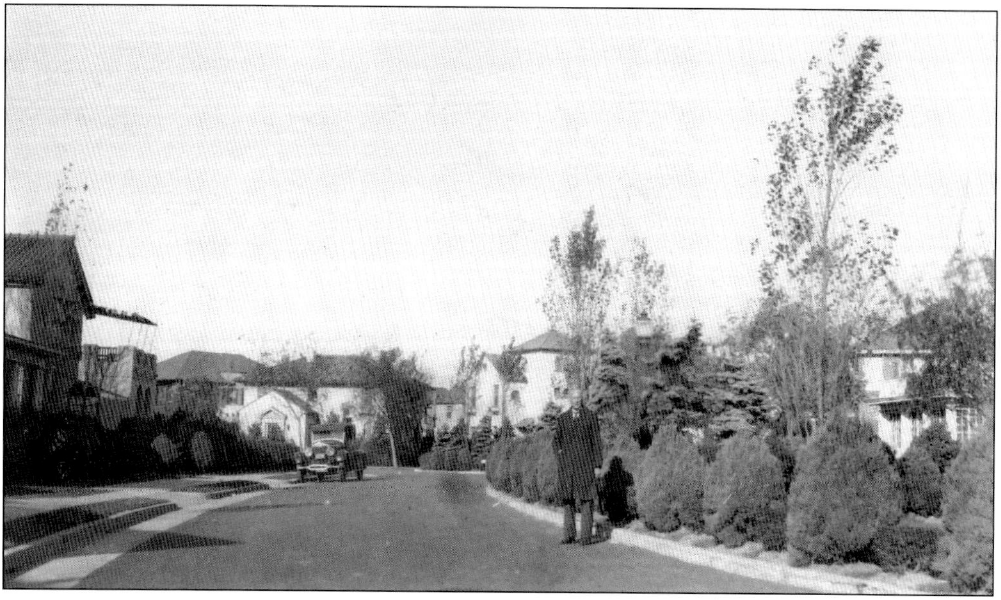

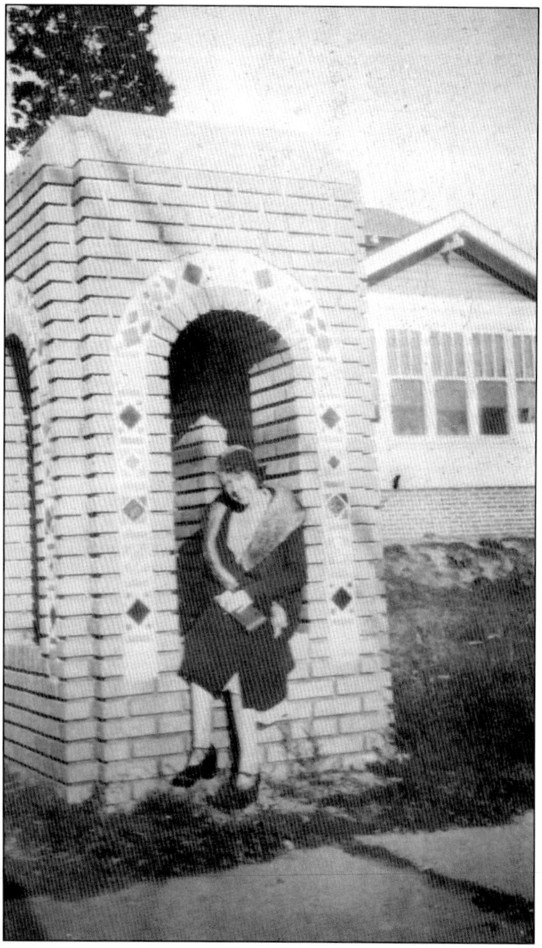

Herman Kirscht stands in front of the East Drive of Marven Gardens. Derived from the first three letters of Margate and Ventnor, this tract is an eclectic mix of Spanish villas, Italian manors, Dutch colonials, and Georgian Revival homes originally costing $18,000 and $25,000. Today, it is considered a well-preserved example of an early 20th-century development and is in the New Jersey Register of Historic Places.

Clara Kirscht poses for her father at the corner of Shore Road and East Edgewood Avenue, Linwood, during another of their many trips in the area. Structures such as this were built to designate the entrances to new developments. This one still stands today.

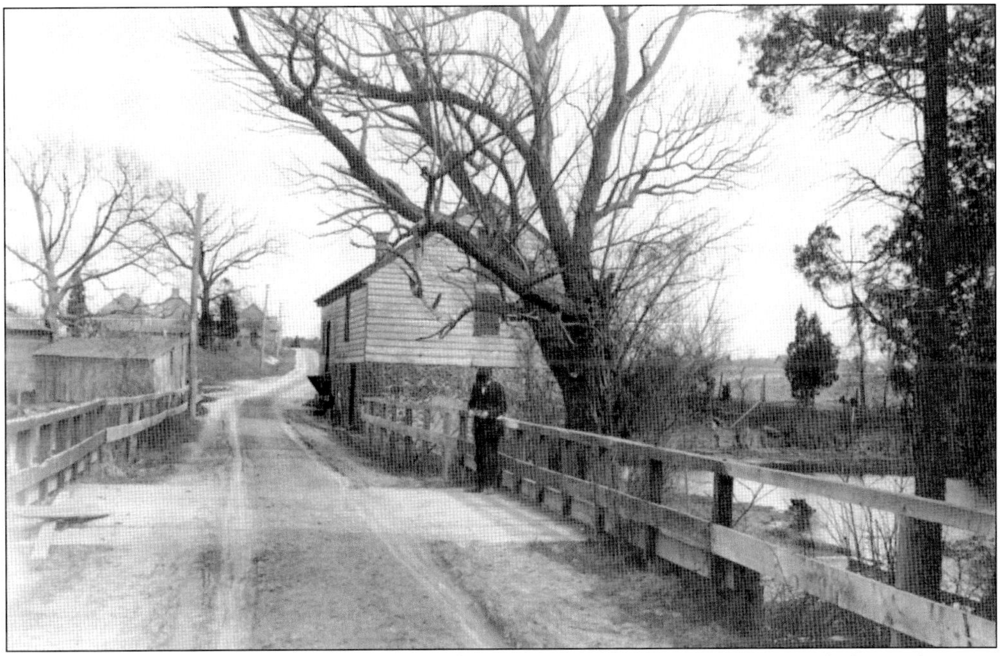

The building on the right in the photograph above is the Bargaintown gristmill, located in Egg Harbor Township. One popular and enduring account of how this community got its name claims that a local landowner told his slaves that if they would build a road in their spare time to traverse a swampy area on his property, he would grant them their freedom. When the road was completed, the landowner granted the slaves their freedom and a piece of land of their own. Hence, the name "Bargaintown." The roadway eventually became known as Central Avenue. Over time, it has been moved and straightened. The photograph above was taken by Max Kirscht. The gentleman in it appears to be his father, Herman Kirscht. The image below is a close-up view of the dam at the Bargaintown millpond. The individual on the cribbing is Benny Clark.

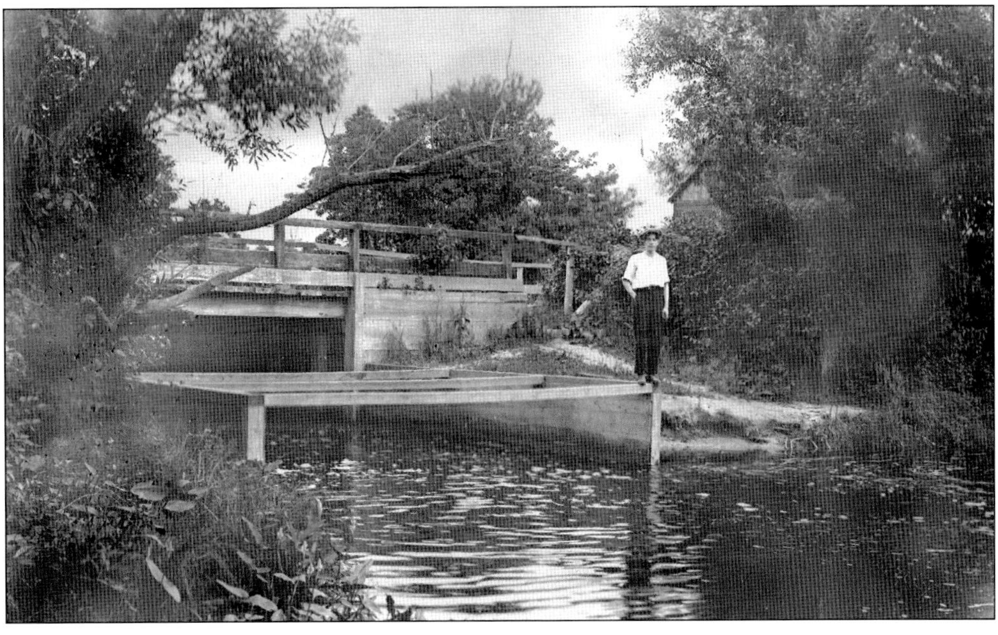

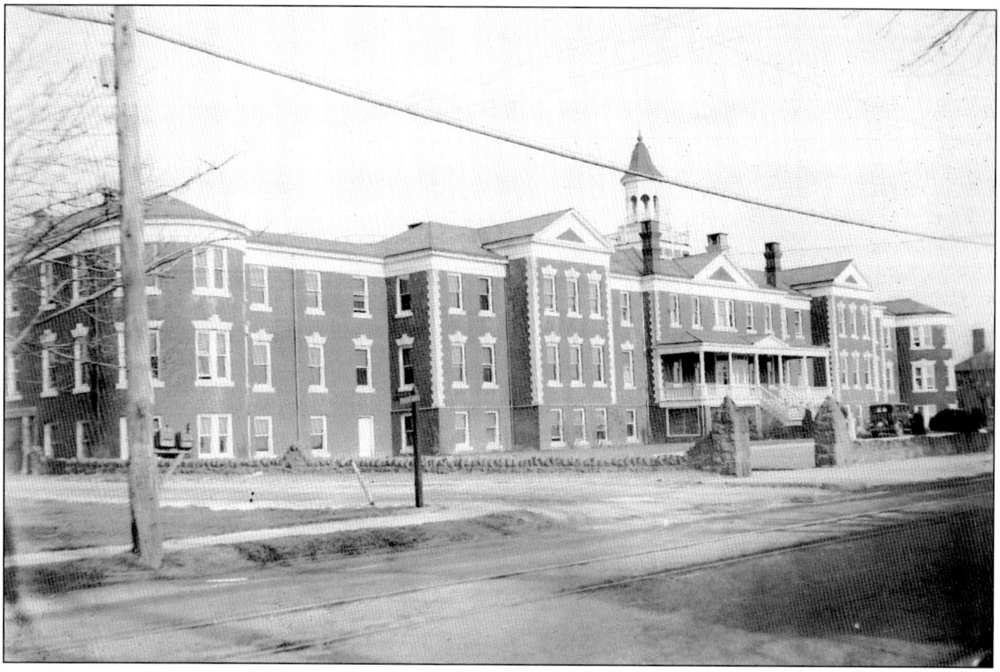

This building was once Atlantic County's insane asylum, built in 1895 at Shore Road and Dolphin Avenue in Northfield. It was constructed to house the mentally ill who had been residing in the almshouse. Today, this building has been renovated and enlarged several times. The Atlantic County Division of Public Health now utilizes much of the building, which is now called the Stillwater Building. The Board of Chosen Freeholders also meets here.

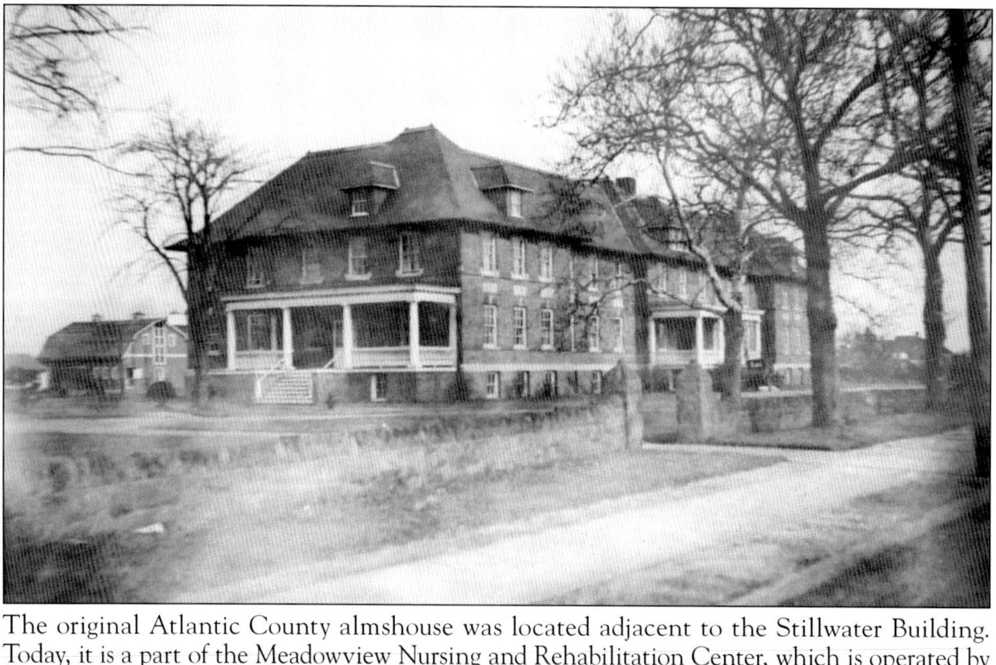

The original Atlantic County almshouse was located adjacent to the Stillwater Building. Today, it is a part of the Meadowview Nursing and Rehabilitation Center, which is operated by Atlantic County. While this building has also been added on to and refurbished over the years, it retains much of its original grandeur.

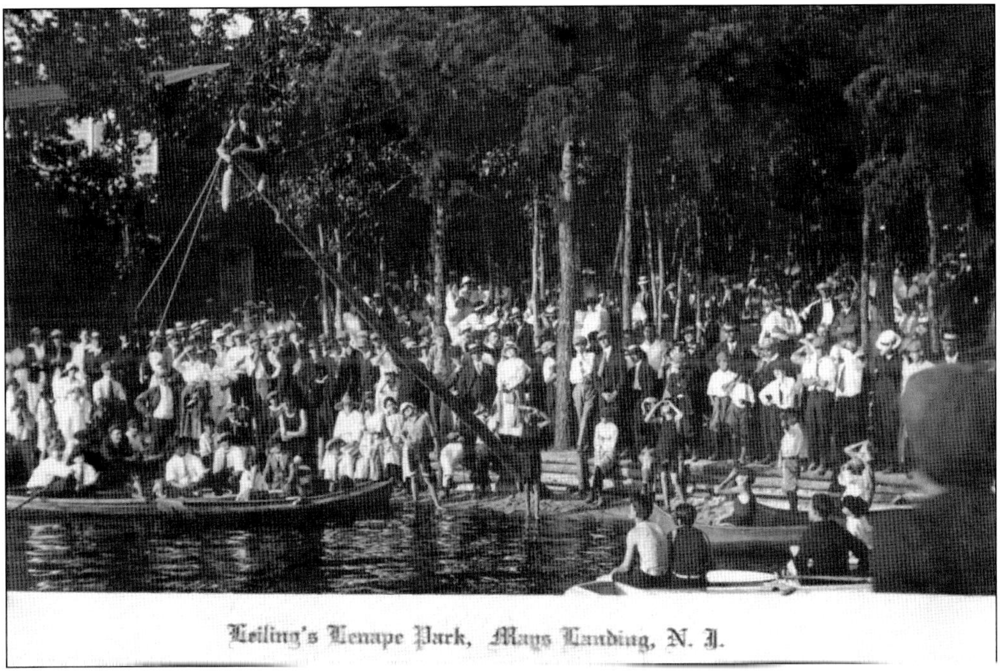

Lorenz Leiling left Germany for the United States in the 1860s. He purchased a farm in Estell Manor in the 1880s. In 1892, he purchased a piece of property along Lake Lenape and operated a dairy and truck farm. With the founding of St. Vincent DePaul Catholic Church in 1906, the pastor sought permission to hold picnics on the Leiling farm. An idea eventually sparked, and Leiling's Lenape Park opened on Memorial Day in 1907. Transportation from the railroad stations to the park was nonexistent until Roy Beach began to convey visitors via boat from his wharf at the end of Main Street to the park. The park was very popular with tourists in the early 1900s, as well as with aquatic clubs from the area. It began to draw even more visitors with the advent of motorboat racing.

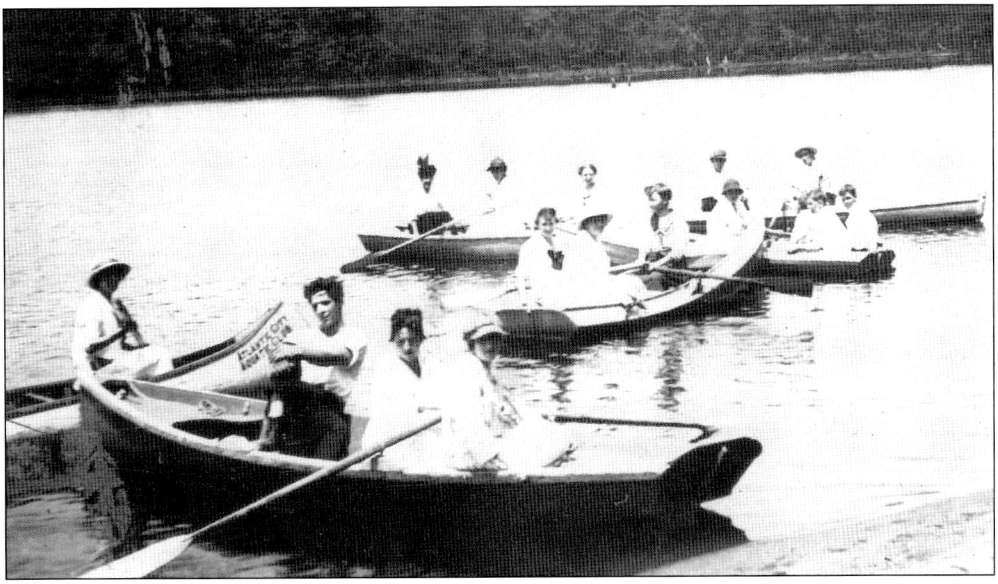

Consistent with our mission to preserve history on a local level, this book was printed in South Carolina on American-made paper and manufactured entirely in the United States. Products carrying the accredited Forest Stewardship Council (FSC) label are printed on 100 percent FSC-certified paper.

MADE IN THE USA